'An interdisciplinary book that will become a must-read for all those working on citizenship, nation, diversity and inequality in Europe. Original in its inception, this book explores how we talk about, contest, practice and also perform our citizenship in the different realms of our social and political activity.'

—**Anna Triandafyllidou**, *Robert Schuman Centre for Advanced Studies, European University Institute*

'This volume re-establishes the conceptual link between citizens and politics and thus revives a classical perspective that today has been mostly lost: as Max Weber famously put it, citizens are occasional politicians (Gelegenheitspolitiker).'

—**Kari Palonen**, *Professor of Political Science, University of Jyväskylä*

'*Shaping Citizenship* is a fine account of the contested nature of citizenship as a political concept and practice. The book provides a comparative appraisal of citizenship ranging from the theoretical controversies around its democratic understanding to the contention surrounding citizenship as a political practice and its centrality in most recent public debates in Europe on immigration and rights.'

—**José María Rosales**, *Professor of Moral and Political Philosophy, University of Málaga*

'Citizenship is probably one of the most politically contested and dynamic fields of research in Europe today. The daily changes in policy and practice, the heated debates, and the triggering events have created a need for understanding and reflection. *Shaping Citizenship* responds to these dynamic issues by addressing the conceptual debates on "inclusion" and "the good enough citizens". It contributes to research on asylum, access and Human Rights and deals with practice in EU innovation, labour migration, dual citizenship and much more. I recommend reading it carefully.'

—**Trond Solhaug**, *Professor, Norwegian University for Science and Technology, NTNU*

Shaping Citizenship

Citizenship is a core concept for the social sciences, and citizenship is also frequently interpreted, challenged and contested in different political arenas. *Shaping Citizenship* explores how the concept is debated and contested, defined and redefined, used and constructed by different agents, at different times, and with regard to both theory and practice.

The book uses a reflexive and constructivist perspective on the concept of citizenship that draws on the theory and methodology of conceptual history. This approach enables a panorama of politically important readings on citizenship that provide an interdisciplinary perspective and help to transcend narrow and simplified views on citizenship. The three parts of the book focus respectively on theories, debates and practices of citizenship. In the chapters, constructions and struggles related to citizenship are approached by experts from different fields. Thematically the chapters focus on political representation, migration, internationalization, sub- and transnationalization as well as the Europeanisation of citizenship.

An indispensable read to scholars and students, *Shaping Citizenship* presents new ways to study the conceptual changes, struggles and debates related to core dimensions of this ever-evolving concept.

Claudia Wiesner is acting professor for comparative politics at Hamburg University and adjunct professor for political science at the University of Jyväskylä.

Anna Björk is a postdoctoral researcher in political science at the Department of Social Sciences and Philosophy, University of Jyväskylä.

Hanna-Mari Kivistö is a postdoctoral researcher in political science at the Department of Social Sciences and Philosophy, University of Jyväskylä.

Katja Mäkinen is a postdoctoral researcher at the Department of Music, Art and Culture Studies, University of Jyväskylä.

Conceptualising Comparative Politics: Polities, Peoples, and Markets
Edited by Anthony Spanakos
(Montclair State University)
and
Francisco Panizza
(London School of Economics)

Conceptualising Comparative Politics seeks to bring a distinctive approach to comparative politics by rediscovering the discipline's rich conceptual tradition and interdisciplinary foundations. It aims to fill out the conceptual framework on which the rest of the subfield draws but to which books only sporadically contribute, and to complement theoretical and conceptual analysis by applying it to deeply explored case studies. The series publishes books that make serious inquiry into fundamental concepts in comparative politics (crisis, legitimacy, credibility, representation, institutions, civil society, reconciliation) through theoretically engaging and empirically deep analysis.

4 **Conceptualizing Comparative Politics**
   Edited by Anthony Petros Spanakos and Francisco Panizza

5 **Migration Governance Across Regions**
   State-Diaspora Relations in the Latin American-Southern Europe Corridor
   Ana Margheritis

6 **What Kind of Democracy?**
   Participation, Inclusiveness and Contestation
   Kateřina Vráblíková

7 **Trust and Terror**
   Social Capital and the Use of Terrorism as a Tool of Resistance
   Ammar Shamaileh

8 **Manipulating Political Decentralisation**
   Africa's Inclusive Autocrats
   Lovise Aalen and Ragnhild L. Muriaas

9 **Shaping Citizenship**
   A Political Concept in Theory, Debate and Practice
   Edited by Claudia Wiesner, Anna Björk, Hanna-Mari Kivistö and Katja Mäkinen

Shaping Citizenship
A Political Concept in Theory, Debate and Practice

Edited by Claudia Wiesner,
Anna Björk, Hanna-Mari Kivistö
and Katja Mäkinen

NEW YORK AND LONDON

First published 2018
by Routledge
711 Third Avenue, New York, NY 10017

and by Routledge
2 Park Square, Milton Park, Abingdon, Oxon, OX14 4RN

Routledge is an imprint of the Taylor & Francis Group, an informa business

© 2018 Taylor & Francis

The right of Claudia Wiesner, Anna Björk, Hanna-Mari Kivistö and Katja Mäkinen to be identified as the authors of the editorial material, and of the authors for their individual chapters, has been asserted in accordance with sections 77 and 78 of the Copyright, Designs and Patents Act 1988.

All rights reserved. No part of this book may be reprinted or reproduced or utilised in any form or by any electronic, mechanical, or other means, now known or hereafter invented, including photocopying and recording, or in any information storage or retrieval system, without permission in writing from the publishers.

Trademark notice: Product or corporate names may be trademarks or registered trademarks, and are used only for identification and explanation without intent to infringe.

Library of Congress Cataloging-in-Publication Data
A catalog record for this book has been requested

ISBN: 978-1-138-73598-9 (hbk)
ISBN: 978-1-315-18621-4 (ebk)

Typeset in Sabon LT Std
by Swales & Willis Ltd, Exeter, Devon, UK

Contents

List of Contributors	x

Introduction: Shaping Citizenship as a
Political Concept 1
CLAUDIA WIESNER, ANNA BJÖRK, HANNA-MARI KIVISTÖ
AND KATJA MÄKINEN

PART I
Theorising Citizenship 17
ANNA BJÖRK, HANNA-MARI KIVISTÖ, KATJA MÄKINEN
AND CLAUDIA WIESNER

1 Prototype Citizenship: Evolving Concepts of
Inclusion and Order 23
MIKHAIL ILYIN

2 The Concept of "Good Enough" Citizen Revisited:
An Exploration of Current Discourses on Political
Participation 39
ELENA GARCÍA-GUITIÁN

3 Citizenship, Democracy and the Iconology of Political
Representation: A Plea for an Iconological Turn in
Democratic Theory 55
HANS J. LIETZMANN

4 Abstaining Citizenship: Deliberative and Epistocratic
Understandings of Refraining from Voting 71
FRANCISCO JAVIER GIL MARTÍN

viii *Contents*

PART II
Debating Citizenship 87
HANNA-MARI KIVISTÖ, ANNA BJÖRK, KATJA MÄKINEN AND
CLAUDIA WIESNER

5 Right of the Politically Persecuted Non-Citizen or
Right of the State? Conceptual Debates on Asylum 93
HANNA-MARI KIVISTÖ

6 Temporality at the Borders of Citizenship: Conditioning
Access in the Case of the United Kingdom 108
ANNA BJÖRK

7 Access to Medical Care: A Citizenship Right or a
Human Right? On Struggles over Rights, Entitlement
and Membership in Contemporary Sweden 123
AMANDA NIELSEN

8 The Non-State Sámi: Struggle for Indigenous
Citizenship in the European North 138
SANNA VALKONEN AND JARNO VALKONEN

PART III
Practising Citizenship 153
KATJA MÄKINEN, ANNA BJÖRK, HANNA-MARI KIVISTÖ AND
CLAUDIA WIESNER

9 Shaping Citizenship Practice through Laws: Rights and
Conceptual Innovations in the EU 159
CLAUDIA WIESNER

10 Practicing European Industrial Citizenship: The
Case of Labour Migration to Germany 175
NATHAN LILLIE AND INES WAGNER

11 "All About Doing Democracy"? Participation and
Citizenship in EU Projects 190
KATJA MÄKINEN

Contents ix

12 Dual Citizenship and Voting Rights: Domestic
Practices and Interstate Tensions 206
HEINO NYYSSÖNEN AND JUSSI METSÄLÄ

Conclusion: Contested Conceptualisations of Citizenship 221
CLAUDIA WIESNER, ANNA BJÖRK, HANNA-MARI KIVISTÖ
AND KATJA MÄKINEN

Index 228

Contributors

Anna Björk is a postdoctoral researcher in political science at the Department of Social Sciences and Philosophy, University of Jyväskylä.

Elena García-Guitián is associate professor at the Department of Political Science, Universidad Autónoma de Madrid.

Francisco Javier Gil Martín is associate professor at the Department of Philosophy, University of Oviedo.

Mikhail Ilyin is tenured professor at Higher School of Economics, National Research University Moscow.

Hanna-Mari Kivistö is a postdoctoral researcher in political science at the Department of Social Sciences and Philosophy, University of Jyväskylä.

Hans J. Lietzmann is Jean-Monnet professor for European studies at the Faculty of Humanities and Social Sciences, Bergische Universität Wuppertal.

Nathan Lillie is a professor at the Department of Social Sciences and Philosophy, University of Jyväskylä.

Katja Mäkinen is a postdoctoral researcher at the Department of Music, Art and Culture Studies, University of Jyväskylä.

Jussi Metsälä is a Ph.D. candidate in International Relations, University of Tampere.

Amanda Nielsen is an acting university lecturer in political science at the Department of Political Science, Linnaeus University.

Heino Nyyssönen is an adjunct professor and a university teacher in political science at the University of Turku.

Jarno Valkonen is a professor at the Faculty of Social Sciences, University of Lapland.

Contributors xi

Sanna Valkonen is an associate professor of Sámi research at the Faculty of Social Sciences, University of Lapland.

Ines Wagner is a senior researcher at the Institute for Social Research, Oslo.

Claudia Wiesner is acting professor for comparative politics at Hamburg University and adjunct professor for political science at the University of Jyväskylä.

Introduction

Shaping Citizenship as a Political Concept

Claudia Wiesner, Anna Björk, Hanna-Mari Kivistö and Katja Mäkinen

This volume focuses on citizenship as a contested concept. We understand citizenship—as well as other key concepts in politics and political science— as objects of interpretative disputes both in their empirical reality and when they are used as analytical categories. This theoretical and methodological perspective on concepts challenges the common understanding and usage of concepts in political science in general, and in comparative politics in particular.

A widely shared understanding in political science is that concepts serve as our tools, or lenses, with which we analyse reality. This is why it is important to carefully reflect on the concepts used. The way we choose and interpret a concept also shapes the lens with which we analyse reality—it shapes our angle, our way of analysis and our research design. The character and properties of the lenses and tools we use affect the way we obtain different views on reality and they can change our analytical results.

To carefully reflect upon a concept is especially important where it is the basis for the comparative method of analysis. This is why a number of renowned comparativists such as Giovanni Sartori (1970) or Philippe Schmitter (2017) have underlined that it is crucial to be precise and reflected in defining and operationalising the research concepts. In a positivist approach, which is not infrequent in comparative politics, a concept then is understood as something that just needs to be defined and operationalised, in order to measure something on this basis.

In this volume we argue contrary to such a positivist and essentialist view and suggest a reflexive and constructivist perspective on concepts instead. This opens up a broader perspective, related to an understanding of concepts that have been opened up in the introductory volume to the book series *Conceptualising Comparative Politics*, where Spanakos (2015, 10–11) argues that researchers can use concepts as lenses, scripts and building blocks in comparative politics. As stated above, concepts are often used as lenses, which affect how things are seen and also make phenomena visible that might not be recognised otherwise. When used as building blocks, concepts serve as tools for categorising the

2 Claudia Wiesner et al.

phenomena under analysis. Concepts can also be understood as scripts, which emphasise the ambiguity, contradiction and change inherent in concepts. Sharing particularly the idea of concepts as scripts, we argue that a concept such as citizenship does not have one single meaning, let alone an essential meaning. Rather, it should be regarded as being socially constructed and used in a reflexive way.

This also means—and it is one of our key points—that a concept is not only a tool for analysis, but can also become an object of political controversy and struggle *itself*. The approach we propose hence does not only entail to reflect upon the usage and understanding of concepts as research instruments and categories of analysis. We also take concepts themselves as research objects and study how they are socially constructed by various actors. Usages, meanings and interpretations of concepts come into focus: how are concepts used in arguments and what is done with and through them? The approach suggested, then, is based on understanding linguistic activity as political activity and vice versa. Therefore, in this book, we analyse citizenship as a concept that is subject to political dispute. The policies related to citizenship, or the political reality, and the political practices that are tied to the concept, vary in different contexts and circumstances, and they are topics of political conflict.

In sum, we are not only interested in citizenship as an analytical lens, a script and a building block of comparative studies, but also as a historical, changing, contested and controversial political concept. We explore how it is constructed through the usages of the concept in various theories, debates and practices.

The Contestedness of Concepts: A Reflexive Approach

We argue that it is important for the usage of concepts in the social sciences and comparative politics in general to study concepts such as citizenship in their contestedness and their various meanings. To regard concepts in terms of their changing character, and also their historicity, entails a reflected and reflexive usage of concepts as categories. This raises a number of crucial points regarding the usage of concepts in the social and political sciences in general that we want to elaborate on with this contribution.

In political science, the most common understanding of concepts is as analytical categories. While we do not share Sartori's (1970, 60) view that a concept can easily be equated with a variable, we agree with him in that concepts serving as analytical categories all too often are not reflected before they are being used:

> Traditional, or the more traditional, type of Political Science inherited a vast array of concepts which had been previously defined and refined—for better and for worse—by generations of philosophers

Introduction: Shaping Citizenship 3

and political theorists. To some extent, therefore, the traditional political scientist could afford to be an "unconscious thinker"—the thinking had already been done for him.

(Sartori 1970, 1033–1034)

Extending Sartori's point further, we regard concepts as being always contingent and controversial in their use, meaning, content, range of reference, normative colour or tone. This goes for both the academic usage of concepts and the everyday language. As mentioned above, there are no essential or exclusive meanings of concepts, but only different potential understandings and usages. It is, therefore, possible to use specific definitions of a concept for analytical purposes, but this means having to choose one meaning of a concept out of a potentially plural set.

We propose discussing concepts in a reflexive, anti-essentialist and constructivist perspective: this perspective allows for the *exploration of potential alternative interpretations of concepts*—such as citizenship and its dimensions in this volume—that could also be used or that have been used. Furthermore, this approach is particularly suited to exploring how a concept is, and has been, defined and redefined, used and constructed—it allows us to analyse the *politics of a concept*. Hence it becomes possible to recognise also less evident power relations, political agencies and loci for politics that are linked to a concept in both theory and practice. Our reflexive and constructivist approach is elaborated in the chapters as a way of analysing, problematising and politicising concepts, which makes the book an important contribution to the field of conceptual studies in political science and comparative politics.

With this perspective, our aim is moreover to take part in the academic debate in two more respects. The book both contributes to the tradition of citizenship studies by analysing the politics of the concept of citizenship through an approach that focuses on the contestedness of concepts and, vice versa, on the tradition of conceptual studies and conceptual history through a conceptual historical exercise focusing on citizenship.

The Reflexive and Constructivist Approach to Concepts: Background

The theoretical and methodological perspective of the book in which concepts are seen as reflexive and socially constructed is inspired by the approach of conceptual history or *Begriffsgeschichte*. This perspective guides us to pay attention precisely to changes and disputes and diverse interpretations, meanings and usages of key political concepts (see Fernández Sebastián 2011 for a recent overview). So far, this approach has not often been applied to the concept of citizenship (for exceptions, see Koselleck 2006; Magnette 2005; Pocock 1998; Skinner 1993).

4   *Claudia Wiesner et al.*

The chapters of the book each apply, in their own ways, heuristic ideas developed in the field of conceptual history.

The field of conceptual history has developed in different strands of thought in political theory and history, namely those around Reinhart Koselleck, on the one hand, and Quentin Skinner, on the other. Quentin Skinner, a British intellectual historian and political theorist, concentrates on what he and others have called a *rhetorical perspective* on conceptual change (Palonen 2003; Skinner 2002a, 179, 182). He insists that language always has two dimensions that must be examined: meaning and linguistic action (Skinner 2002b, 3). For Skinner, concepts are tools in political debates and also tools for viewing and conceptualising reality:

> I wanted to treat the understanding of concepts as always, in part, a matter of understanding what can be done with them in argument. [. . .] In announcing this belief I declared my allegiance to one particular tradition of twentieth-century social thought. [. . .] It is characterized by the belief that our concepts not only alter over time, but are incapable of providing us with anything more than a series of changing perspectives on the world in which we live and have our being. Our concepts form part of what we bring to the world in our efforts to understand it. The shifting conceptualisations to which this process gives rise constitute the very stuff of ideological debate, so that it makes no more sense to regret than to deny that such conceptual changes continually take place.
>
> (Skinner 1999, 62)

In his work, Skinner mainly applied this perspective to analyses of texts in political theory, arguing that theorists always take part in political controversies with their texts and that, hence, they have to refer to the background of the value systems, beliefs and dominant ideas of their time (Skinner 2002c).

Another key strand in conceptual history is offered by Reinhart Koselleck, a German historian, and the other editors of the first major work of conceptual history, *Geschichtliche Grundbegriffe* (*GG, Basic Concepts in History*). They wanted to grasp the interrelations of social and political changes and the meanings attributed to key concepts which were both brought about by and encouraging the development of a modern nation state in Germany. This strand can be termed the *temporal perspective* on conceptual change.

The GG team famously termed the relevant time period *Sattelzeit* (*saddle period*; Koselleck 1967, 82) because they argued that the old world broke down and a new world developed (in the German case between 1750 and 1850, following the GG authors). They wanted to understand this process by grasping its mental and linguistic conceptualisation, and hence by analysing the key concepts that preceded, described and

Introduction: Shaping Citizenship   5

followed the changes under way (Koselleck 1967, 81). Using a concept in this context always means to refer to previous and more historical layers of meaning that have been attached to the concept as well.

Following a broadly Koselleckian line, several teams have been studying the conceptual histories of other nation states. These examples include France (Reichardt 1985–1996), Finland (Hyvärinen et al. 2003) and the Netherlands (Tilmans 2012). Furthermore, a project which attempts a European overview has recently been undertaken (European Conceptual History Project 2012) and the first volume on "Parliamentarism" has just been published (Ihalainen, Ilie and Palonen 2016).

What has just been said about rhetorical and temporal perspectives to conceptual change does not imply a clear-cut division. Rather, we suggest that the two approaches can be integrated (Palonen 2004; Richter 1995), as they open up a broad horizon of analytical and interpretative perspectives on conceptual change (Palonen 2004, 13). The rhetorical perspective concentrates rather on short-term processes, rhetorical and contextual studies, and the role of key actors, thus concerning the micro-aspects of conceptual change. The temporal perspective, on the other hand, is focused on mid-term and long-term processes and temporal and structural aspects of conceptual change and, hence, the macro-aspects. Both strands emphasise the importance of context: as the concepts are always fought over, debated and interpreted differently, they must be analysed against their specific intellectual and historical background (Skinner 2002a; Koselleck 1996; Palonen 1997).

Today, research based on the conceptual historical approach has not only become increasingly common, but also pluridisciplinary. An international research network on conceptual history began to develop around the History of Political and Social Concepts Group (since 2012 History of Concepts Group), founded in 1998 by Melvin Richter and Kari Palonen (see Palonen 2005). In 2015, a Standing Group on "Political Concepts" was set up in the European Consortium of Political Research (ECPR), chaired by Claudia Wiesner and Kari Palonen, and the approach was thus also established in political science. Several chapters in this volume originated in the sections organised by the Standing Group in the recent ECPR General Conferences.

The Added Value of Our Reflexive and Constructivist Approach to Concepts

We argue that to apply the resources of the conceptual-historical approach in political science and its usage of concepts can be especially fruitful for a number of reasons.

First, the perspective of conceptual history *focuses on the interrelations of political, institutional and social changes in the material world, and changes in the meaning of concepts* (Ball and Pocock 1988;

6 *Claudia Wiesner et al.*

Koselleck 1996, 65; Palonen 1997, 64; Skinner 1999, 60). Concepts can be seen as nodal points of these changes, because they both influence and indicate institutional, political and social changes. Concepts serve as pivots, or factors, and indicators (Koselleck 1996, 61–62) for controversies, conflicts and changes under way in material, social and political reality. In that context, changed interpretations of key concepts are both reflecting and encouraging political, social and value changes. The related controversies are, hence, situated at the intersection of empirical changes and changes of meaning of concepts (Koselleck 1996, 61, 65), both influencing the changes in question before they occur as well as possibly legitimising them afterwards (Skinner 2002c; Koselleck 1967). Conceptual history offers a methodology that was explicitly designed for studying the conceptual consequences of the establishment of new political spaces (Koselleck 1967, 81).

Second, *conceptual history as a theoretical and methodological approach explicitly focuses on the linguistic activities* that occur in processes of social, institutional and political changes in the material world. It highlights the debates, conflicts and differences that are related to these changes, and the ways they are driven by the respective actors and their interests, using specific arguments and rhetorical moves (Skinner 2002a; Koselleck 1996; Palonen 1997).

Third, this view *is a fruitful frame for analysing* how the legitimacy of ideas and institutions can be constructed, as it is through concepts that meaning is associated to a certain state, or a citizenship (Skinner 1999, 66–67).

Fourth, conceptual history offers heuristic tools for analysing how institutional and conceptual change are related in different patterns and ways. A concrete example is provided by Koselleck (2006, 62) and Schulz (1979), who distinguish four possible interrelations between institutional and conceptual changes: (1) Both political, institutional and social reality and the meaning of the respective concepts stay the same (i.e., no change). (2) There is change of political, institutional and social reality before or without conceptual change. (3) There is conceptual change before change of political, institutional and social reality: this case mainly occurs when concepts are invented with the purpose of transporting a certain meaning, or to create legitimacy. Conceptual innovation is often shaped by key actors, "innovating ideologists" (Skinner 2002b, 148) aiming to create positive expectations with regard to future developments (*Vorgriffe*, Koselleck 1997). 4) Political, institutional and social reality and concepts can go in opposite directions: new concepts are coined but they are not (yet) related to reality, or reality changes and old concepts no longer fit.

Importantly, the relation between institutional and conceptual change does not imply causal relation, but mainly a temporal one: it allows for a distinction to be made as to whether a concept was first invented or changed or institutions changed first and the conceptualisation followed.

Introduction: Shaping Citizenship 7

Therefore, the interrelation between conceptual and institutional change can be of a different character. It can be direct, when a concept is invented and then put into practice; it can be mediated, when concepts are factors of change or influence institutional change; and it can be indirect, when conceptual change indicates institutional changes. But it is difficult to fix the moment or the amount of change that marks that a "change" has indeed occurred. Interpretative techniques only provide the means to study dominant interpretations as well as changes in the institutional practice, but they do not allow for measurement of whether and to what degree a conceptual change is, e.g., supported by the citizens. A way to close that gap can be to use micro-data (see Zvereva 2014 for an exemplary study). Finally, in addition to the types of temporal interrelations between institutional and conceptual change, different directions of the interrelations between conceptual and material world changes can be distinguished: top-down, bottom-up and sideways.

In sum, the added value of the reflexive perspective on concepts we suggest is that it not only allows us to reflect on the conceptual resources and lenses that we employ in our analyses, but it also offers us the theoretical and methodological background and the heuristic tools for systematically tracing and using the different understandings of a concept in a research design, in political theory, and as an object of political controversy. Thus, the approach systematically opens up a panorama of different possibilities of understanding a concept, to see how a concept is understood and interpreted in various ways in theory and practice, and to study how it is contested and controversial in both. This also includes the historical usages of a concept—Quentin Skinner (2009) in this context termed the notion of "genealogy" of a concept. To acknowledge that there is a huge treasure of different possible understandings of a concept helps to sharpen or change our analytical lenses, and also to adapt them to new realities. The chapters of the book will each apply parts of this methodological and heuristic toolkit that had just been described.

Dimensions of Citizenship as Sites for Controversy

Citizenship is one of these ever-contested concepts. During the centuries, definitions and criteria of citizenship have been contested both in political theory, and in political and social practice (e.g., Clarke et al. 2014). If citizenship is thus ever-contested, it may seem difficult to pinpoint exactly what is left to mark it out, except for the fact that it defines the relation between a citizen and a polity. More concretely: if there are so many different understandings, controversies and contestations, is there anything left that conceptions of citizenship have in common?

In both theory and practice of citizenship in Western Europe, there are arguably four dimensions that shape most conceptions of citizenship:

8   *Claudia Wiesner et al.*

access, rights, duties and the active content of citizenship, which in the following we term "political activity". The four dimensions are covered by most national concepts of citizenship which define conditions of *access* (i.e., mostly nationality rules and the related laws); the legal consequences of citizenship in the sense of a citizen's *rights* and a citizen's *duties*; and how citizen's *political activity* is carried out.

These four dimensions, then, are also at the core of studying citizenship in comparative politics, as they have manifold practical and normative implications for shaping and realising the relationship between citizens and a polity. The dimensions are also relevant for analysing the changes and struggles around the concept of citizenship as they have been the classical foci of conceptual controversies. The chapters in this volume will each take up one or more dimensions.

The dimension of *access* to citizenship is key to the whole concept (Brubaker 1994; Gosewinkel 2001). Most of the common interpretations of citizenship agree that it defines the *demos* (or the democratic subject, or the sovereign) in a polity, drawing a border with regard to who is a citizen and who is not. Access to citizenship and the related rights is usually formalised in nationality laws. Access criteria also entail demarcating between "us and them", concerning both citizens and non-citizens, and referring to the normativity and legitimation of political and cultural ideals behind them. Thus, citizenship is also governance of the population through categorisation, exclusion and inclusion (see Ilyin in this volume).

The definitions of who should be considered a full citizen have changed over the centuries in the history of democratisation and democratic theory: in antiquity, only a small group of wealthy men were entitled to citizenship. Women and unfree men were excluded until the 20th century in most Western representative democracies (see in detail Wiesner 2007). These exclusions became foci of political struggle: Key conflicts turned around the inclusion of women and foreigners in a formally male-oriented concept of citizenship that was related to different ideas of a nation (see, e.g., Gosewinkel 2001 for a detailed study of the German case). Such struggles drove the development of citizenship while nation states developed into representative democracies over a long period (see, e.g., Weber 1979; Marshall 1950).

In today's reality, nationality laws define access to nation state citizenship. Even in the European Union it is the sole access criterion to Union citizenship to be a member state national, as there is no EU nationality. National regulations range from *ius sanguinis*, conceptualised around an ethnic concept of nationality, to *ius soli*, related to a political concept of nationality. Naturalisation has raised political debates in most representative democracies in recent years. One outcome has been the growing number of integration courses and tests for immigrants which have been introduced all over Europe within the past ten years (see Björk in this volume).

Introduction: Shaping Citizenship   9

Rights linked to citizenship have been developing—mainly due to conflicts and struggles over an extension of democratic and citizenship rights—in relation to and during the processes of democratisation, and especially the establishment of representative democracy. A classical distinction made by T. H. Marshall (1950) differentiates between three types of rights: freedom rights, political rights such as the right to elect and to be elected, and social rights. We suggest expanding the list to include rights that belong to the next generation after Marshall, *cultural rights* (see, e.g., Kymlicka 2002; Young 1990) and also a *right to protection through the state* (internal security), which can be regarded as one of the oldest rights of citizenship, although omitted by Marshall (Wiesner and Björk 2014).

Marshall's categories are both broadly used by social scientists as well as critiqued by them (see Turner 1997 for an overview) because his division relies on 1940s Western nation states and employs their norms in terms of gender and ethnicity. However, Marshall emphasises several important points: citizenship rights are multi-dimensional, they are political constructions, and they are intermediate outcomes of historical processes, conflicts and practices (on these aspects see Kivistö; Nielsen; Nyyssönen and Metsälä; and Wiesner in this volume). Moreover, citizenship rights are not uniform and they refer to different domains of an individual's relation to a polity (see Lillie and Wagner, and Wiesner in this volume).

Over the course of centuries and up until the present day, therefore, the widening of citizenship rights has been related to significant political controversy, exemplified among others by the fight for women's suffrage and the feminist movement, as well as in the civil rights movement. Current debates on these issues include the claim to rights by non-citizens, or the recognition of particular rights (see Björk; Kivistö; Nielsen; and Valkonen and Valkonen in this volume), as do new theoretical conceptions of what ensues from the right to political activity (see García-Guitián and Gil in this volume).

Citizen's *duties*, such as the duty to go to school, to do military service, or to pay taxes, are the third conceptual dimension classically associated with citizenship in representative democracies (Brubaker 1994; Weber 1979; Gosewinkel 2001). Both military service and schooling have been important for developing the figure of the loyal citizen, decisive for the ideal of nation states (Brubaker 1994; Weber 1979), and taxation constitutes the basis for modern welfare systems. Nevertheless, the duties pertaining to citizenship have been seldom studied, although this topic seems to be on the rise in current political theory (see García-Guitián and Gil in this volume).

Finally, *political activity* refers to the question of *what the demos does*, and includes a variety of activities from participation in elections to political protest. In contemporary democratic theory, the catchword

10   *Claudia Wiesner et al.*

of "participatory turn" has become one of the new key terms, as the forms of participation are constantly developing (see García-Guitián; Gil; Lietzmann; and Mäkinen in this volume) through new technologies and social engagements, as well as new international institutions and supra-nationalisation.

As such, citizenship in all its dimensions is never neutral, but positioned. Citizenship intersects with various factors and various types of belonging, such as class, ethnicity, indigeneity, gender and age (Yuval-Davis 2003; Yuval-Davis 2011). These aspects all lead to the overarching area of questions about diversity, difference, and recognition (Bauböck 2008; Kraus 2008; Parekh 2006; Taylor 1994; Tully 1995). Diversified identifications may serve as a base for political action (Connolly 1992; Isin and Wood 1999; Parekh 2008). Thus citizenship can be seen as a relational "act", also involving statelessness and non-citizenship, rather than as a fixed structure (Clarke et al. 2014; Isin and Nielsen 2008). The chapters of the book will discuss questions and situations where different kinds of belonging intersect with citizenship, with regard to migrants (Björk; Kivistö; Lillie and Wagner; Nielsen), ethnic minorities (Valkonen and Valkonen) and class (Lillie and Wagner). New constellations of citizenship set old conceptions and categories in motion, and into more diversified frameworks. Changes in the national and international setting for citizenship, such as European integration, regionalism, globalisation and increasing mobility, have been recognised by several scholars (Bellamy and Warleigh 1998; Ibid. 2001; Benhabib 2006; Soysal 1996; Delanty 2002; Isin and Turner 2002; Joppke 2010), but thus far, an explicit account of a conceptual analysis remains to be undertaken.

Citizenship as a Contested Concept: Case Selection and the Contents of the Book

As has been said, citizenship is a key category in the political and social sciences in general and in comparative politics in particular in numerous respects. The cases of the book are selected in such a way that they provide crucial and illustrative examples as according to where the debate on the concept of citizenship currently stands (a) in political theory, (b) regarding real-life debates around citizenship and (c) regarding changes in current citizenship practices and policies.

The book's regional focus is set on Europe, where many crucial developments of modern Western citizenship took place: it was in Europe where the ancient *poleis* have been situated, and where subjects successively developed into citizens. In Europe a "citizenship acquis" developed that became central for a generalised understanding of citizenship, and it was also in Europe that many of the battles over inclusion and exclusion regarding citizenship have been fought. Hence, conceptual changes and conflicts around citizenship have been a central issue in the political and

Introduction: Shaping Citizenship 11

conceptual history of the democratisation of European nation states. A recent conceptual innovation in Europe is citizenship of the European Union, and at present, citizenship is also reinterpreted in the context of migration and globalisation.

For this book, therefore, we have selected studies which illustrate and analyse these changes. The cases focus on representation and participation, migration and mobility, as well as transnational forms of citizenship. These three topics are central in current academic research and theorisation regarding citizenship, but also in political debates and practices.

Citizenship is a core concept for conceptualising democracy: in democratic nation states, citizenship relates closely to the democratic subject, the *demos*, or the sovereign in a legal and political sense. As it defines the demos, it also predestines who may participate in elections or political parties and organisations and, thus, conceptualising citizenship is essential in the measurement of the quality of democracy or the comparative analysis of welfare states. Citizenship development also indicates successes in democratisation as the admission of new population groups to full citizenship rights and political participation is a classical indicator here (see Dahl 1971). In the current "participation-boom" participation is given new and increasingly diverse interpretations. Its ongoing, both qualitative and quantitative, changes regard forms, channels and effects of participation as well as supranational contexts of participation, and they raise questions on representation: all forms of participation are not automatically representative, which has important implications on democracy. Participation and its connections to citizenship are discussed in this volume by García-Guitián. Electoral participation is the topic of the chapters by Gil and Nyyssönen and Metsälä, and participatory governance is discussed by Mäkinen. Lietzmann specifically addresses representation.

In today's Europe, citizenship is increasingly debated in the context of migration and mobility. There are heated political debates about the real-life implications of migration to citizenship, and academic research focuses on how different forms of migration and mobility diversify the conceptions of citizenship. The chapters by Björk, Kivistö and Nielsen discuss how citizenship is shaped in different ways in the context of immigration, refugees, asylum and naturalisation. Through boundaries drawn in these contexts, new categories regarding citizenship are created, such as non-citizens, irregular migrants or permanent residents. Paying attention to those excluded or marginalised from (full) citizenship increases our understanding of citizenship and the demarcations it includes.

Citizenship is more and more discussed in contexts that transcend nation states. Multilevel and complex governance and many other international and subnational transformation processes—such as globalisation, regionalism, localisation, European integration, migration and the changing significance of nation states, all of which are also core questions in comparative politics—have transformed the contexts of citizenship and

12   *Claudia Wiesner et al.*

the concept itself. Citizenship has been both down-scaled and up-scaled; we talk about local citizenship, global citizenship and multilayered or multilevel citizenship, for instance. Citizenship may hence be attached to various territorial and administrative layers simultaneously. Therefore, some of the cases in this volume indicate how citizenship is practised beyond the nation state. The chapter by Nyyssönen and Metsälä focuses on voting practices of dual citizens across state borders. Indigenous citizenship of the Sámi people living in the area of several states is analysed in the chapter by Valkonen and Valkonen.

One of the new frameworks of citizenship is the European Union. At present, all nationals of one of the member states are also "Union Citizens", but there are ongoing debates related to the rights and rights claims of non-EU citizens regarding what kind of positive rights "third country nationals" should have in the EU (Bauböck 2006; Kostakopoulou 2002; Maas 2008; Rigo 2009; Vink 2005). The Europeanisation of citizenship challenges the national concepts of citizenship and the practices of citizenship in the member states (Wiesner 2007). It also offers new territorial and administrative layers to which formal definitions of citizenship and citizens' practical experiences of rights and participation, as well as individual identifications, can be attached. Transnational forms of citizenship in the context of the European Union are discussed in the chapters by Wiesner, Lillie and Wagner and Mäkinen. These chapters show how mobility in the EU context can have most varied implications for different people in terms of citizenship and hence for the concept of citizenship.

Each chapter thus approaches citizenship in a specific context. The reflexive approach to concepts requires sensitivity towards these specific contexts and their languages which often means concentrating on one demonstrative case in a single study. The approach nevertheless is inherently comparative since it focuses on similarities, novelties or commonalities of each of the cases, as well as their histories. It is then the common analytical lens that will bring the specialised analyses together: rather than exercising a more traditional comparative method of discussing two or more cases together with shared variables, the different aspects of citizenship will be studied comparatively through the reflective approach to concepts and the heuristic tools that were just presented. The point is to identify links and differences in usage as well as continuities and changes in the conceptual development between the cases, in a way that allows a comparative reading of the different cases, materials and contexts. The composition of the book moreover opens a comparative perspective insofar as it explicitly combines national level analyses with theoretical and supranational insights.

The politics of the concept of citizenship, hence, in this book are explored by studying how the concept of citizenship is used and shaped

Introduction: Shaping Citizenship 13

by, and through, theories, debates and practices. Access, rights, duties and political participation in this context have a crosscutting function in the structure of the book. They are to be interpreted as both heuristic dimensions of the concept of citizenship and as foci of the controversies in theory, debate and practice.

The *theory* section, relating to normative ideas on what citizenship in representative democracy should be, will show that the concept is contested in itself, as are the areas that are thought to be relevant. The contributions focus on the conceptual history of citizenship and its link to democracy, participation and representation.

The chapters analysing *debates* on citizenship examine current political debates and struggles over the concept of citizenship in different arenas and show how new questions have come into focus. They study parliamentary, political and mediated debates on what should be happening in citizenship policies. Special attention is given to the margins of citizenship, i.e., on the inclusions and exclusions of citizenship and the conditions of access. The chapters thus show that concepts have a function in political real-life, and that the debates around interpretations of concepts center on both empirical realities of a concept and normative ideas about what the reality should be.

The section discussing *practices*, finally, will show that empirical reality sometimes challenges mainstream interpretations of concepts. It underlines that we need to rethink our analytical categories in order to grasp these changes. A special emphasis is put on a new political space, the European Union, and the question of how new practices regarding mobility, labour and participatory governance interact with new and established usages and meanings of the concept of citizenship.

Acknowledgement

The book has been edited with the support of the following research projects: "Legitimation of European cultural heritage and the dynamics of identity politics in the EU" (EUROHERIT), funded by the European Research Council (grant number 636177); the Finnish Distinguished Professorship Project "Transformations of Concepts and Institutions in the European Polity" (TRACE), funded by the Academy of Finland; and "Politics of human rights: conceptual and rhetorical reading of the post-war debates", funded by the KONE Foundation.

References

Ball, Terence, and John Pocock, ed. 1988. *Conceptual Change and the Constitution*. Lawrence: University Press of Kansas.
Bauböck, Rainer, ed. 2006. *Migration and Citizenship: Legal Status, Rights and Political Participation*. Amsterdam: Amsterdam University Press.

14 *Claudia Wiesner et al.*

———. 2008. "Beyond Culturalism and Statism: Liberal Responses to Diversity." *Eurosphere Working Paper Series.* Online working paper no. 06.

Bellamy, Richard, and Alex Warleigh. 1998. "From an Ethics of Integration to an Ethics of Participation: Citizenship and the Future of the European Union." *Millennium* 27:447–470.

———. 2001. "Introduction: The Puzzle of EU Citizenship." In *Citizenship and Governance in the European Union,* edited by Richard Bellamy and Alex Warleigh, 3–18. London & New York: Continuum.

Benhabib, Seyla. 2006. *Another Cosmopolitanism.* Oxford & New York: Oxford University Press.

Brubaker, Rogers. 1994. *Staats-Bürger: Deutschland und Frankreich im historischen Vergleich.* Hamburg: Junius.

Clarke, John, Kathleen Coll, Evelina Dagnino, and Catherine Neveu. 2014. *Disputing Citizenship.* Bristol: Policy Press.

Connolly, William E. 1992. *Identity/Difference: Democratic Negotiations of Political Paradox.* Ithaca & London: Cornell University Press.

Dahl, Robert A. 1971. *Polyarchy: Participation and Opposition.* New Haven, CT: Yale University Press.

Delanty, Gerard. [2000] 2002. *Citizenship in a Global Age: Society, Culture, Politics.* Buckingham & Philadelphia, PA: Open University Press.

European Conceptual History Project. 2012. "Mission Statement." www.javi erfsebastian.es/images/mission_statement_ECHP.pdf. Accessed September 21, 2012.

Fernández Sebastián, Javier, ed. 2011. *Political Concepts and Time: New Approaches to Conceptual History.* Santander, Spain: Cantabria University Press and McGraw-Hill.

Gosewinkel, Dieter. 2001. *Einbürgern und Ausschließen.* Göttingen: Vandenhoeck & Ruprecht.

Hyvärinen, Matti, Jussi Kurunmäki, Kari Palonen, Tuija Pulkkinen, and Henrik Stenius, ed. 2003. *Käsitteet liikkeessä: Suomen poliittisen kulttuurin käsitehistoria.* Tampere, Finland: Vastapaino.

Ihalainen, Pasi, Cornelia Ilie, and Kari Palonen, ed. 2016. *Parliament and Parlimentarism: A Comparative History of a European Concept.* New York: Berghahn Books.

Isin, Engin, and Greg Nielsen, ed. 2008. *Acts of Citizenship.* New York: Palgrave Macmillan.

Isin, Engin, and Brian S. Turner, ed. 2002. *Handbook of Citizenship Studies.* London: SAGE.

Isin, Engin, and Patricia Wood. 1999. *Citizenship and Identity.* London: SAGE.

Joppke, Christian. 2010. *Citizenship and Immigration.* Cambridge: Polity.

Koselleck, Reinhart. 1967. "Richtlinien für das Lexikon politisch-sozialer Begriffe der Neuzeit." *Archiv für Begriffsgeschichte* 11:81–99.

———. 1996. "A Response to a Comment on Geschichtliche Grundbegriffe." In *The Meaning of Historical Terms and Concepts: New Studies on Begriffsgeschichte,* edited by Hartmut Lehmann and Melvin Richter, 59–70. Washington, DC: German Historical Institute.

———. 1997. "The Temporalisation of Concepts." *Redescriptions (Finnish Yearbook of Political Thought)* 1(1):16–24.

Introduction: Shaping Citizenship 15

———. 2006. "Drei bürgerliche Welten. Zur vergleichenden Semantik der bürgerlichen Gesellschaft in Deutschland, Frankreich und England." In *Begriffsgeschichten: Studien zur Semantik und Pragmatik der politischen und sozialen Sprache*, 402–463. Frankfurt am Main: Suhrkamp.

Kostakopoulou, Theodora. 2002. "'Integrating' Non-EU Migrants in the European Union: Ambivalent Legacies and Mutating Paradigms." *Columbia Journal of European Law* 8:1–21.

Kraus, Peter. 2008. *Union of Diversity: Language, Identity and Polity Building.* New York: Cambridge University Press.

Kymlicka, Will. 2002. "Citizenship Theory." In *Contemporary Political Philosophy*, edited by Will Kymlicka, 284–326. Oxford & New York: Oxford University Press.

Maas, Willem. 2008. "Migrants, States, and EU Sitizenship's Unfulfilled Promise." *Citizenship Studies* 12:583–596.

Magnette, Paul. 2005. *Citizenship: The History of an Idea.* ECPR monographs. Colchester: ECPR.

Marshall, Thomas. 1950. *Citizenship and Social Class: And Other Essays.* Cambridge: Cambridge University Press.

Palonen, Kari. 1997. "An Application of Conceptual History to Itself: From Method to Theory in Reinhart Koselleck's Begriffsgeschichte." *Redescriptions (Finnish Yearbook of Political Thought)* 1:39–69.

———. 2003. *Quentin Skinner: History, Politics, Rhetoric.* Oxford: Polity.

———. 2004. *Die Entzauberung der Begriffe. Das Umschreiben der politischen Begriffe bei Quentin Skinner und Reinhart Koselleck.* Münster: LIT.

———. 2005. "The Politics of Conceptual History." *Contributions to the History of Concepts* 1:37–50.

Parekh, Bhikhu. [2000] 2006. *Rethinking Multiculturalism: Cultural Diversity and Political Theory.* Hampshire: Palgrave Macmillan.

———. 2008. *A New Politics of Identity: Political Principles for an Interdependent World.* Hampshire: Palgrave Macmillan.

Pocock, John. 1998. "The Ideal of Citizenship since Classical Times." In *The Citizenship Debates: A Reader*, edited by Gershon Shafir, 31–41. Minneapolis: University of Minnesota Press.

Reichardt, Rolf, ed. 1985–1996. *Handbuch politisch-sozialer Grundbegriffe in Frankreich 1680–1820.* München: Oldenbourg.

Richter, Melvin. 1995. *The History of Political and Social Concepts: A Critical Introduction.* New York: Oxford University Press.

Rigo, Enrica. 2009. *Rajojen Eurooppa* [*Europa di confine: trasformazioni della cittadinanza nell'Unione allargata*]. Finnish translation by Antti Paakkari, Taina Rajanti, Miika Saukkonen, and Eetu Viren. Helsinki: Like.

Sartori, Giovanni. 1970. "Concept Misformation in Comparative Politics." *American Political Science Review* LXIV:1033–1053.

Schmitter, Philippe C. 2017. "Politics as a Science, aka Politology." www.eui.eu/Documents/DepartmentsCentres/SPS/Profiles/Schmitter/Politics-as-a-science.pdf. Accessed July 3, 2017.

Schulz, Heiner. 1979. "Begriffsgeschichte und Argumentationsgeschichte." In *Historische Semantik und Begriffsgeschichte*, edited by Reinhart Koselleck, 43–74. Stuttgart: Klett-Cotta.

16 Claudia Wiesner et al.

Skinner, Quentin. 1993. "Two Concepts of Citizenship." *Tijdschrift voor Filosofie* 55:403–419.

———. 1999. "Rhetoric and Conceptual Change." *Redescriptions (Finnish Yearbook of Political Thought)* 60–73.

———. 2002a. "Retrospect: Studying Rhetoric and Conceptual Change." In *Visions of Politics. Vol. 1: Regarding Method*, 175–187. Cambridge: Cambridge University Press.

———. 2002b. "Introduction: Seeing Things Their Way." In *Visions of Politics. Vol. 1: Regarding Method*, 1–7. Cambridge: Cambridge University Press.

———. 2002c. "Moral Principles and Social Change." In *Visions of Politics. Vol. 1: Regarding Method*, 145–157. Cambridge: Cambridge University Press.

———. 2009. "A Genealogy of the Modern State: British Academy Lectures." *Proceedings of the British Academy* 162:325–370.

Soysal, Yasemin Nuhogly. 1996. "Changing Citizenship in Europe." In *Citizenship, Nationality and Migration in Europe*, edited by Mary Cesarani and David Fulbrook. London: Routledge.

Spanakos, Anthony Petros. 2015. "Conceptualising Comparative Politics: A Framework." In *Conceptualising Comparative Politics*, edited by Anthony Petros Spanakos and Francisco Panizza, 1–23. New York: Routledge.

Taylor, Charles. 1994. "The Politics of Recognition." In *Multiculturalism: Examining the Politics of Recognition*, edited by Amy Gutmann, 25–74. Princeton, NJ: Princeton University Press.

Tilmans, Karin. 2012. "Applying Begriffsgeschichte to Dutch History: Progress Report on the Dutch National Conceptual History Project." http://dare.uva.nl/document/43514. Accessed September 21, 2012.

Tully, James. 1995. *Strange Multiplicity: Constitutionalism in an Age of Diversity*. Cambridge: Cambridge University Press.

Turner, Bryan S. 1997. "Citizenship Studies: A General Theory." *Citizenship Studies* 1:5–18.

Vink, Maarten. 2005. *Limits of European Citizenship: European Integration and Domestic Immigration Policies*. Hampshire: Palgrave Macmillan.

Weber, Eugene. 1979. *Peasants into Frenchmen: Modernization of Rural France 1870–1914*. Palo Alto, CA: Stanford University Press.

Wiesner, Claudia. 2007. *Bürgerschaft und Demokratie in der EU*. Münster: LIT.

Wiesner, Claudia, and Anna Björk. 2014. "Introduction: Citizenship in Europe after World War II." *Contributions to the History of Concepts* 9:50–59.

Young, Iris M. 1990. *Justice and the Politics of Difference*. Princeton, NJ: Princeton University Press.

Yuval-Davis, Nira. 2003. "Citizenship, Territoriality and the Gendered Construction of Difference." In *State/Space: A Reader*, edited by Neil Brenner, Bob Jessop, Martin Jones, and Gordon Macleod, 309–325. Malden, MA: Blackwell.

———. 2011. *Power, Intersectionality and the Politics of Belonging*. FREIA Working Paper Series. Working paper no. 75. FREIA—Feminist Research Center in Aalborg. Denmark: Aalborg University.

Zvereva, Galina. 2014. "Shaping New Russian Identity: Discourses of 'Inclusion/ Exclusion in Europe'." In *The Meanings of Europe*, edited by Claudia Wiesner and Meike Schmidt-Gleim, 221–235. London: Routledge.

Part I

Theorising Citizenship

Anna Björk, Hanna-Mari Kivistö,
Katja Mäkinen and Claudia Wiesner

The following chapters discuss how contemporary challenges to citizenship have been taken on in political and democratic *theory*. There, the role of the citizen was to some extent forgotten for a longer period and explicitly reintroduced only in the 1960s following the discussion in T. H. Marshall (1950), after which the discussion on citizenship heated up in the 1980s and the 1990s (Magnette 2005, 1–2). As Skinner notes, "political life itself sets the problems for the political theorist" (Skinner 1978, Preface, xi), and so developments concerning citizenship also require further theoretical insights when, for example, migration and transnational democratic institutions set new questions for defining citizenship.

The chapters take up a number of current debates in political theory and their linkages to the concept of citizenship, discussing the dimensions of rights together with duties, and active participation (García-Guitián, Lietzmann and Gil). The framework for these contemporary theoretical insights is set by an introduction to the development of the concept of citizenship from a long-term perspective (Ilyin). Ilyin's chapter outlines tendencies of the history of the concept of citizenship and sketches the conceptual approaches to citizenship over time: Greek vs. Roman; civic vs. ethnic; liberal vs. republican. The core ideas of these traditions continue to both echo in the background of contemporary citizenship debates and are debated as prominent theories of citizenship.

Following Ilyin's analysis of historical dichotomies, García-Guitián, Lietzmann and Gil discuss the impact of political theory for the concept of citizenship from the contemporary perspective of democratic theory. Definitions and different interpretations of the (supposed) relationship between the citizen and the state vary in Western political and democratic thought. The main traditions—liberalism, republicanism and communitarianism—each approach citizenship differently, in regard to which aspects of it are emphasised. In liberalism, the key to citizenship is access to rights, after which the realisation of one's citizenship is in the hands of the individual. Republicanism, on the other hand, stresses active participation, whereas communitarian theories embrace the idea of belonging as a key aspect of citizenship.

18 *Anna Björk et al.*

The liberal view is the most common understanding of citizenship in Western countries today. Common for liberal theories is that the relationship between the citizen and the state in its ideal form is kept as light as possible (see, e.g., Schumpeter 1994 as a prominent case of a "thin" idea of democracy). Here, the possibility of practising citizenship remains with the individual and is ensured without any emphasis on citizen's duties. In liberal models, then, citizenship is primarily a legal status guaranteeing access to rights.

In the republican tradition, the focus is on active engagement with the polity's life as a key aspect to citizenship. Theories stemming from this tradition emphasise the need for participation almost to the point of obligation. The roots of the republican tradition are in the Athenian *polis*, where full citizens were both entitled and expected to participate in public life. Following this republican strand of ideas, Skinner (1993) has argued that active engagement by citizens in the polity is a prerequisite for maximising individual's liberty because an involved citizen is less likely to have their will subjected to the domination of others. In his essay "Two Concepts of Citizenship" (1993), he discusses the possibility of using the law as a tool for enforcing civic duties, which would mean using law as a means for producing liberty and not merely securing it. When it comes to putting such ideas into practice, it turns out that only a few democratic states in Europe have introduced political citizenship duties such as obligatory voting (with a few exceptions; see Malkopoulou 2015). Active participation, nevertheless, has become one of the dominant debating points in the contemporary discourses on citizenship.

In the communitarian tradition, citizens' ties to communities play a central role which raises the question of community, its definition and conditions. In this tradition, the concept of identity is linked with citizenship (e.g., Delanty 2002; Etzioni 1995; Walzer 1994 and 2005). "Identity" here refers to what is also called "group identities", as the communal ties often presuppose the notion of cultural and historical belongings. The question of community has been, and still is, one of the key features of debates concerning naturalisation.

These theories form the background against which to read contemporary debates in democratic theory and their links to the concept of citizenship. Again, Ilyin opens up the panorama by introducing a range of historical concepts of citizenship extending up to today's understanding of multiple citizenships. The basis is on prototypical distinctions that are related to the concept of citizenship, but Ilyin takes us a step further from the conventional canon when he discusses the logic of dichotomies and imaginaries that the historical concepts of citizenship hint at. The chapter gives examples of conceptual analysis at work: linking historical and contemporary sources, theoretical insights and common expressions with extensive meanings, it shows the interconnectedness of past and present interpretations of concepts.

Ilyin's outline of the historically constructed meanings of citizenship and its dimensions opens up the field and leads to the present-day examples of modern representative democratic systems, which have citizenship at their core and which are discussed in the remaining chapters by García-Guitián and Lietzmann. In these chapters, the conceptual approach is turned around: instead of having the concept of citizenship at the heart of their conceptual operations, the authors approach citizenship from the perspective of the key concept of representation, central to modern democratic theory. The same turn is taken in Gil's chapter, but, instead of the concept of representation, the focus of the chapter is on voting.

The focus of the chapters by García-Guitián, Lietzmann and Gil is hence on aspects that are currently crucial both in democratic theory and in politics: voting, participation and the crisis of democracy. They show that there are a number of issues under scrutiny during processes of change when representative democratic citizenship is theorised. The interpretations of participation, rights and representation show the complexity of the relations between political involvement, citizenship and democracy.

García-Guitián analyses how different modes of *political activity* imply different ideas of citizenship and different notions of democracy. She argues that the diversity of political behaviour among citizens supports a mode of theorising of citizen participation which differs from the idealised view of the active citizen and which can be conceived as a source of diverse and complementary (non-electoral) forms of political representation. She discusses the figure of a "good enough" citizen as a reaction to the contemporary cries for the crisis of representative democracy and the need for innovation. The debates about the ideal typical citizenship rewrite the concept from the perspective of participation, asking the important question of when a citizen is doing enough in terms of political activity—when he or she is being a "good enough" citizen.

In that context, García-Guitián criticises the sharp division between representative and participatory democracy common in modern democratic theory, and discusses the multiple changes in ways and degrees of citizen involvement and interest in politics. These changes have the potential to renew democracy and improve the deliberative character of democracies as well as transform representative democracies into participatory democracies. The idea is that the complex forms of citizen participation should be viewed as part of political representation. García-Guitián argues for a diversity of citizenship types: critical, even anti-establishment citizens are important for renewing democracy, yet they should not dominate. Rather, the new forms of participation are present along with the traditional ones (such as voting).

Lietzmann continues to discuss the possible crisis of representation. He, however, analyses the representative systems and their legitimacy by raising the issue of the symbolic dimension of the concept of representation.

20 *Anna Björk et al.*

Political representation is the primary way of linking citizens to parliaments and governments, where different ideas and arrangements formulate the relations between citizens and polities. Lietzmann asks whether current changes in the practice of political participation and representation really represent a "crisis", or rather, whether they lead to a claim for an icono-logic turn in democratic theory. The iconological perspective means that citizens are the main actors in the belief in, and the legitimacy of, political representation. According to Lietzmann, the crisis of legitimacy regarding the representative forms of democracy would benefit from a visual reading of the concept of representation in political theory. This is, he states, because the traditional concept of representation no longer fits the present social and political realities. On the other hand, whereas the old concepts of representation fail, new ones are opening up—such as the iconological concept of representation.

Finally, Gil also places representative democracy at the centre of his discussion of citizenship. His perspective on citizen participation is through voting, which he analyses from the point of view of abstention. This question of "abstaining citizenship" ties together the three dimensions of (voting) rights, duties and active participation. Gil argues that abstaining from voting should be taken seriously as a form of political action, at least potentially, and that as a conscious choice, refraining from voting should be interpreted as more than mere passivity. Rather, Gil argues that abstaining potentially serves as a means of exercising political power, even if it is an ambiguous move because it does not express clear political preferences. He criticizes both the claim that only qualified citizens should be allowed to vote and that those who are incompetent had a moral duty not to vote in order to avoid outcomes that have negative effects on others. His main example of such thinking is James Brennan, whose views Gil traces back to Mill's analyses of an ethics of voting. Gil, thus, problematises the concept of abstention through a reading of Brennan and Mill, providing an insight to the concept of citizenship through political philosophy.

New practices and modes of participation in decision-making in representative democracies, such as the deliberative mini-publics mentioned by Gil, or the participatory practices organised by administration, as discussed in the chapter by Mäkinen, construct new types of relations between citizens and polities and new ways of citizen involvement. Both types of participation contribute to diversifying the idea of citizenship and the citizens' relation to the polity, although sometimes the outcome is a limited degree of guided and organised participation. As mentioned above in the case of political activity discussed by García-Guitián, different ideas and forms of citizenship have different implications for democracy.

Finally, the chapters in the theory section also open a perspective onto the further chapters of the book: Ilyin discusses the dichotomies and logics which resonate with the divisions between citizens and non-citizens, thus echoing with the chapters authored by Björk, Kivistö and Nielsen. Furthermore, García-Guitián gives an introduction to the more empirical chapter about participation by Mäkinen, and Gil provides an introduction to the more empirical chapters about rights by Kivistö, Nielsen, Nyyssönen and Metsälä.

References

Delanty, Gerard. 2002. *Citizenship in a Global Age: Society, Culture, Politics.* Buckingham & Philadelphia, PA: Open University Press. Original 2000.

Etzioni, Amitai. 1995. *The Spirit of Community: Rights, Responsibilities and the Communitarian Agenda.* London: Fontana Press.

Magnette, Paul. 2005. *Citizenship: The History of an Idea.* ECPR monographs. Colchester: ECPR.

Malkopoulou, Anthoula. 2015. *The History of Compulsory Voting in Europe: Democracy's Duty?* New York: Routledge.

Marshall, Thomas. 1950. *Citizenship and Social Class: And Other Essays.* Cambridge: Cambridge University Press.

Schumpeter, Joseph A. 1994. *Capitalism, Socialism, Democracy.* Fourth edition. London: Routledge.

Skinner, Quentin. 1978. *The Foundations of Modern Political Thought I.* Cambridge: Cambridge University Press.

———. 1993. "Two Concepts of Citizenship." *Tijdschrift voor Filosofie* 55: 403–419.

Walzer, Michael. 1994. *Thick and Thin: Moral Argument at Home and Abroad.* Notre Dame, IN: University of Notre Dame Press.

———. 2005. *Politics and Passion: Toward a More Egalitarian Liberalism.* Hartford, CT: Yale University Press.

1 Prototype Citizenship
Evolving Concepts of Inclusion and Order

Mikhail Ilyin

The purpose of this chapter is to explore internal connections between various ways of conceptualizing citizenship. The domain of conceptualization is an interface between two alternatives—diverse terminological usage and consistent cognitive design—that ultimately match fundamental Fregean discrimination of *Bedeutung* (reference) and *Zinn* (sense). Overlapping areas expand with shuttle movements from an infinite plethora of citizenship-bounded phenomena (and respective terminological references) to their universal comprehension (cognitive schemata) and back. This chapter seeks to single out major field lines of reference/sense polarity as they are displayed in the conceptual history of citizenship and the models and usages of the concept of citizenship, as well as the conceptual developments linking models with their usage.

Specific vector field lines or strands match institutional and behavioural varieties of political and social association that in some ways correspond to, or concur with, citizenship. The central vector is that of a classical nation state citizenship. Parallel, or rather complementary, strands connect verbal practices, political institutions and cognitive designs typical for contemporary multiple citizenship, polis citizenship or more subtle varieties of association with empires, guilds, orders, tribes and other similar entities.

The chapter refers to selected cases of conceptual analyses and presents their outcomes. Reconstructions of respective cognitive schemata are crucial. Whereas their shared schematic denominator emerges as the ultimate cognitive scheme of inclusion/exclusion, in each case specific nuances are critically significant. Thus, distinctions of varieties of inclusion in terms of kinship, lineage, hospitality, blood oath, filiation and adoption, camaraderie, companionship, patrimonial inheritance—authentic or imaginary, actual participation, formal membership, affiliation, individual selection, belonging etc.—become analytically visible in each case of our conceptual histories.

Reconstruction of cognitive schemata rest on analysis of inner forms of selected usages. Typically, it reveals characteristic metaphors, their patterns and eventually etymons or primary mental representations.

24   *Mikhail Ilyin*

Etymological discussions help to decipher respective cognitive schemata. Such reconstructions are the ultimate results of this chapter's conceptual and cognitive analysis. It begins with a general overview of contemporary or historically recent verbal practices and terminological usages.

Current Usages

Just a glimpse at current usage of the term *citizenship* would allow one to say that the core meanings reflect legal aspects of personal membership in a nation state. This is overwhelmingly the case in current political science literature. It is also typical of everyday English language communication, although British legal discourse provides an array of terminological options. Depending on the context, the idea of nation state legal membership may be rendered in English as *subject* (British subject), or *national* (EU nationals) or *citizen*. There is a variety of legally fixed denominations like *British Citizens, British Overseas Territories Citizens, British Overseas Citizens, British Nationals, British subjects without citizenship* and even *British Protected Persons* among a few other legal terms.

This terminological core—reflecting legal aspects of personal membership in a nation state—is surrounded by the fuzzy bunches of meanings of belonging to a variety of groups. It is possible to speak of corporate, social, monastic, republican, imperial, liberal, democratic, fascist and all manner of other 'citizenships'. Metaphorical shifts of meanings may be concealed or overtly expressed but they are always in force and provide an assortment of conceptual foci expected to grasp very specific phenomena.

The term *citizen* has two major foci. A more evident one is linked with formal membership of the nation state whereas another is linked with social and cultural belonging to a city. The two cores are surrounded by a wide-ranging and lopsided area of expanding metaphorical usages. Its extent may range from *citizen of the Heavenly Jerusalem* to *citizen of the World*, or from *citizen of hope* to *citizen of despair*, or from *citizen of faith* to *citizens of disbelief* or even *citizen of hell*.

In many other languages, the situation looks fairly similar, particularly the Romance languages where the terms sound quite similar because of their Latin base: *civilitas* (qualities of a true Roman that distinguish him from a barbarian), *civitas* (civic community and civic qualities), *civis* (Roman citizen and particularly primary community member of Rome).

The common lexical core of the Romance languages and of the deeply Romanized English language share not only common roots but also the mutual conceptual history of citizenship. Although the word *citizen* was borrowed by English from French in the 14th century to name a city dweller, "it was only around the time of the French revolution that the word takes the meaning of belonging to a sovereign state" (Magnette 2005, 5).

Prototype Citizenship 25

The change is already noticeable in the 'Eastern wing' of Romano-Germanic Europe. Thus, the German terms for citizenship are *Staatsbürgerschaft, Bürgerschaft, Staatsangehörigkeit* with extra specific terms in Austrian and Swiss legal traditions. Respectively, the terms for a citizen are *Staatsangehöriger* along with *Bürger* and *Mitbürger* and until recently *Untertan*. But city-dwellers are called by an analogous but distinctly different term, that of *Stadtbürger*.

Moving further east and away from the primary domain of Roman Law we discover greater diversity. The Hungarian term for citizen, *polgár*, is a word borrowed from German. Hungarians borrowed the term in the 13th century from a Middle High German dialect where it sounded like *purgæer*. A similar loan can be found in Croatian. Citizen is called *pùrgar* (Cyrillic spelling *пургар*). The word *burgher* designated a citizen of Zagreb, whereas a common term for a city-dweller is *građanin*.

In other Slavic languages, respective terms vary and provide an assortment of rather specific derivations. The Russian term *гражданство* (grazhdanstvo) and *гражданин* (grazhdanin) derive from *grad*, city, whereas in Polish *obywatelstwo* and *obywatel* derive from the root meaning 'to live' and prefix 'close by, around'. Czech *občanství* and *občan* derive from the notion of community. In Ukrainian, the situation is similar. The terms *громадянство* and *громадянин* are derived from *громада*, a standard term for community. In Czech, however, the difference is quite evident. Whereas Czechs refer to something common, Ukrainians conceptualize community, *громада* (hromada), as something being great (*громадно*, hromadno), i.e., something greater than person. The Slovene term *državljanstvo* implies a link with a great power or originally with the idea 'holding together'.

The Finnish conceptual history of key political concepts was mapped by the *Käsitteet Liikkeessä* project (Hyvärinen et al. 2003). Finns readily linked the idea of citizen, *kansalainen*, and citizenship, *kansalaisuus*, with that of people, *kansa*. In the early 19th century, some Fennoman writers used the word *kansalainen* to differentiate a subject and 'a member of the people'. Other contemporary options for translation of the Latin *civis* are: *porvari* (bourgeois), *kunnastolainen* (member of municipality), *kansakuntalainen* (member of a nation), *maamies* (a countryman with agrarian connotations). Somewhat later, in the 1870s, *yhteiskuntalainen* (member of the society, *yhteiskunta*) was suggested, but none of those actually survived. A person who lives in a city is *kaupunkilainen*, referring to *kaupunki* (a city or a town).

The Estonian concept has nothing to do with either a city or people. It looks very unusual since it links *kodanik* (citizen) and *kodakondsus* (citizenship) with an archaic form of the word for building, *koda*. But the logic is clear. The property ownership (building) is an implied qualification for being a citizen first of a municipality and then of a country. *Kodakondus* is a status (with rights and duties) of those who possess

26   *Mikhail Ilyin*

property, 'building owners'. Estonians clearly differentiate citizens from city dwellers who are called *linlased* or *linnakodanikud* from *linn* (city).

Neighbouring Baltic people used the IE root *plh_1* related both to Greek πόλις and Indian Sanskrit पुर (pura). The root initially referred to a cliff, then to a stronghold, a fortification and a city. In Lithuanian and Latvian the respective terms are *pilis* (in Modern Lithuanian the borrowed Slavic term *miestas* is used) and *pils* (where the modern Latvian term is *pilsēta*). Corresponding terms for citizen and citizenship are *pilietis, pilietybė* (Lith.) and *pilsonis, pilsonība* (Latv.).

In sharp contrast, modern Greeks choose to 'forget' the classical terms πολίτης (citizen), and πολιτεία (things pertaining to polis, e.g., order, dignity or identity of polis) and use two terms for citizen, ιθαγενής and υπήκοος, and for citizenship, ιθαγένεια and υπηκοότητα. Whereas the words ιθαγενής and υπήκοος may be occasionally recorded in Modern Greek, the terms for citizenship were devised during the liberation struggle. First the term υπηκοότητα was introduced in 1831 as the equivalent of the term *citizenship*. Then the term ιθαγενεια was introduced in 1848 as the equivalent of the French term *nationalité*. Currently, the differences in connotations are very slight. In legal terms, they are perfect synonyms. The Ancient word δημος is the current term for a city or town. A city dweller is called δημότης, and municipal citizenship is called δημοτικότητα.

When we move further East to Turkey a new conceptual model is used. It is based on a word, *vatan*, borrowed from Arabic وطن meaning 'birthplace'. *Vatandaş* formerly meant a 'local person' until political reforms in the 1860s led to *vatan* being used as an equivalent for the French *patrie* and *vatandaş* for compatriot. It was only later that *vatan*, and its close synonyms *yurt* and *memleket*, received the new referent of 'the state' and the terms for citizen finally emerged: *vatandaş, yurttaş* or sometimes *yurtdaş* and only rarely *memleketdaş*. *Vatandaşlık* and *yurttaşlık* are the current legal terms for citizenship. City dweller is called *şehirli* or *kentli* from synonyms for a city (*şehir* and *kent*). In the Arab world the same word وطن (*vatan*) was used as a conceptual source for citizenship. The core meaning of the term for citizen (*muvatyn*) is a local person, fellow countryman, compatriot. Citizenship is *muvatana*.

The overview ends here on the Eastern fringes of Europe where common traditions of conceptual history citizenship—central for this book—start to fizzle out.

Cognitive Schemata, Prototypes and Invariants

Diversity seems to complicate our understanding of what a citizen is: "Is it possible to be citizens at all within polities which are still ghosts of premodern empires: the Commonwealth of Independent States, the United Kingdom, Japan, dare one say it, the People's Republic of China?" (Dunn 2005, no page).

Prototype Citizenship 27

The doubts look convincing only inasmuch as we tend to stick to a core schemata of conceptualization that the political science lingua franca and *Franglais plus* tradition impose upon us. A broader horizon may not only complicate but also liberate our thinking and vision, thus we should be able to adequately assess as many uses and misuses of these terms as possible along with their correspondence to citizenship-related phenomena.

Paul Magnette, who mostly sticks to *Franglais plus* mainstream, recognizes the universal implications of citizenship (Magnette 2005, 4). Suppose we choose to face the challenge outlined by Paul Magnette. Then, points of view and horizons of vision would multiply progressively. Is there any chance to withstand such snowballing? Yes, if we intellectually equip ourselves to make our units of investigation comparable. Comparative approaches and morphological methods come to our aid. They reduce the boundless plethora of usages and practices, ideas and mental entities, to comparable forms. With all their blurred overlapping and ambiguous variance, they nonetheless reveal their similarities: homology, homeology, homodynamy and other morphological properties. One can morphologically fix their overall configurations, internal setups and external frames. One can analytically shape their dynamics into divergence and convergence.

Morphological inquiry is as old as comparisons. It is our innate proficiency. However, morphology as a distinct branch of science emerged in 1790 when Goethe published his "Essay on Metamorphosis of Plants". In this celebrated oeuvre, he described *Urpflanze* (protoplants) as a kind procreative model, fundamental morphological universal for all and any plant. Later Goethe and his followers developed a far more abstract construct of *Urphänomen* (protophenomenon), or an ultimate abstract representation of phenomena.

Both Urpflanze and the ultimate cognitive scheme are purely theoretical generalizations. In actual research, genera and species, ideal types and concepts, replace abstractions. Moreover, each genus or type embraces further units providing their nested succession up to a single organism or word use.

Some species are more typical than others. Oak is a more typical tree than willow or baobab. A robin is a more typical bird than a penguin or ostrich. In other words, oaks and robins serve as prototypes of a large class of creatures (Roesch 1975). In a similar way, we may associate ancient polis citizenship with its Athenian precedent and modern citizenship with the French one. Conceptual historians focus on prototypes of citizenships when they study word uses.

It would not be an easy task to find a shared quality that underlies all the diversity of phenomena associated with citizenship. One can think of intellectual vehicles like belonging, inclusion or membership. They are universal, or at least widespread and recurrent. Paul Magnette has

28 *Mikhail Ilyin*

proposed the following: "Two contrasts form the continuous basis, and permanent structure, of citizenship. First of all: exclusion. [. . .] The second constant element of the concept of citizenship is legality" (Magnette 2005, 182). This 'contrast' implies exclusion and thus also inclusion. Using the notion of legality, the author, in my view, focuses on the acceptability or unacceptability of inclusion or exclusion and related practices and norms. In this sense, the 'contrast' could be better represented by the pair order and disorder.

To formalize Magnette's idea let us fix two 'contrasts' of inclusion/exclusion and order/disorder. These two conceptual instruments sound far less charged with nuances and undertones than citizenship, but with all their generalizing potential the proposed notions still have a specific semantic or connotative foci. One can try again to reduce their divergence and variance with a kind of 'lowest common denominator'. In my view, the best candidate would be the cognitive scheme embedded in orientation metaphor in/out or rather 'to be in'/'to be out' (Lakoff and Johnson 1980).

Specific modes of social authorization emerge and become ingrained at successive stages of social evolution. In his foreword, John Dunn asks a question, "What does citizenship really consists in?" (Magnette 2005). One answer may be: the order. Whereas inclusion may be primarily linked to the form of citizenship, it is the order that provides substance. Furthermore, the very question may be amended. What does citizenship really consist of? The overall fundamental order or cosmology of citizenship rests on three structural domains: (1) inside order and networks that structure it, (2) limits of order or boundaries between the inside networks and (3) outside disorder and agency destructive to internal networks and the entire order of citizenship.

The universal scheme of citizenship order can essentially be described as human conditions that match up dissent living with your own 'fellow citizens', whoever they me be—compatriots, kin, neighbours or members of some other community. Proto-Indo-European conceptualization of such human conditions is reconstructed as *priyo*. Its later derivatives are freedom, peace and friendship. It is opposed to active destructive agency of war and the inactive influence of need. This schematic opposition of human/inhuman works as the conceptual base of the order/disorder opposition. Inclusion works to safeguard essential human conditions of peace and freedom while inhuman influence over war and need is excluded. This pattern manifests in all citizenship-like phenomena.

The universal principle of inclusion/exclusion could produce a number of prototypes depending on the scope and media of inclusion, its agency and manner, as well as the character of the results achieved or pertaining order. Thus, scope and media are interrelated. The greater the scope of inclusion the more advanced the medium of communication it provides, ranging from oral speech to global electronic networks of communication.

Prototype Citizenship 29

The agency and manner of inclusion indicate who decides whom to include and what procedures are used, e.g., coercion or consent. The character of the established order may be centripetal or centrifugal, heterogeneous or homogeneous, egalitarian or stratified.

Clear-cut and simple inclusion is rare. Far more common are the intricate spin-off groups that coexist, intersect and even integrate with each other. Their prototypes are those of multiple inclusion. Some variants of inclusion are possible only with individuals and groups that have undergone primary inclusion at an earlier stage. Thus, building the polis or community implies primary inclusion of tribes, common-ancestry lineages (φ(ρ)ατρίαι) and extended families (γένη). Secondary inclusion in an existing polis is the artificial creation of pseudo-natural groups like deme or trittyes (τριττύες). Equally, inclusion in the nation state implies that you integrate people who are already members of estates, social orders, corporations, municipalities.

There is little doubt that today's modern European ideas of citizenship are the most advanced manifestation of a broader effort "to find the meaning of living in a community and to protect themselves from injustice" (Magnette 2005, 4). But we cannot and should not disregard the more general human endeavour to live together in peace, security and pursuit of happiness. A truly universal story of this quest is as long as the very timeline of social evolution, or some 15 hundred to 17 hundred human generations.

We cannot reconstruct and interpret all the phenomena of the entire 50 millennia of social evolution but we can carefully investigate those that are available in the background of overall social evolution. The simplest initial prototype is characterized by closed access and vocal communication restricted by the ability to hear and interact with each other. Primordial inclusion and order emerged some 15 hundred to 17 hundred generations before present (BP) with the so-called Great Leap Forward (Diamond 1999, 39) or the Upper Paleolithic Revolution. It was the focal period when steady long-term accumulation of knowledge and the interaction between skills and frames, resulted in a momentary interface that produced sophisticated enough human language along with cultural universals like burials, art, game playing, cooking, long-distance barter and exchange between groups, and probably humour. In short, the universals are described as behavioural Bs: blades, beads, burials, bone tool-making and beauty (Calvin 2004).

Those self-enclosed enclaves numbered a few dozen people and were maintained by their mode of biological reproduction inherited from pre-human primates. They also developed the first proto-human, and then increasingly human, social reproduction fashioned by immediate vocal interaction and a daily routine of playing procreation roles. Vocal speech and lineage were essential tools of communication and governance. Morphologically, the closed human communities were reproduced by the

30 Mikhail Ilyin

'blueprints' or memes of ancestral lore transmitted by oral narrative and familial rites. The participation of individual humans in their common customary routine would not even imply any distinction among rights and duties.

Initial patterns of inclusion and order are well entrenched in our current politics, which is little wonder as they have been practised for a thousand and a half generations without an alternative, and followed by another five hundred generations within overlapping orders of multiple inclusion. They are represented by a wide assortment of small-scale forms of inclusion and order, such as cliques, bus parties or even early citizen initiatives.

Demand for Novel Ways of Inclusion, Modes of Communication and Resultant Orders

Extending tribal, chiefdom communities and their alliances could not rely on the patterns of direct rule of kinship genes or even tribes. New and indirect ways of maintaining order were required. There was the need for something that was not immediate but stable, that would transcend everyday contextualized father–son transactions and turn them into structural relations of multitudes of fathers and sons. Such structural relations could be mediated by something that transcends contextual everyday relations and direct communication by a grand and transpersonal medium. Such a medium was common heritage or patrimonium of many generations transpersonalized by acting through the medium of miraculous agency such as Gods, Ancestors, Muse in a poetic and ritualized lore.

Common patrimonium was a thing that would involve generations and imply stability and the essential link between fathers and sons. It represented institutionalized links in the form of customs of maintaining depersonalized generational order and the agents that acted as mediators between the generations as well between the ruler(s) and the ruled.

The gradual development of homogeneous and egalitarian primitive bands into heterogeneous and stratified asymmetrical chiefdoms produced new options. Structural and morphological developments were triggered respectively by the need to maintain order when direct verbal communication—and to this effect, getting input in working out common goals—to give orders and check their implementation became highly problematic or even impossible. The authority was de facto structurally detached from the general populace and often dispersed over sizeable territories.

A morphological solution to the problem was quite self-explanatory and straightforward. It was the creation of a link or medium between the authority and the entire populace. Specifically, a patrimonial solution

Prototype Citizenship   31

for the problem of polity overextension reshaped tripartite division, as essential unity of the prevailing authority (quasi-patriarch, master of the household) and the entire populace (quasi-kinship, kinsfolk, domestics, householders) provided the linkage between them (quasi-household, its instrumental aspects and symbolic representations as common legacy). The last component worked as a crucial integrative device.

The prototype of patrimonial brotherhood did not replace the primordial one but supplemented and integrated it. It was a first instance of multiple inclusion and compound order. The further institutional innovations and arrangements followed this precedent.

Each of the structural units of patrimonial brotherhood—authority, medium and populace—actually utilized the primordial approach to inclusion. Further integration of patrimonial prototypes with more advanced and complex arrangements produced far more assorted and divergent patterns of organization. The patrimonial component in such cases served an important function to compensate the structural and managerial gaps that cropped up with political transformations and growth.

A number of historical types with distinct patrimonial input were described by Max Weber under the rubric of patrimonialism (Weber 2002). They include traditional patrimonialism (*Patrimonialismus*), sultanism (*Sultanismus*), estate domination (*ständische Herrschaft*), as well as the more recent Caesarismus (*Cäsarismus*), rule of officials (*Beamtenherrschaft*) and plebiscitary domination (*plebiszitäre Herrschaft*).

There is abundant literature on neo-patrimonialism. Views on the ability of patrimonial orders or rather the patrimonial component of complex orders to serve as a vehicle for modernization and even democratization are quite controversial. The majority of authors stress dysfunctionality of neo-patrimonialism. On the other hand, there are authors who recognize its functionality, particularly in the context of reforms. Christian von Soest, e.g., insists that some patrimonial regimes are fairly accountable to public opinion and promote efficiency reforms (Soest 2007). Furthermore, in his article "Can Neopatrimonialism Dissolve into Democracy?" Mamoudou Gazibo fairly convincingly showed that neopatrimonialism could fuse with democracy within hybrid regimes of 'new democracies' in the post-Communist space or 'third wave democracies' in Latin America (Gazibo 2012).

Polis Citizenship

Patrimonial brotherhood greatly augmented the growth of archaic societies which soon led to the onset of growth along two distinct tracks. One was further external broadening of patrimonial inclusion beyond old limitations into a greater scope of widespread despotic rule. Another was the internal concentration of overlapping inclusions within densely

32 Mikhail Ilyin

populated settlements. The former relied on centrifugal expansion. Another resorted to centripetal contraction. One produced a would-be subject of despotic (domestic) rule. The other led to the appearance of the citizen.

The first poleis surfaced with the Urban Revolution about 300 generations BP. They integrated assemblages of chiefdoms and tribal leagues with the help of the so-called co-habitation or synoikesis (συνοικησισ). This new system of synoikismos (συνοικισμός) was a response to the challenge of the gradual growth of populations and corresponding social networks and other structures. Up to this point, their enlargement threatened the limits of the closed primordial and even patrimonial systems. They continued to rest essentially on primary inclusion with minor divergences. The growth was outbound and uneasy external enclosures were highly problematic. With co-habitation, inclusion could turn both ways, outside and inside. Co-habitating chiefdoms and tribal leagues would partially reside within an urban settlement whereas their peripheral edges would cover the surrounding area.

There are historical records on the transformation of old primordial kinship into citizenship dating back to the reforms of Urukagina, Lagash and Solon. When Solon launched his campaign for *seisachtheia* (σεισάχθεια) reforms he expressed concern over the violation of old traditions of kinship and brotherhood. Many free Athenians became *hektemoroi* (ηεκτεμοροι), i.e., serfs who cultivated what used to be their own land and gave one sixth of the produce to their creditors.

All fellow city dwellers are a kind of 'kin' linked not by blood but by political (polis-based) bonds which, nonetheless, led to the development of the concept of citizenship.

The creation of 'artificial' kinship/citizenship and further 'artificial' divisions into demes and tritties actually opened up the possibilities for access to those units. Previous units were closed by lineage, both actual and imaginary. Now new units could be created by political decision that also set up procedures of inclusion.

Another important achievement was the gradual transformation of customs into rights and duties of citizens. Rights and duties were inseparable but contextually people developed the ability to interpret them and to implant them with personal participatory meaning.

Parallel to the polis there was the development of despotic units. It relied not on polis-like contraction but on the further extension of alliances of chiefdoms and tribal federation.

Hegemony of a single chiefdom had been a key structural condition. To that effect its chief transformed into a despot. It was an advanced version of a patrimonial order reinforced by despotic or domestic rule. Each and every one was included in this order as the 'children' of a 'home master'. They were nothing but the domestics (δμῶάς < IE *dems) of a domestic ruler (δέσποτις < IE *dems + pot).

Imperial Civility and Subsidiarity

Growth of the polis and despotic hegemonies allowed for the integration of populations and territories on an unprecedented scale. During and after the Civilization Revolution that took place about 120 generations BP, a new prototype of inclusion and order emerged. It combined explicitly open access and communication networks with all the previous prototypes: primordial and patrimonial, as well as the polis and its despotic variant. Writing provides opportunities to communicate and organize against the restraints of time and place. Political and communication hierarchies could extend infinitely in would-be universal empires unless they faced a lack of resources and malfunctions of their relay junctures and transmission links. Here, it is vital that this open-access order includes closed-access orders in the form of corporate and local bodies. So historical empires and civilizations are, in fact, generally open frameworks with closed units inside them. This amalgamation of openness and closedness may explain internal tensions and the historical instability of empires and civilizations.

New political systems and their civilizations promoted the new and unifying appeal of civility. It was referred to differently in various languages using metaphors ranging from excellence to urbanity and from good manners to peace. In the Roman tradition, civility rested on three central notions: *civilitas* (qualities of a true Roman that distinguish him from a barbarian), *civitas* (civic community and civic qualities) and *civis* (Roman citizen). The etymology has informal and emotional connotations. The word *civis* had been derived from IE *$keiuo$—"intimately close, familial" (Benveniste 1969). *Civitas* is primarily the attachment to one's own, to *cives*, intimate fellow-cohorts. Such well-trusted fellows first built the city of Rome then created a huge empire and finally established *Pax Romana*.

The political form of an empire as an open system includes a dominant centre, typically the Eternal City (Urbs Aeterna) extending its political, military and cultural control over vast surrounding areas. It is an open system because vast resources of civility outnumber barbarian potential. Limes (Lat.) or borderlands served as a transition zone from civility to barbarity and back.

Other important features of imperial order were hierarchy and indirect rule. Imperial inclusion rested on networks of loyalty with authoritative functional subordinations that are centripetally focused on a complex hierarchy. Loyalty to the empire and allegiance to the civilization were primary imperatives for an imperial subject. Although Roman *civis* is traditionally translated as citizen, such a rendition is true only vis-à-vis Republican times. In imperial times interpretation of the term is that of a subject, highly valued and even privileged, but still a subject.

34 *Mikhail Ilyin*

Institutionally and conceptually, the imperial transformation of civic (polis) rights and duties into liberties and responsibilities that were granted was a radical innovation and followed from the extension of politics and the distances between the seat of authority and individual subjects. The ensuing problems could only partially be coped with under the patrimonial model. A more stable and subtle mode was that of establishing hierarchies and subordination.

An important innovation was the development of the imperial virtues of civility and liberality. The imperial mission was to extend the liberality of free people to the uncivil world of barbarians and to liberate all those who were able to civilize.

The theocratic form of imperial rule doubled dimensions of inclusion by converging empires and world religions. The theocratic prototype was soon modified by feudalizing the profane or horizontal dimension whereas the sacral or vertical dimension remained intact. This modification led to the outburst of multiple citizenship in European Respublica Christiana, which had existed for a millennium since its formation during the 5th to 15th centuries. Within Respublica Christiana, there appeared a great range of corporate structures, including monastic and chivalrous orders, guilds and partnerships, universities and confraternities. The development of such corporate bodies was accompanied by the regulation of inclusion and the emergence of various "citizenships" in monastic and other orders.

It was in the early 16th century that the Respublica Christiana collapsed and split into an array of territorial units that multiplied and privatized the former sacral (vertical) dimension. This was the story of a new form: nation state citizenship.

Nation State Membership

Citizenship in its narrow sense of membership in a nation state is quite new, both as a phenomenon and a notion. "It was only in 1792 that it (the word *citizen*—M.I.) was first used to a member of a state" (Magnette 2005, 5). The term *citizenship* designating nation state membership is still more recent:

> A few decades later appeared the *citizenry* derivative (1819), which means the civic body, and *citizenhood* (1871), synonymous with what we call today citizenship. It is only in the second half of the second half of the twentieth century, and even more so since the 70s, that the word is in constant use and that it has taken on a clearly political meaning. The same evolution is found in other European languages.
>
> (Magnette 2005, 5)

Nation states are also recent phenomena. The term implies the combination of a nation and a state. Such blends have been very uneasy products of the two parallel processes of nation-building and state formation. The interrelation and relative autonomy of those two processes was clearly identified in political science only in the 1960s, but they actually started much earlier, at least as far back as the European Renaissance. The consolidation of sizable linguo-cultural communities within Respublica Christiana was re-conceptualized in terms of a common 'origin' or nation. Just as the polis transformation was imagined as the artificial re-creation of kinship on the scale of the city, the modern overhaul was thought of as a similar development on much greater territorial scale.

This new scale of nations did not automatically coincide with new political frameworks of sovereign domination. Early Modern times gives examples of states within nations and nations within states. It was only in the 19th century, in particular, with the unification of Germany and Italy, that the nation state configuration gained prominence.

The word *state* appeared some time in the 16th century (Skinner 1989, 2010). But even then, it referred not so much to a distinct morphological unit of politics but rather to assorted territorial units of very diverse nature that strived to build up partnerships for mutual survival. To that effect, they recognized the legal equality and ultimate authority of each other along with fixed boarders. Such an experiment initially took place in Italy after the Peace of Lodi in 1456 and helped to interrupt a long sequence of wars for the next four decades. Many parties to the Peace of Westphalia would not pass even very modern criteria for statehood. It was only after the Vienna Congress that the structural affinities developed by participants of a successive international system made them look like states. So, it is not by chance that *citizenry* entered English political vocabulary just after the Congress of Vienna, *citizenhood* after modifications to the Vienna system in 1871, and *citizenship* was firmly established only in the 20th century.

All through the nascent period of nation states persons belonging to these first territorial units were called, and treated as, subjects. Imperial, patrimonial and other old-fashioned constituents of modern political forms and corresponding concepts dominated long into the next century. They are still apparent and effectual even with much advanced democracies. With autocracies, anocracies and many new democracies that emerged only in recent decades, patrimonial and imperial patterns often continue to prevail. They are still apparent and effectual even within advanced democracies. In actual fact, nation states have always been, and still are, assorted patchworks of overlapping configurations of inclusion, as heterogeneous countries like Switzerland and Belgium clearly prove. But a closer look at 'homogeneous' countries like Denmark or Portugal also confirms a multiplicity of inclusions and specific 'citizenships' (corporate, neighborhood, etc.).

36 *Mikhail Ilyin*

With all the intricacy of multiple citizenships and patterns of inclusion, it is the legal bond with territorially defined domains of power that plays the key role. The territorial borders of states work essentially to establish crucial distinguishing factors. This simplifies and rationalizes inclusion, but at the same time complicates it. In fact, the distinction between internal and external is ambiguous because each individual state has its own perspective and point of departure. States may have shared segments of their borders, but they often operate quite differently from their opposing sides.

Nation state citizen corps can be defined as networks of formal depersonalized contractual partnerships. Such citizenship networks are autonomous to varying degrees but they make up authoritative functional hierarchies with a seat of common sovereign authority at the top acting on behalf of the whole national body. In its turn, the interdependent territorial frameworks for overlapping citizenship networks were conceptualized as sovereign states.

The modern concept of citizenship is based on the principle of autonomy. The emergence of an autonomous possessive individual—epitomized, e.g., by Robinson Crusoe—was only a beginning. It was coupled with new reconceptualization of rights and duties. Citizens could be considered equal subjects of the sovereign state entitled to a set of granted rights by virtue of inclusion, or autonomous participants that can gain civil (political) rights by virtue of qualified participation in the state-size networks of trust. During the Putney debates, the first option was advocated by a 'democratic' colonel, Tom Rainsborough, and the second by 'autocratic' general, Henry Ireton. Analytically, one can consider whether rights qualify the nature of inclusion or if inclusion provides rights. Equally, long estranged rights and duties could be interpreted as the one conditioning the other, or vice versa.

Those analytic distinctions lay at the bottom of the conflict of republican (civic) and liberal (imperial) orders. As Michael Walzer shrewdly noted, the current and most widespread meaning of being a citizen implies a "particular dualism of republican and imperial or liberal citizenship" (Walzer 1989, 216). In his definition, "a citizen is, most simply, a member of a political community, entitled to whatever prerogatives and encumbered with whatever responsibilities attached to membership" (Walzer 1989, 211).

Does it mean that we can employ two prototypes, republican and imperial, to make a dualistic conceptual device to arrange all specific cases within a bipolar scale? Yes, it is possible, as Walzer himself demonstrates in his chapter on citizenship in a classic volume on political innovation and conceptual change (Walzer 1989, 216). It is a step which is certainly justified from the point of view of the current dilemmas and contradictions of citizenship and ambiguities of civic participation.

Conclusion: Multiple Citizenships, Old and New

European and other multiple citizenships provide a major theoretical challenge for political science. There is nothing special in sharing inclusions and the multiplication of orders. On the basis that citizenship must also include all other historical types and prototypes in its form then the concept of citizenship must be multiple. So multiple citizenship is not something exceptionally recent and outlandish, as is often claimed, but still quite common and widespread many generations ago.

Multiple citizenship is not something that developed by putting together separate national citizenships which then add up to the EU or some other supranational jurisdiction. Rather, those are national citizenships that gradually evolved and split up from an overlapping citizenship of Early Modern polities of Western Europe. The Holy Roman Empire is probably a prototype. But in the case of the unitary Kingdom of France—with its distinct dukedoms and counties having their own parliaments, privileges and political identities recognized by the central authorities in Paris—subnational collective identities were coupled with personal political identities that amalgamated with those of French subjects. The situation in Spain and many other parts of Europe was not much different. Interestingly enough, common Italian identity coupled with personal identities of belonging to the Italian nation developed well into the Renaissance, despite the fact that central political authority was missing. Since the time of Saint Constantine, Europeans combined loyalties to all kinds of authorities with their Christian allegiance. Jurisdiction of the Holy See was central for maintenance of *Res publica Christiana*.

Virtually any kind of citizenship, save for the most elementary forms of inclusion, has always been multiple. So the issue is not multiplication *per se*; the problem is rather the immense scope of inclusion coupled with the contradictory qualities of the ensuing political orders at various levels.

Acknowledgement

This work is supported by the Russian Science Foundation under grant 17-18-01536 "Knowledge transfer and convergence of methodological practices: cases of interdisciplinary integration of political, biological and linguistic research."

References

Benveniste, E. 1969. *Le vocabulaire des institutions Indo-Européennes 1*. Paris: Les Editions de Minuit.

Calvin, W. 2004. *A Brief History of the Mind*. Oxford: Oxford University Press.

38 Mikhail Ilyin

Diamond, J. 1999. *Guns, Germs, and Steel: The Fate of Human Societies.* New York: Norton.

Dunn, J. 2005. "Foreword." In *Citizenship: The History of an Idea*, by P. Magnette. Colchester: ECPR Press.

Gazibo, Mamoudou. 2012. "Can Neopatrimonialism Dissolve into Democracy?" In *Neopatrimonialism in Africa and Beyond*, edited by Daniel Bach and Mamoudou Gazibo, 79–89. London and New York: Routledge.

Hyvärinen, Matti, Jussi Kurunmäki, Kari Palonen, Tuija Pulkkinen, and Henrik Stenius. 2003. *Käsitteet Liikkeessä: Suomen Poliittisen Kulttuurin Käsitehistoria.* Tampere, Finland: Vastapaino.

Lakoff, G., and M. Johnson. 1980. *Metaphors We Live By.* Chicago, IL: University of Chicago Press.

Magnette, P. 2005. *Citizenship: The History of an Idea.* Colchester: ECPR Press.

Roesch, E. 1975. "Cognitive Representations of Semantic Categories." *Journal of Experimental Psychology: General* 104:192–233.

Skinner, Q. 1989. "The State." In *Political Innovation and Conceptual Change*, edited by Terence Ball, James Farr, and Russell L. Hanson, 90–131. Cambridge: Cambridge University Press.

———. 2010. "A Genealogy of the Modern State." *Proceedings of the British Academy* 162:352–370.

Soest von, C. 2007. "How Does Neopatrimonialism Affect the African State? The Case of Tax Collection in Zambia." *Journal of Modern African Studies* 45:621–645.

Walzer, M. 1989. "Citizenship." In *Political Innovation and Conceptual Change*, edited by Terence Ball, James Farr, and Russell L. Hanson, 211–219. Cambridge: Cambridge University Press.

Weber, M. 2002. *Wirtschaft und Gesellschaft: Grundriss der verstehenden Soziologie.* Mohr: Siebeck.

2 The Concept of "Good Enough" Citizen Revisited

An Exploration of Current Discourses on Political Participation

Elena García-Guitián

Within the context of the current economic crisis, the literature on politics reflects an enlargement of a discourse on the crisis of representation which is equated with a crisis of representative democracy. This latter, according to the debates, can be overcome only by a deep transformation of the democratic model. It would require a conversion of representative democracies into real participatory democracies, giving a leading role to the direct involvement of citizens. This view, therefore, sets the context where new oppositional uses of the 'representative versus participatory' dichotomy are confronted.

The conceptual historical analysis highlights the continuities and ruptures in this debate which is at the core of the institutionalization of modern democracies (Urbinati 2006), and which has, from the outset, determined the construction of its models (Held 1996). It provides us with an understanding of the roots of this confrontation that is far from new, the particular embodiment of different historical periods and contexts, and the specific meanings attributed to the key concepts used to support present political debates.

However, although this dichotomy—representative versus participatory democracy—links and gives meaning to the basic concepts of our political vocabulary—such as democracy, representation, or sovereignty—its current usages mainly stresses the alternative views of citizenship. Here citizenship is understood as (Macpherson 1977) a depiction of real citizens and their potentialities that is at the core of all normative views of democracy and constitutes a central element for assessing the legitimacy of real democratic regimes (Dalton 2009). From this perspective, the dichotomy can be approached as an opposition of two types of citizen: the individual that pursues his/her interests through voting in elections and the conscious citizen that attains self-determination through political participation.

Some years ago, Dahl (1992) tried to defend an intermediate vision of the citizen in contemporary democracies located between the 'good citizen' depicted in classical theory and the rational egoist who played the leading role in some contemporary views. His description of the

40 *Elena García-Guitián*

'good-enough' citizen sought to adjust the gap between the real political behaviour of citizens and the normative expectations attributed to them. He provided us, therefore, with a viewpoint that supports the critique of some uses of the representative/participatory opposition that current empirical research seems to reinforce, offering various descriptions of citizens that force us to adopt plural views of 'the citizen' to sustain our proposals.

In what follows, there is a reflection on the way this dichotomy is portrayed, stressing its excessive simplicity and its political usage in the context of the crisis. It is based on a restrictive description of representative democracy equivalent to its 'minimal' account, which is opposed to promising participatory models founded on the potential development of new forms and spaces of citizen participation, presented as an alternative vision of citizenship. To analyse all its implications it is necessary, first, to question the opposition between representation and participation that has permeated political language but that has been challenged in contemporary political theory through the idea of the system or representation (Urbinati 2006). Second, although this opposition has a long genealogy in political thought providing the building blocks for its contemporary use, it tends to be justified using as one of the opposite discourses Schumpeter's vision of democracy. This is a controversial equation of the 'representative model' with what is considered its 'minimal' version that has to be acknowledged. Third, to understand its current usages, it is important to point out the idea of citizenship they envisage. Participatory versions tend to disregard the importance of voting and traditional political activism as extended forms of citizen participation, ignoring the 'good-enough' citizens, and identifying 'the citizen' with the considered 'critical' ones. Yet the diversity of citizen profiles provided by empirical research supports a different way of theorizing citizen participation conceived instead as a source of diverse and complementary (non-electoral) forms of political representation. This requires us to leave aside the proposal of alternative (always partial) models of democracy that pretend to go beyond representative democracy and fully envision the way complex forms of citizen participation can be a part of an enhanced system of representation.

Crisis of Representation as a Crisis of Representative Democracy

To announce a crisis of representation is not surprising in democratic theory, but in the present circumstances it has (once again) surpassed the academic discussion to become the main subject matter in the public sphere, fuelling the birth of successful new populist parties and social movements (from the extreme right to left-wing radicals) and raising new hopes for the therapeutic effects of citizen participation. Their common core is a criticism of 'traditional' political parties in the hands of a

The Concept of "Good Enough" Citizen 41

'political class' or 'caste' and always prone to pursue its own political and economic interests. It is a monopoly of parties over democratic representation, as compulsory intermediaries, which has been challenged as they are considered unable to fulfil the expectations derived from the different normative exigencies of the representative ideal.

The embodiment of the representative system has always been a controversial issue. Its main component is the relation established between citizens and those elected to form part of a collective assembly, notwithstanding that in democratic systems there are other forms of political representation. But this institutional core has determined the normative content of the concept of representation. To try to articulate it, after an exhaustive exploration of central theories and historical debates, Pitkin (1967) identified five dimensions of its formulation which help us to determine its contours: (a) authorization; (b) accountability; (c) representativeness; (d) symbolic identification; and (e) 'acting for'.

Present-day diagnosis of an analysis of representation from these various perspectives supports the perception of a crisis based on the following assumptions:

First, the formal dimension of authorization (i.e., to represent implies being authorized by someone to act on his or her behalf) is challenged by the critique of existing electoral systems believed to be unfair and instrumental in guaranteeing the domain of traditional party elites who avail themselves of the system to maintain the status quo.

Second, the dimension of accountability (i.e., to represent involves a duty to justify what has been done to the represented, who can assess the performance mainly through new elections) is contested for being poorly institutionalized in contemporary democracies. Periodic elections and traditional checks and balances can no longer fulfill their function, giving too much power to partial majorities for an excessive period (the legislative terms). They are inadequate to force the responsiveness of representatives.

Third, the descriptive dimension (i.e., to represent presupposes a share of some objective traits: territorial, identitarian, or corporative, with the represented) is questioned when accepting the obvious differentiation of a ruling political class, unable to be representative of ordinary citizens.

Fourth, from the symbolic dimension (i.e., to represent demands a certain emotional connection with the represented which certifies the authenticity of the link) the increased distrust of professional politicians seems to impede any possibility of an emotive identification. This explains why the term 'political disaffection' is so widely used in the academic diagnosis and political debates around the present situation of contemporary democracies, very often wrongly understood simply as a personal emotional rejection of party politicians.

Fifth, the compromise that results from the substantive dimension (i.e., to represent means acting on behalf of the represented and being

42   Elena García-Guitián

responsive to their demands) is believed to have been betrayed, as there is a widespread view of parties as defenders of their own or dominant economic interests—rather than the common good—not being responsive at all to citizen claims. From these diverse perspectives offered by a comprehensive analysis incorporating all the dimensions of the concept of representation, only negative conclusions are drawn which therefore gives rise to a deep feeling of crisis (for a more complex development of this perspective see Lietzmann's chapter in this volume). As the representative link is generated through its acceptance by an audience (Saward 2010), there is the risk of transforming this perception into the foundation of a discourse on the crisis of democracy.

Nevertheless, both this simplistic diagnosis and its consequent advanced solutions take on a different appearance when seen through the lens of political theory. As it has been stressed (Saward 2010), the institutionally embodied representative claim is always experiencing the assault of other claims—of political and social representation as well as of alternative institutional embodiments—generating tensions often solved through a political reform (changes in electoral rules, processes of decentralization).

The challenge is to identify the real cause of present discomfort and to give a convincing answer to the hopes of citizens. That is the reason for the insistence on differentiating institutional structural deficits from their contextual malfunctioning which in some political systems, particularly those experiencing the worst economic crisis, has fuelled the critics and has urged the proposals for a democratic renewal. But the so-considered permanent shortfalls should orientate the solutions, not the specific (although scandalous) poor performances.

For some analysts, then, this renewal can be undertaken simply through standard institutional reforms such as forcing changes to dominant parties to make them more capable of representing citizens (compulsory primaries); changing electoral rules (individual candidatures); or expanding controls (neutral institutions). For others, this democratic deficit, perceived as a crisis of representation, can only be surpassed by a deeper transformation of the democratic model. It would require a radical conversion of representative democracy into a real participatory one, giving a leading role to the direct involvement of citizens. This view, therefore, establishes a context where new oppositional uses of the representative versus participatory dichotomy are confronted. Some academics today, as well as political movements, have adopted this last approach opposing representative and participatory democracy. Even some of their names—such as the Spanish 'Real Democracy Now' movement—evoke the theme of transforming present representative systems which are considered to be non-authentically democratic. Political scientists studying these movements also tend to highlight efforts at envisioning a different democracy. As Della Porta (2012, 33), e.g., has stated:

The Concept of "Good Enough" Citizen   43

"These movements conceptualize and practice different democratic models that emphasize participation over delegation and deliberation over majority voting".

Without attempting to develop a full analysis of contemporary models of democracy and a diagnosis about their flaws, it is important to highlight the way the 'representative versus participatory dichotomy' is being used to criticize present-day democracies, and the descriptions of citizens it envisages—both empirical and normative. This approach justifies the need to change our way of theorizing citizen participation, leaving aside proposals for alternative (limited) models of democracy differentiated by the use of diverse and creative labels, and to locate it within a comprehensive conception of representative democracy (Plotke 1997; Saward 2010; Warren 2012).

The Dichotomy of Representative versus Participatory Democracy

Political crisis is often presented as the natural outcome of the obvious pitfalls of the present model of democracy identified with 'liberal democracy', 'elitist democracy', 'minimalist democracy', 'traditional democracy', 'electoral democracy', 'pluralist democracy', or just, as described above, representative democracy. The alternative seems to insist on a participatory model which is regarded by some as synonymous with 'direct democracy' or 'deliberative democracy'.

There is a continuous temptation to present them, in academic as well as political debates, as two basic models founded on opposed characteristics. Each one is portrayed as having some well-defined traits, sketched by notorious theorists with whom they are identified. This is clear in the case of the account of the 'representative model', whose specific components are too often extracted from Schumpeter's (1942) description of democracy. The first characteristic of this model is based on his critique of what he called 'classical normative models' of democracy, which he regarded as founded on unrealistic approaches that presupposed the possibility of defining a common good, and attributed non-existent political (good) qualities to citizens. He opposed to it a more realistic account of real citizens, described as ignorant and slightly interested in politics, far away from the idealized individuals envisioned by normative theory. Democracy is thus best understood as the political system that puts the selection of the political elite in the hands of citizens, via voting, without expecting anything else from them. In the genealogy of this vision of democracy, it is common to find other authors as Dahl (1956) or Sartori (1987), whose defence of representation as the pillar of democracy is taken as a proof of their elitism and distrust of ordinary citizens.

Contrasting the participatory model, authors include descriptions which stress the relevance of direct citizen involvement in politics.

44 *Elena García-Guitián*

But the list of names identified with this model changes depending on the specific type of participation they put emphasis on. When speaking about the participatory model (considered the more radical one, as it presupposes direct forms of citizen involvement), Barber (1984) or Pateman (1970) are most frequently cited, always under Rousseau's shadow (but also with frequent appeals to liberals as Tocqueville or Mill). When the alternative is the deliberative model, then Habermas (1996) and all those authors self-identified with this discourse are the point of reference.

To clarify these descriptions, it is important, first, to identify various theoretical debates which have to be distinguished for analytical purposes. On the core of this dichotomy lies the old polemic located at the birth of modern democracy: representation versus direct participation. Appealing to an idealized version of classical Athenian democracy or to a depiction of Rousseau's critique of representation (Urbinati 2000, 763), representative systems are often considered fake substitutions for real democracy. Through the misuse of the term democracy they hide its real aristocratic character (Manin 1997). But contemporary debates on democracy do not really question representative democracies, just what can be considered its 'minimal conception'. Even in the so-called radical alternative versions, mechanisms of citizen participation appear as complements of the core representative institutions, not as their substitutes (Pateman 1970, 42; Barber 1984, 262).

Secondly, the dichotomy is too simplistic and does not take into account the continuity of debates around the proposal of different models of democracy. Moreover, it ignores that all of them generally show some flaws when trying to fix their specific core components. One of their clearest differences is the way they envisage citizen participation and propose mechanisms to make it effective. But models and typologies are far from offering clear articulations of democratic institutions, apart from generic depictions of the preferred public sphere and designs of very specific participative mechanisms. In doing so, many theorists tend to misrepresent the vote in elections as the core and more extended form of citizen participation, and obscure the fact that not all these mechanisms (consultation, referendum, deliberative forums, etc.) fulfil the same roles and satisfy the same normative expectations. This has given rise to a current and somewhat confusing debate about models of democracy: pluralist, associative, participatory, deliberative, direct, adversary, advocacy, monitorial, and so on, as it is by labelling a model that theorists express their differences—although they theorize the totality by depicting only a part.

Thirdly, to understand this dichotomy it is also instructive to explore the constitutive disputes about the shortcomings, weaknesses, and performance of real democratic systems, showing their unavoidable normative concerns. This is the theoretical level on which the report

The Concept of "Good Enough" Citizen   45

The Crisis of Democracy (Crozier, Huntington, and Watanuki 1975) took place during the 1970s, inspiring many proposals for democratic innovation. From this perspective, citizen participation is a tool to improve the democratic performance of institutions and to make good governance possible. Today, generalized discontent with democracies is considered a given fact that has multiplied the efforts to develop strategies aiming to improve existing institutions through new forms of citizen participation. Nevertheless, these reforms have been approached from different perspectives linked to the normative expectations articulated in the theorctical models.

All too often this binary classification is described in very simplistic terms, becoming a useful political weapon which finds increasing support in the context of the crisis as it has proved to be both very popular and effective. Its assertion constitutes a departure point for sketching different normative proposals, aiming to extend and institutionalize citizen participation, providing an alternative (to the existing) model of democracy.

From the participatory perspective, as articulated by Pateman (1970), representative democracy uncritically restricts itself to becoming a system based on competitive leadership, delegation of power to an elite, and the majority as the decision-making principle. In this portrayal of the representative model participation is seen in instrumental terms as a way to protect citizens from governors and make democratic institutions work, disconnected from its classical function of guaranteeing good government and facilitating self-determination. Moreover, what this highlights is that some accounts (e.g., Crozier, Huntington, and Watanuki, 1975) have come to consider massive participation a danger for democracy, one that is prone to produce an overload of demands, collapse responsiveness, and unbalance the system. This conservative diagnosis has validated the conviction that democracy is capable of functioning with wide levels of political apathy, as real citizens are uninterested in politics and highly involved citizens always constitute a minority.

On the contrary, participatory theories emphasize that the real meaning of democracy is citizens' self-government, although the specific content is far from being clear. Whereas the starting point seems to be the representative model, different discourses articulate explicit traits as a complement, stressing diverse forms of citizens' involvement. Even if in their analysis many authors speak indistinctly of participatory, deliberative, or direct democracy as compatible proposals, there are not specific alternative institutional designs capable of making their different normative expectations compatible (Pettit 2001).

In his description of the evolution of liberal democracies, Macpherson (1977) emphasized that the design of models of democracy always involves a conception of human nature expressed in a depiction of real citizens (through the analysis of their historical and current relations) and their potentialities (through changes in social/economical/political

46 Elena García-Guitián

relations). People's beliefs about the political system and what they could become are thus a part of the political system.

This is reflected in controversies about models where there is a tendency to misrepresent the position of rival theories by focusing on their description of citizens and their political competence. But behind it we also find the well-known polemics between empirical (real) versus normative (ideal) theories, which highlights an unavoidable tension that is at the core of any institutional design.

This tension was transcended by Schumpeter (1942) in his description of democracy. Real citizens should condition our normative idea, as idealized forms subvert real democracies by establishing unattainably high standards. His popular definition of democracy was based on a critique of what he considered to be the main presumptions contained in the eighteenth-century theory of democracy, which implied that there is a 'common good' and a 'volonté générale' articulated through the representation of a previously predefined individual will.

His emphasis on competitive leadership as the core element of modern democracies, and his descriptions of the cognitive and emotional limitations of ordinary citizens—from whom nothing should be expected except their contribution to fuelling elite competition through voting—made him the best reference for critics of representative democracy. Nevertheless, his minimal conception cannot be equated with that of generic representative democracy which has many diverse accounts (all of them including forms of representation/participation through different institutions and mechanisms). To refer to Schumpeter's definition, therefore, has a political purpose: to overstress the scope of contributions made by other proposals.

Other references commonly used to describe the failures of the representative model include the popular task force promoted by the Trilateral Commission in the 1970's within a context of a perceived crisis of democracy which bore similarities to today. In their report, Crozier, Huntington, and Watanuki (1975) analysed the pessimism pervading the democratic systems of the United States, Japan, and some European countries, to try to make an accurate diagnosis and propose concrete targets to stop the perceived decline of democracy.

The principal risk outlined was the rise of anomic democracies (Crozier, Huntington, and Watanuki 1975, 161), due to the continuous growth of citizen dissatisfaction and the lack of institutional confidence following from the loss of common purposes. The causes of their dysfunction were diverse and complex (economic, social, and political factors), but in this analysis special emphasis was put on the pernicious effects caused by the expansion of citizen participation: an unavoidable fragmentation and growth of demands that generated a huge increase in public expenditure overloading democratic governments which were unable to satisfy the demands of citizens and consequently became unresponsive.

The Concept of "Good Enough" Citizen 47

The report contained studies of several countries showing a variety of situations which precluded the possibility of achieving common conclusions. Nevertheless, Huntington's analysis of the American case was widely cited and had more room on the final comments, what gave a conservative character to the entire work. But his admonition about the dangers of massive participation had to be located in a political context characterized by an extensive mobilization of citizens through groups. The increasing disaggregation of interests and constitution of groups defending their particularity in a political system characterized by weak parties and the accessibility of group demands by institutions was perceived as a dysfunctional tendency of the American democracy of the time.

However, the report also stressed that it was not a diagnosis that could be generalized, as such, to include other countries, as was the case with Japan, which, on the contrary, was considered too elitist and in need of more citizen participation in order to become more democratic. The common recommendations for all were, among others, a re-empowerment of parliaments, adaptation of weakened political parties to the new context—i.e., to become more trustful and able to articulate fragmented demands in a common project—and a reform of public administrations and local governments with a view to democratizing them.

The report, therefore, was not conceived as a sketch of a theoretical model of democracy or citizen participation, but rather it evolved out of a concern about democratic governability: it tried to analyse the problems democracies were facing in the context of the deep economic crisis of the 1970s.

This diagnosis basically matches up with present concerns (Dalton, Scarrow, and Cain 2004), although the context has once again been transformed. Now it seems that the growing dissatisfaction and sense of underperformance of institutions is widespread, but new changes have also been introduced in real democracies to curb these developments.

In their analysis of eighteen European countries, Bedock, Mair, and Wilson (2012) concluded that since the 1980s there have been many diverse institutional reforms (electoral, parliamentarian, territorial decentralization, funding of political parties, election of executives, suffrage, citizen participation mechanisms) mainly intended to "open-up the process of decision-making to the citizen" as part of a wider process of change. The outcome has been a huge increase in mechanisms and opportunities for citizen participation, which, nonetheless, continues to be despised in many discourses on participation that refer to theoretical descriptions of previous decades using the representative/participative dichotomy.

To appreciate and assess these discourses, a more accurate description of the reality of citizens' political behaviour in present democracies is needed.

48 *Elena García-Guitián*

Depictions of Democratic Citizens: The Notion of 'Good-Enough' Citizen Revisited

The analysis of citizens' political behaviour and their forms of participation is a well-developed area of political science. It has produced different depictions of democratic citizens, as well as assessments of their potential influence in the proper functioning of democracy, considering that the actual citizens are the product of an endlessly contested political system and could, therefore, be otherwise.

The main normative question traditionally approached from this perspective has been the type of involvement of actual citizens (mainly, but not only, in terms of voter turnout) and their impact on the performance of democratic systems. What are the forms and numbers that contribute to legitimize a democracy and improve its quality? Which, if any, are considered disruptive?

In democratic theory, there has always been a concern to try to determine when citizens' rates of involvement would cease to be supportive of the system. It covers forms of participation in the widest sense—from voting in elections, to signing petitions, or manifestos; from participation in demonstrations, to involvement in social movements—and stresses that modern democracies have developed a wide legislation both to guarantee it and to fix its limits. We have, then, a huge academic literature devoted to analysing its content and figures, but also its impact on the performance of democracy (Oñate 2013).

What this literature shows is the growing uneasiness with voter turnout and decreasing activism in traditional institutions such as political parties, trade unions, or social organizations, triggering alarms about the repercussions for the legitimation of democracies (Macedo 2005). But empirical research (Dalton 2008; Norris 2003) also reveals that more citizens are politically engaged in different forms of political action than ever before, and this is a common trend that should have reduced the anxiety generated by the advance of political disaffection (Merkel 2014). Participation has noticeably increased in terms of direct action and volunteering, but has declined in terms of direct membership in political parties and campaign mobilization—although there are significant differences between countries (Montero et al. 2016). A common conclusion is that democracies count on an enlarged group of 'engaged' citizens, highly discontent with the performance of democracies and distrustful of institutions, but still interested in politics and ready to participate—although in some other way (Dalton 2009).

When making our judgements about citizens' involvement, we should reflect this diversity instead of appealing to a single idealized conception of citizen. From this perspective, empirical analysis (Montero et al. 2016) identifies at least four types of citizens:

The Concept of "Good Enough" Citizen 49

1 Cives: who are those that show institutional confidence and political interest.
2 Deferential: those who show institutional confidence but have no political interest.
3 Critical: those who show political interest but have no confidence in institutions.
4 Disaffected: those who show no political interest and no confidence in institutions.

These distinctions give rise to different normative expectations, but how can we then characterize the average (ordinary, lay, normal) citizen?

Many years ago, Dahl (1992, 47) stated that empirical evidence confirmed that the majority of citizens have just an occasional interest in politics, and that they are intermittent, part-time citizens. From this reality, he described the 'good-enough citizen' as the one having a minimal political competence (who does not fit the classical vision of good citizen, nor the narrow view which sees him/her as a rational self-interested individual).

Good-enough citizens are those who "would posses sufficiently strong incentives to gain a modicum of knowledge of their own interests and of the political choices most likely to advance them, as well as sufficiently strong incentives to act on behalf of these choices" (Dahl 1992, 48). In Dahl's view, their competence ought to be developed through formal education, relevant and low-cost information through media, and party competition. But he also warned that the increase of complexity and scale was changing democratic politics and reinforcing the role of experts, giving rise to new demands on the level of competence of citizens that this model would have problems incorporating.

More than a decade later, Warren (2009) observed a widespread citizen malaise towards democratic political institutions that underperform. Governing had become a more technical, complex and multilevel matter, giving a leading role to experts and, at the same time, generating a growing discontent and distrust on the part of citizens.

This author insisted on the fact that people like neither politics nor conflict and would prefer to delegate it to politicians. They have no interest in detailing and passing on their preferences to their representatives, nor in actively controlling them. They prefer to trust them whereas also assuming that this would be frustrating most of the time. Therefore, Warren (2009) concluded that the competence a good democracy should promote among its citizens is the optimization of their political resources via voting or joining associations. Citizens will participate on relevant issues when they believe that their involvement can influence the outcome. Is this, then, a return of the 'good-enough citizen'? Descriptions of citizens thus show a variety of types, but the interpretation of their potentialities changes the normative conclusions used to support theories of citizen participation. Although this is a polemic without end—is this behaviour constitutive of the citizens or an outcome of the system? —the role attributed to them nonetheless sets up a normative discourse.

The idea of citizenship, understood as a "shared set of expectations about the citizen's role in politics" (Dalton 2009, 20), is a central element of any political culture and influences the assessment of the whole political system. It endorses visions of citizen participation, standards of institutional legitimacy, and principles of justice.

What the empirical analysis seems to prove is a progressive conversion from a 'duty-based citizenship' to an 'engaged citizenship' that is mainly the product of a change in patterns of socialization among young people. The normative aftermath is a tendency to see engaged citizens as real promoters of a renewal of democracy. This perspective (Dalton 2008) stresses that their involvement helps to: (a) counteract the fear of citizens' disaffection as one of contemporary democracy's maladies; (b) boost new social movements that play a function of control and construction of critical trust (Della Porta 2012, 42); and (c) fuel participation in inclusive and plural public spheres, thus improving the deliberative character of democracies.

But what about its relation with the other types? Whereas 'disaffected' citizens (whose number has progressively grown in current democracies) appear as the real problem, the 'deferential' (who had the leading role in 'minimalist' theories of democracy) also lack a good reputation. Their respect for authority as well as their limited involvement give them a conservative character, but there are also interesting differences in what concerns the 'cives' (those who have traditionally participated in political organizations and institutional mechanisms) whose compromise with present democratic institutions seems to depict them as too conformist. Nonetheless, a part of these 'engaged' citizens can be included under the 'cives' type, whereas others join the numbers of 'critical' citizens.

We can identify, then, a first theoretical approach incorporating a weak presumption: critical citizens act joining progressive social movements, creating spaces of public deliberation that will lead the fight against neo-liberalism and economic inequalities (Della Porta 2012). Indeed, their anti-establishment role will transform representative democracies into participatory democracies.

Yet as Urbinati (2012, 70) has pointed out, this perspective shows a "distaste for ordinary politics" which is typical in many of these analyses. In addition, citizen participation should not be seen as an alternative to political representation (Plotke 1997), whereas radical citizens should not monopolize the leading role.

Other perspectives centred on the improved performance of present democracies in terms of good governance put the accent on the

The Concept of "Good Enough" Citizen   51

involvement of those citizens affected by political decisions. They assume that a collection of mechanisms of direct participation accessible for diverse types of citizens (experts, lay, active), and adapted to the specificity of the concrete issue, can reinforce political representation and improve public administration, giving rise to better political outcomes.

As Fung (2006, 66) has accurately stated, "whether public institutions and decision-making processes should treat members of the public as consumers, clients, or citizens depends partly on the context and problem in question". This perspective involves a decision about three types of questions: Who participates (representativeness)? Which mechanism (processes)? What is the scope of the decision (extent of authority)?

This approach would be useful in solving problems of legitimacy, justice and the effectiveness of public action, all of which are in need of different strategies, participants and procedures (see Mäkinen's chapter in this volume).

Thereby, this second approach rejects simplistic discourses that regard direct control by citizens as the most authentic and developed form of citizen participation (real embodiment of the idea of self-government), as was implied, e.g., by Arnstein's (1969) popular typology. On her 'ladder of participation', the quality of citizen participation was determined by a ranking of its different forms, from the lower level of mere information about politics, to consultation or partnership, with self-management on the top position.

A third perspective can be added, that of particular democratic models based on the prioritization of normative goals which imply the fostering of the type of participative mechanisms that best fit their proposal. We can think of participatory discourses that equate real democracy with direct instruments for ordinary citizens' participation (referendums, open assemblies, on-line forums), but also of deliberative theories that promote the extension of precise deliberative procedures (deliberative polls or fora). Often, in their anxiety to locate themselves as alternative to representative democracy, they hide the fact clearly expressed by Plotke (1997, 24) that "rather than opposing participation to representation we should try to improve and expand representative practices. On that basis, a number of the most valuable aspects of participation should be considered as part of a reformed scheme of representation".

Perhaps the best way to approach the complexity of contemporary democracies is leaving aside the limited lenses offered by specific models of democracy (Warren 2012) that are unable to present an integrated conception of the whole democratic system. In this sense, Habermas's (1996) systems approach or Warren's (2012) so-called problem-based, functional approach can be much more fruitful in understanding the reality of participation in present democracies and its connections with complex forms of social and political representation.

52 *Elena García-Guitián*

Conclusion

The widespread use of the representative versus participatory dichotomy in both academic work and political debates requires an explicit rejection of its application to present democracies. Its theoretical weakness and unsuitability for understanding the complexity of our political systems contributes to the delegitimation of representative institutions without offering a real feasible alternative.

The historical analysis of the description of the citizen provides us with a better understanding of the debate, tracing its historical roots (the origins of representative government); describing the particular understanding of it in today's context of crisis (inspired in the debates that took place in the seventies of past century); and outlining the specific meanings attributed to the key concepts used to support it.

This dichotomy is based on a simplistic account that mistakenly identifies the representative model with a minimalist theoretical model, such as the one offered by Schumpeter. Nevertheless, there are many other accounts, both normative and institutionally embodied, that contain and promote diverse forms of citizen involvement (apart from mere electoral voting), believed to be a constitutive element of representative democracies.

Behind the strategy of using this dichotomy lies a political discourse that certifies the present-day crisis of representation and of representative democracy, offering the development of a (real) participatory democracy as a remedy.

But this tension between representation and the direct involvement of citizens should be softened. Empirical analyses show the growing complexity of citizens' political behaviour. They help to depict different types of citizens, each one playing diverse roles in the system, without identifying citizens with specific critical categories. This reality throws doubt on the suitability of democracy models based on the ideal of citizen self-government through an individual's direct involvement and the rejection of representative institutions. On the contrary, current theories of participation should rely on a more precise description of real citizens and their potentialities, and encompass the specific mechanisms to make such participation feasible within the system of representation.

Moreover, we should change the mode of theorizing about citizen participation, leaving aside the proposal of specific and limited models, and situate it in a more comprehensive conception of representative democracy. Mechanisms of citizen participation should be viewed not in opposition to political representation, but as a part of it.

Acknowledgement

This research has been funded by the grant CSO2013-48641-C2-1-R, Spanish Ministry of Economy and Competitiveness, project: A new local architecture: efficiency, dimension, and democracy.

References

Arnstein, S. 1969. "A Ladder of Citizen Participation." *Journal of the American Institute of Planners* 35(4): 216–224.

Barber, B. 1984. *Strong Democracy: Participatory Politics for a New Age.* Berkeley, CA: Berkeley University Press.

Bedock, C., P. Mair, and A. Wilson. 2012. "Institutional Change in Advanced European Democracies: An Exploratory Assessment." Robert Schuman Centre for Advanced Studies. European Union Democracy Observatory. European University Institute. http://cadmus.eui.eu/bitstream/handle/1814/20817/RSCAS_2012_11.pdf?sequence=1n. Accessed 14 February 2017.

Crozier, M. J., S. P. Huntington, and J. Watanuki. 1975. *The Crisis of Democracy: Report on the Governability of Democracies to the Trilateral Commission.* New York: New York University Press.

Dahl, R. 1956. *A Preface to Democratic Theory.* Chicago, IL: University of Chicago Press.

———. 1992. "The Problem of Civic Competence." *Journal of Democracy* 3(4):45–59.

Dalton, R. J. 2008. "Citizenship Norms and the Expansion of Political Participation." *Political Studies* 56:76–98.

———. 2009. *The Good Citizen: How a Younger Generation is Reshaping American Politics.* Washington, DC: CQ Press.

Dalton, R. J., S. E. Scarrow, and B. E Cain. 2004. "Advanced Democracies and the New Politics." *Journal of Democracy* 15(1):124–138.

Della Porta, D. 2012. "Critical Trust: Social Movements and Democracy in Times of Crisis." *Cambio* 2(4):33–43.

Fung, A. 2006. "Varieties of Participation in Complex Governance". *Public Administration Review* 66:66–75.

Habermas, J. 1996. *Between Facts and Norms: Contributions to a Discourse Theory of Law and Democracy.* Cambridge: Cambridge University Press.

Held, D. 1996. *Models of Democracy.* London: Polity and Stanford University Press.

Macedo, S. 2005. *Democracy at Risk.* Washington, DC: Brookings Institution Press.

Macpherson, C. B. 1977. *The Life and Times of Liberal Democracy.* Oxford: Oxford University Press.

Manin, B. 1997. *The Principles of Representative Government.* Cambridge: Cambridge University Press.

Merkel, W. 2014. "Is There a Crisis of Democracy?" *Democratic Theory* 1(2):11–25.

Montero, J. R, A. Sanz and R. M. Navarrete. 2016. "La democracia en tiempo de crisis: legitimidad, descontento, desafección." In *Participación, representación y democracia*, edited by J. L. Cascajo and A. Martín de la Vega, 15–66. Valencia, Spain: Tirant lo Blanch.

Norris, P. 2003. *Democratic Phoenix: Reinventing Political Activism.* Cambridge: Cambridge University Press.

Oñate, P. 2013. "La movilización ciudadana en los albores del siglo XXI: una contextualización para el debate." *Revista Española de ciencia política* 33:33–51.

54 Elena García-Guitián

Pateman, C. 1970. *Participation and Democratic Theory*. Cambridge: Cambridge University Press.

Pettit, P. 2001. "Deliberative Democracy and the Case for Depoliticising Government." *UNSW Law JI* 24(3):724–736.

Pitkin, H. F. 1967. *The Concept of Representation*. Berkeley, CA: University of California Press.

Plotke, D. 1997. "Representation is Democracy." *Constellations* 4(1):19–34.

Sartori, G. 1987. *The Theory of Democracy Revisited*. Chatham, NJ: Chatham House.

Saward, M. 2010. *The Representative Claim*. Oxford: Oxford University Press.

Schumpeter, J. A. [1942] 1976. *Capitalism, Socialism and Democracy*. London: Allen & Unwin.

Urbinati, N. 2000. "Representation as Advocacy: A Study of Democratic Deliberation." *Political Theory* 28(6):758–786.

———. 2006. *Representative Democracy: Principles and Genealogy*. Chicago, IL: University of Chicago Press.

———. 2012. "Unpolitical Democracy." *Political Theory* 38:65–92.

Warren, M. 2009. "Citizen Participation and Democratic Deficits: Considerations from the Perspective of Democracy." In *Activating the Citizen: Dilemmas of Participation in Europe and Canada*, edited by J. DeBardeleben and J. H. Pammet, 17–40. London: Palgrave Macmillan.

———. 2012. "When, Where and Why Do We Need Deliberation, Voting and Other Means of Organizing Democracy? A Problem-Based Approach to Democratic Systems." APSA 2012 Annual Meeting Paper. https://ssrn.com/abstract=2104566. Accessed 15 February 2017.

3 Citizenship, Democracy and the Iconology of Political Representation

A Plea for an Iconological Turn in Democratic Theory

Hans J. Lietzmann

The social perception of political representation in Europe changed dramatically during the last fifty years, prominently underlining the role of citizenship in the process of representation. Originating from a predominantly government-focused and parliament-oriented conception of political representation, new forms of a non-parliamentary, direct, deliberative and participative democracy evolved which have proved to be more efficacious in the current political and cultural context. New forms of democracy were accompanied by new understandings of citizenship in which the role of citizens is now required to be more active.

In most European countries these developments are reflected in both the national development of procedures for direct democracy since the mid-1980s, and to some extent in the regionalist bottom-up movements of citizens themselves. Recent developments in participative democracy and the call for civil participation in all fields of planning and development (see Mäkinen in this volume) have to be understood in this sense as a fundamental renewal of the social perspective on presentation and re-presentation in the sphere of politics (Lietzmann 2014).

These developments did not occur suddenly, but evolved gradually over long periods of the 20th century: in the process of the formation of elected governments, political parties, interest groups, citizen-initiatives and ethics commissions. However, it is only now that these processes have resulted in an omnipresent 'crisis of representation', in a visible 'reformulation of representation' and in a fundamentally transformed 'scenography' (Lietzmann 2012; Hénaff 2014).

Nevertheless, these developments continue to be discussed within the scope of the conventional paradigms foremost in political and socio-scientific research. However, this institutional and rationally oriented debate does not capture significant changes which are founded on the transformation of the social imagination of political representation by the citizens, and with the change in perspective of the presentation of democratic representation. The current research focuses on the 'political

56   *Hans J. Lietzmann*

representation' mainly as the institutional action of political representatives, but not as a specific, mutual process of the public's imaginative perception of politics and their institutional presentation.

This 'symbolic representation' is still recognized as irrational, affective and somewhat illegitimate within the political system (Pitkin 1967, 108; cf. Budde 2013; Hénaff 2014). Even in studies which are more open-minded and ambitious, political representation is defined as a top-down process. So far, there is no evidence of scientific approaches to political representation in the perspective of their societal reception and construction (see Mansbridge 2011; Saward 2010; Manow 2006).

The political representation of citizenship is not an established institutional framework, but arises from societal construction (Berger and Luckmann 1969; Ankersmit 2002). It is therefore a part of general social transformation and participates directly in the change of the societal perspective of citizens and their own creativity. Its characteristic, form and transformation are directly subject to an 'iconology of cultures'—every political culture evolves its own roles, figures and iconic performances (Belting 2009, 10). The approaches to how societies regard their (political) representation, i.e., the view of key players and the execution of political power, lead us analytically directly to the centre of their (political) thinking (Hénaff 2014, 89). According to this, political representation within the organizational framework of the political regime poses a cultural technology (Krämer and Bredekamp 2003), which clearly and concisely symbolizes the political perception in which the critique and approval of the prevailing institutions are vitally expressed, and which transforms itself in the context of the individual social perspective. We are currently witnessing a profound cognitive transformation of political society and its perception of policy. Citizens change their attitude intuitively towards political processes, the organization of the 'political' or towards the symbolic location of the political representation.

The Representation of a "Mental Image" and the "Iconic Belief" of Citizens

Political presentation and re-presentation are figure-based perceptual concepts (Boehm 2001; 2007). They characterize the impression which the political society has of the decision-making structures. This concept is anchored in objective political structures and it is demonstrated in its rich content by the 'sensual presence' of these structures in the societal perspective.

The visual comprehension of a metaphor appears in a directly political way in the thinking of an era: How are these political structures intuitively understood? How are they interpreted? The logic of these mental pictures consists, thus, of concrete historical experiences and cultural contexts, as well as of expectations which can exceed reality (see, the project of an 'iconic episteme', Boehm 2007). In this 'mental image' the acute perception of the representative practice gets a living expression. In the ways these 'mental images' change we can follow the transformation and renovation of the social process of politics. Consequently, it can be shown how closely allied are the figure-based perceptual concepts, viz. the 'representation' and the 'presentation' of policy.

The recurring question is whether, and in which appropriate forms, the perspective of both the current and status quo transcending comprehension of political representation could be described by means of the concept of an iconologic 'image'. The political science perspective of this central issue is the concept of the '(societal) imaginary' (Castoriadis 1984; Hénaff 2014; Kamper 1986). Castoriadis combines—in one of the expressions of Jacques Rancière (2009, 133)—"the verbal and the visible [. . .] (the) evolvement of the schemes of the mind and of the sensual phenomena"; he defines this as the 'representative regime'.

In contrast, there is the concept of a 'mental image' in the discipline of visual culture which can be operationalized and used (see Belting 2007, 49; Mitchell 2009; already actually Sartres 1971, 205, 'images mentales'). Within this concept, the internal representations of external circumstances are introduced. The substantive image of political representation is understood as "two different facets" that are attributed to "the same process as the one of acquisition of world experience" (Belting 2007, 14). The mental image of political representation is not solely a reflection but an action itself: it is involved in the social construction of political representation. It appears as an 'image' (Bredekamp 2010).

For this, the construct of an 'iconic belief' (*Bildglauben*) is essential (Belting 2007, 50) because such an 'iconic belief' of the citizenship is crucially confronted with 'democratic representation' and its underlying specific socio-political mentality. This concept can be used for the clarification of the phenomenon that the rational images and manifestations of the representative political structures are filled and enriched with intuitive contents. Citizens follow a pattern of an 'imaginary-supply' which supplies the social community with the principle of 'political representation' and, simultaneously, society delivers this representation with its genuine social and continuous new meaning (Tisseron 2007, 308; Kruse 2010, 215–216). Such an 'iconic belief' is a real part of understanding 'political and democratic representation' and forms its specific character.

Therefore, the contextualization of the theoretical concept of the 'iconic belief' and the social-scientific concept of the 'political legitimacy-belief' have a special significance. This concept, most extensively developed by Max Weber in his modernization theory (Weber 1988), deals with the interaction between political systems and their mental acceptance, shared and granted 'legitimacy' by societies.

The presentation of Weber's specific 'forms of the legitimate political power' refers explicitly to the intentional reception of techniques

58   *Hans J. Lietzmann*

of government, the power structures and their normative justification by the people (Palonen 1998; Hennis 1987; 1996). A regime is classified as 'legitimate', but not until it is *regarded* as legitimate. Firstly, the 'belief' in legitimacy is what legitimates the regime as a socially feasible ensemble. Moreover, Weber's legitimacy is considered to be dependent on the sensual political process of believing; it is primarily the sensual, affective and emotional perspective of political legitimacy that creates and reshapes this believed political legitimacy. Here, it is useful to confront the concept of the 'iconic belief' with the theory of democratic representation.

Political Representation as a 'Symbolic Form'

Political representation is a social construction. It describes an assumption by society about the legitimacy of political procedures, which evolves from 'the image' or the view of political practice and in the context of expectations about its forms. In this image the official myths and the social dreams of citizens are blended with real political life into a sort of an amalgam. Here, an aspiring theory of political culture differentiates between an official culture of 'interpretation' and a socially emerging 'socio'-culture (Rohe 1990; 1996, 8). Thus, we experience a 'world view', a 'world image' (Rohe) or a 'world feeling' (Panofsky 1927). All these concepts stand for a 'real irreality' (Boehm 2008), which floats between pure facts, official (re-)presentation and their social reception. The intention now is to define these facts with regard to political representation in respect of hermeneutics and its concepts.

If a consistent analysis of the current social perspective of political representation is being considered, the question of its temporal condition arises. On the basis of current ideas about representativeness, there is an indirect conclusion about the current societal, political and social imaginations. Comprehension of the political representation is, therefore, a "key to the culture-specific habits of thinking" (Belting 2009) of each era under consideration. The way of thinking of each era contributes to the potential imaginations of the citizenship and their expectations on political representation (Boehm 2008, 46).

In this respect, there is a parallel with the views of Erwin Panofsky and his 1927 study about "perspective as a symbolic form". In the same way as perspective (view) is defined by Panofsky, a change of political representation may be deduced from a transformation of societal imaginations concerning representation and the expectations of the representatives.

In Panofsky's view of Cassirer's 'symbolic form', 'political representation' is not considered to be a "*Wertmoment* (value moment)", but a "*Stilmoment* (style moment)" (Panofsky 1927, 108), by means of which a specific connotation to a specific mental image is connected and a specific comprehension is attributed. In this sense, individual epochs can be distinguished and classified, not solely by the fact of their correspondence to a specific imagination, but additionally by means of the 'symbolic form' and its specific features: how much they correspond to the fact of being viewed as their own, and how far they are affectively accepted, as such, or 'believed'.

At the same time, the research focus is regularly posed to substantive but not mental images. Remarkable shifts can be observed in the field of political approaches towards (political) presentations and re-presentation (see Bredekamp and Schneider 2005; Koschorke 2002; Manow 2008; Hénaff 2014). In political science, we speak of the "Machiavellian Moment" (Pocock 1975), in the science of history about the "*Sattelzeit* (saddle period)" (Koselleck 1979): a reorganization of the 'political' and a reorientation of patterns of cultural thinking. Besides the imagination of representation there is a continued stagnation of the central perspectives of political representation towards the 20th century. "The seats of the old power are from the start taken by the ones, who are elected by the people [in the 17th century, H.J.L.] [. . .] The (mental) images of the democratic sovereignty have been quite exactly formed into a casting mould of the traditional sovereignty" (Hénaff 2014, 93).

Political representation is still considered to be equivalent to actions of the 'government'. What is required is a new research focus on the current transformation using iconological methods and the instruments of visual culture. What, e.g., distinguishes contemporary cultural technology, the societal construction of political representation, which increasingly consists of a civic pluralization of strategic political planning and decision-making? Which (patterns of) imaginations are relevant in respect of the current crisis of political representation that is currently under discussion? Of what does the new attribution and the new imaginative interpretation, which is subject to the political representation, consist? What focus is applied to the newly 'symbolic form' of democratic representation?

The Question of Representations in Political Theory

Political representation represents the culminating point of political societies and their virtual political self-organization and hence thematises the link between citizens and their representatives: how should the process of political leadership be organized? How can political organization and the willingness to follow a political leadership be theoretically guaranteed? How should the political decision-making process look in order to be perceived as legitimate by all citizens?

Different historical forms of representation build the basis of the self-interpretation of a society in the context of political action. Societies constitute and symbolize themselves, in particular, by the way the

60   Hans J. Lietzmann

representation of political leadership is organized, demonstrated and observed. So it can be said that what lies behind the representative institutions is a symbolic order and a symbolic self-perception which is historically contingent and subject to conceptual change.

A political society 'articulates' its political and symbolic self-perception through the form of its political representation (Voegelin 1959, 78). In other words, the institutions and their change 'express' the reality of a political society through the conceptual form of representation and decision.

It is therefore most important not to understand the function of politics only in the sense of producing collectively binding decisions, but rather we need to take into account the 'social accountability and visibility' of politics. Decisions will only be regarded as binding by those who perceive themselves as a community. 'Political visibility' will only be established by 'the construction of social spaces' or, to put it another way, "by the simulation of social spaces" (Nassehi 2002, 46) within political decisions will be acknowledged to be binding.

In conclusion, representation is a historically contingent concept for symbolically organizing the visibility and accountability of concrete political spaces. Only within these spaces is politics and political leadership culturally recognized by the subjects and therefore realized. This is a fluid, precarious and dynamic process of social and cultural recognition.

The 'Standard Account' of Political Representation and its Remarkable 'Crisis'

The usual debate in political science continuously deals with a 'Standard Account' of representation (Urbinati and Warren 2008, 389). This 'Standard Account' is defined in the writings of Hannah Fenichel Pitkin (1967). Based on the constitutional debate of forms of political representation in the 20th century (Leibholz 1973; 1965; Schmitt 1928, 209), Pitkin says that "representation, taken generally, means the making present in some sense of something which is nevertheless not present literally or in fact" (Pitkin 1967, 8). She defines representation as "a principal-agent relationship" in which a representative stands and acts for those he or she represents. It becomes evident that the recent debate is focused on the question of a representative democracy and its organizational forms. It can even be said that the debate mainly understands representation as a form of representative democracy.

The widely discussed 'Standard Account' of political representation includes a dimension of strong national sovereignty, as "the sovereignty of the people identifies with the state power" (Urbinati and Warren 2008, 389), as well as a legitimization guaranteed by the "responsiveness by electoral mechanisms" (also see Urbinati and Warren 2008).

Citizenship, Democracy 61

As a response to the so-called crisis of representation 'complements', variations and expansions of the traditional forms of democratic and national politics are discussed. These include new strategic options for actors (Saward 2010; Blühdorn 2011; Jentges 2010); modified competences for independent and fair administrations and constitutional courts (Rosanvallon 2010); enhanced activation of "self-authorized representatives" (Urbinati and Warren 2008, 403); the implementation of "citizens' juries", and "mini-publics" (Fung and Wright 2003; Fung 2006); as well as other forms of "citizen representatives" (Brown 2006; Stephan 2004; Dalton 2007; Urbinati and Warren 2008, 405f); and a completely new strategy of "political representation as a democratic process" (Urbinati 2006b).

Nevertheless, a wide public and scientific discussion has taken place, concluding that representation and its institutions are in a dramatic crisis, and not only in Europe (Dalton 2004; Saward 2010; Mansbridge 2003). Many European societies feel they are not being effectively lead by their governments (Kohler-Koch 2010; Rosanvallon 2010; Saward 2011). Moreover, almost all political parties (i.e., the political representatives) are losing members. Even lobby associations, trade unions and entrepreneur associations complain about losing their ability to mobilize citizens. We can observe a demobilization of citizens in the established institutions of current political systems. Thus far, scholars have concluded three possible reasons for this crisis of representation.

Many scholars think that the institutions are in a crisis (Pollak 2007; Warren 2008; Linden and Thaa 2011). They say that the institutional arrangements of political systems have lost their operational capability, their connectivity, and their responsibility and accountability. Many institutions no longer represent the manifold structures of a modern society. The conclusion is that an institutional reset and organizational reform is necessary.

Another debate observes a general crisis of trust leading to an erosion of the willingness to follow the leadership of institutions. The social individualization and the destruction of general social, ideological and religious contexts have eroded the cohesiveness of modern societies. Traditional political systems are unable to cope with the structures of modern societies. Political representation can no longer be guaranteed under the pluralistic circumstances of modern societies. For these reasons, representation is doomed to fail.

Finally, the general frameworks of modern politics are held responsible for the decline of political representation; the transnationalization and the globalization of politics have contributed to the failure of representation of the political and of citizens. The contingency of today's modernity, as well as the transnational structure of decision-making processes, have made political representation impossible.

62 Hans J. Lietzmann

Can the Iconological Concept of Political Representation be Particularly Useful?

"The concept of political representation is misleadingly simple: everyone seems to know what it is" (Dovi 2011, 1). This also holds true for the reality of political representation: it is almost impossible to gain a clear impression of it. Although several attempts have been made to describe this reality in a comprehensive way, these descriptions reflect completely different social and political processes (Pitkin 1967; Ginzburg 1999; Urbinati 2006a; Manow 2006; Göhler 2007; Pollak 2007; Saward 2010). The iconological approach highlights dramatically these heterogeneous political and cultural practices.

The medieval imaginative procedure to keep the pictures of defunct lords and kings alive, e.g., in the form of puppets made from wax, wood or leather, and to demonstrate their 'presence' in the time of the interregnum has been considered as 'represéntacion' in many different political cultures (Spain 1291/ England 1327/ France 1422) (Ginzburg 1999, 97–98).

Later, this practice continued the well-known frontispiece of Hobbes's 'Leviathan' where we can see an absolute sovereign who is constituted by a number of civic bodies; the "mortal God" that Hobbes defines as the ruler of the people is a figure made by humans but seems at the same time to be somehow supernatural and "able to fulfill enormous doings" (Patrizi 1593, 69; cited in Bredekamp 2012, 66). During civil war, no stable political rule survives, and people come back to the virtual power of a new imaginative (!) representation of the societal will. The execution of Louis XIV in France and his replacement by a new representative 'corps législatif' strongly confirms representative practices by the democratic revolutionists: representation by the body of the monarch was replaced by the image of a "great citizen body and [. . .] the assembly of representatives, the double body of political representation" (Baecque 1997, 9; cited in Manow 2006, 153).

American colonial history and its separation from English superiority tells us another story. The slogan "No taxation without representation" rejecting the claim to power of the British Empire, was the founding cry of an American 'representative republic' with its own imaginative visibility (Göhler 2007).

According to Kantorowicz' well-known study on "The king's two bodies", the representative puppets of the Middle Ages stand for an early form of the eternal shape of the enduring dignified kingdom. The description of claims to power in abstract institutions therefore has a long tradition.

These ritual eternalizations were made to keep the claim to power present. They can be described as "fictions post mortem" (Ginzburg 1999, 101) and they are used when power cannot be executed. They are

Citizenship, Democracy 63

"doubles" and "ritual substitutes" (ibid., 103). Their existence contributes to the imagination that they replace the real execution of power. It does not mean that they 'describe' or 'narrate' power, but they symbolize the leadership in situations when the leadership itself is unable to execute power—e.g., when the king is dead or when the leadership seems too amorphous or abstract (in the sense of a 'people' or a 'nation'). It could also be the case when the leadership has to be reconstituted in fixed intervals over a certain period of time as it is with kingdoms and with parliaments. These are the periods in which the political leadership needs an "artificially constructed leader" (Bredekamp 1998, 106) to guarantee its continuity.

In this context, representation is a "cultural technique" (Bredekamp and Schneider 2005, 9) that has been used throughout all phases of Enlightenment and through the antagonisms of the times of transition from the early modern to modern times. It has been used in spite of all processes of secularization and deconstruction in a number of myths.

As representation is a social ritual practice that has been used through all times, it can be said that a practised representation is a "psychological category" (just like a dream or any other supernatural appearance) (Gombrich 1999, 105). Through representation, a society comes into contact with an abstract power and turns it into something that can be experienced in real life!

Similar processes can be observed in the cults centred around Christian pictures and relics. These do not point to a Christian foundation of politics as whole (Duso 2005, 177ff; Voegelin 1959), but they show the common idolatrous basis of religion and political socialization. They point out the common mystifying nucleus of religious and political practice—as incomprehensible as this may seem, this is the picture we have of this world which clearly influences our social actions.

A Dynamic and Iconic Understanding of Democratic and Citizens' Representation

Recent theories in the pictorial field of social science make reference to representation and imagination indicating an ontological structure of the pictorial quality of our social actions (Kruse 2010; Belting 2007; Boehm 2007; Tisseron 2007). Imagination is part of the human mind and therefore of civic societies which are always in search of imaginations and autonomously react to any stimulation of imagination. They respond to the practice of their outside world and they illustrate their experiences in their perception. These imagined pictures become the action paradigm for citizens' political and everyday thinking and behaviour. The image of being 'represented' is the matrix guiding them to 'automatically' understand daily information and experiences. As Sartre (1971, 205ff) says, these mental imaginations guide our social consciousness.

64   *Hans J. Lietzmann*

The power that these imaginations have lies "in their function of enwrapping and encasing. By stimulating our empathy through emotional and sensual impulses, they respond to the wish of entering an imaginary reality" (Kruse 2010, 216). The emotional and political profit is that they synthesize the innumerable impressions which assail us in the external political world. The unification and simplification of this world view provides social and emotional relief and, at the same time, represents the function of the actual execution of power. The picture we have of the reality of representation therefore reflects our strong belief in a virtual reality, but it is also a persistent projection screen for our understanding of reality. It helps the subjective worldview and the objective living conditions to survive (Kruse 2010, 217; Tisseron 2007, 314).

Citizens also use their image of 'representation' with a 'destroying passion'. Humans are determined by the ambivalence between worldview and view of politics. In contrast, they also sense that these views might only be images and impressions. They question their views and observe carefully whether they correspond to reality. If the mismatch between imaginary perceived representation and actually experienced representation gets too wide, the imagined representation will immediately be dropped. "We are immediately ready to condemn it: it is always their guilt!" (Tisseron 2007, 314).

The more recent theory of representation does not take pictorial sciences and the imagination of political representation into account. There are some important concepts of political representation as a question of social dynamics. These concepts try to release the question of political representation from a pure institutional point of view and they pick out the conceptual change as a question of political and social action (Urbinati 2006a; 2006b; Castiglione and Warren 2006; Pollak 2007; Thaa 2008; 2013). However, these approaches follow a normative conceptual line of argument: they 'compose' pictures of political representation which they hope political societies follow.

With the help of these theories, we can prove to what extent the prevailing images of political representation have been discredited. These political theories are the seismograph of a growing discontent with the prevailing imaginations of political representation; they demonstrate that the image, the demand and the reality of political representation are distant from each other and are the legitimate attempt to create new imaginations. Even if the "diffuse, aesthetic potentiality" of political representation within societies is taken into account (Saward 2010), it remains true that politicians are defined as the actors, and citizens as the observing public. Even if these theorists point out the "cultural dimensions of representation" (Thompson 2012, 112) and the fact that "political representation is a creative activity" (Disch 2012), many (including Saward) neglect the performative circumstances of the perception by society.

In contrast to Bourdieu (1991) who gives cultural representation the power of a real agent theory, in which professional politicians produce images of leadership and charisma as they like (cf. Jentges 2010, 62), Jentges' description is somehow more flexible, although he nevertheless follows the picture of a cultural representation as a top-down process. At this point, it needs to be emphasized that representation is a process of recognizing structures and institutions by citizens. It can even be argued that they only become 'representative' through the recognition by citizens. Representation is a social process and its success is determined by polities. In this sense—as Max Weber shows by taking legitimacy as an example (Weber 1972, 122–128; Palonen 1998)—representation is not produced by the leaders but it rather comes into being by the citizens' belief in the legitimacy of the leadership. Representation does not emerge from the 'top-down', but from being believed from the 'bottom-up'. It needs to be accepted by all citizens as their own re-presentation and it requires a positive perspective and the active development of society. This social practice of representation, its creation, is a practice of social individuals, not a practice of the institutional actors. Representation is born out of a social process which "takes into consideration all humans as the producers of their way of living" (Horkheimer 1937, 625). Today, representation always remains an object of this process of creation. These "objects and the way they are being perceived, the question and the sense of its answer show human activity and the degree of its power" (ibid.).

These creations require a number of "regulative fictions" helping citizens to produce a picture of itself (Koschorke 2002, 77). As long as citizens act politically and decide politically, daily myths, staging and rituals will be part of that every day practice; politics always make use of metaphysical understandings, symbolic forms and emotional attributions. These attributions depict the imaginary "sense of reality" of each society (Diers 1992, 31). They form the hybrid character of every society (Latour 2008, 18ff; see also Lietzmann 2012). What remains an exciting and extremely important question is how they develop and how they change.

Conclusion

If representation means that a small group of citizens acts on behalf of the rest of the citizenry, the core questions include who are the represented and which claims and voices are represented in the representative arenas, and how? These crucial questions must be addressed from the perspective of the represented citizens, because any representative structures and institutions are based on a societal process to the extent that it is recognized as such by those it is supposed to represent. Hence, the question of representation is closely connected to different interpretations of the scope and meaning of citizenship. Understanding representation as an

66 Hans J. Lietzmann

iconological concept can shed new light to the complexities of representation in current conditions which are in flux in several ways.

Changing subjectivity and the general alteration of conditions lead to a shifting self-perception by the people in modern societies and modify the imagination of political representation. The mimetic potential has shifted and no longer corresponds to the traditional modes of representative politics. Therein lies no 'crisis of representation', but the decline of a traditional kind of representation and the nucleus of a new one. The legitimacy of traditional politics erodes in the course of social change. Recent social changes imply a conceptual change of representation: more individual and self-determined self-perceptions—which already put national representation under pressure because of its lack of differentiation—replace the traditional image of representation in the sense of a 'representatio singulariter' characterized by national or federal modes of representation.

Most modern societies still do not have a real response to these developments. Due to its genealogy, it relies on the opposite of representation and, for now, does not have any imaginative power at its disposal to raise awareness of its role, its function and its importance as the alter ego of the self-perception of citizens. The 'iconic belief' currently does not correspond closely enough to images and political representations such that it functions as a representation of the represented.

References

Ankersmit, Frank. 2002. *Political Representation*. Stanford, CA: Stanford University Press.

Belting, Hans. 2007. "Eine Herausforderung der Bilder." In *Bilderfragen*, edited by Hans Belting, 1–26. München: Fink.

———. 2009. "Zu einer Ikonologie der Kulturen. Die Perspektive als Bildfrage." In *Ikonologie der Gegenwart*, edited by Gottfried Boehm and Horst Bredekamp, 9–20. München: Fink.

Berger, Peter L., and Thomas Luckmann. 1969. *Die gesellschaftliche Konstruktion der Wirklichkeit*. German translation: Monika Plessner. Frankfurt am Main: Fischer Taschenbuch Verlag. [1966. *The Social Construction of Reality*. New York: Penguin Books.]

Blühdorn, Ingolfur. 2011. "Das postdemokratische Doppeldilemma." In *Krise und Reform der politischen Repräsentation*, edited by Markus Linden and Winfried Thaa, 45–74. Baden-Baden: Nomos.

Boehm, Gottfried. 2001. "Präsentation–Repräsentation—Präsenz. Auf den Spuren des homo pictor." In *Homo Pictor*, edited by Gottfried Böhm, 3–13. München & Leipzig: Saur.

———. 2007. "Das Paradigma 'Bild'. Die Tragweite der ikonischen Episteme." In *Bilderfragen. Die Bildwissenschaft im Aufbruch*, edited by Hans Belting, 77–82. München: Fink.

———. 2008. "Jenseits der Sprache? Anmerkungen zur Logik der Bilder." In *Wie Bilder Sinn erzeugen*, edited by Gottfried Boehm, 34–53. Berlin: Berlin University Press.

Citizenship, Democracy   67

Bourdieu, Pierre. 1991. *Language and Symbolic Power*. Edited and introduced by John B. Thompson. Translated by Gino Raymond and Matthew Adamson. Cambridge: Polity Press.

Bredekamp, Horst. 1998. "Politische Zeit: Die zwei Körper von Thomas Hobbes' Leviathan." In *Geschichtskörper*, edited by W. Ernst and C. Vismann, 105–118. München: Fink.

———. 2010. *Theorie des Bildakts. Frankfurter Adorno-Vorlesungen*. Berlin: Suhrkamp.

———. 2012. *Thomas Hobbes Der Leviathan. Das Urbild des modernen Staates und seine Gegenbilder 1651 2001*. Berlin: Akademie.

Bredekamp, Horst, and Pablo Schneider. 2005. "Visuelle Argumentationen – Die Mysterien der Repräsentation und die Berechenbarkeit der Welt." In *Visuelle Argumentationen*, edited by Horst Bredekamp and Pablo Schneider, 7–10. München: Fink.

Brown, Mark B. 2006. "Citizen Panels and the Concept of Representation." *Journal of Political Philosophy* 14:203–225.

Budde, David. 2013. "Formen der Repräsentation und ihre Legitimation." Working Paper no. 3. Arbeitsbereich Politische Theorie und Ideengeschichte/ FU Berlin.

Castiglione, Dario, and Mark E. Warren. 2006. "Rethinking Democratic Representation: Eight Theoretical Issues." Paper presented at the Centre of the Study of Democratic Institutions. Vancouver, Canada, May.

Castoriadis, Cornelius. 1984. *Gesellschaft als imaginäre Institution*. Frankfurt: Suhrkamp. [1975. *L'institution imaginaire de la société*. Paris: Seuil.]

Dalton, Russell D. 2004. *Democratic Challenges, Democratic Choices: The Erosion of Political Support in Advanced Industrial Democracies*. Oxford: Oxford University Press.

———. 2007. *The Good Citizen: How a Younger Generation is Reshaping American Politics*. Washington, DC: CQ Press.

Diers, Michael. 1992. "Von der Ideologie- zur Ikonologiekritik." In *Frankfurter Schule und Kunstgeschichte*, edited by A. Bernd, 19–40. Berlin: Reimer.

Disch, Lisa. 2012. "The 'Constructivist Turn' in Political Representation." *Contemporary Political Theory* 11:114–118.

Dovi, Suzanne. 2011. "Political Representation." *Stanford Encyclopedia of Philosophy*. http://plato.stanford.edu/entries/political-representation/. Accessed February 15, 2017.

Duso, Giuseppe. 2005. *Die moderne politische Repräsentation: Entstehung und Krise des Begriffs*. Berlin: Duncker+Humblodt.

Fung, Archon. 2006. "Democratizing the Political Process." In *The Oxford Handbook of Public Policy*, edited by R. Goodin, M. Moran and M. Rein, 667–683. Oxford: Oxford University Press.

Fung, Archon, and Erik Olin Wright. 2003. *Deepening Democracy: Institutional Innovations in Empowered Participatory Governance*. London: Verso Press.

Ginzburg, Carlo. 1999. *Holzaugen: Über Nähe und Distanz*, 97–119. Berlin: Wagenbach.

Göhler, Gerhard. 2007. "Deliberative Demokratie und symbolische Repräsentation." In *Inklusion durch Repräsentation*, edited by Winfried Thaa, 109–125. Baden-Baden: Nomos.

Gombrich, Ernst Hans. 1999. *The Uses of Images: Studies in the Social Function of Art and Visual Communication*. London: Phaidon.

68   *Hans J. Lietzmann*

Hénaff, Marcel. 2014. "Die Bühne der Macht: Die Inszenierung der Politik – Über sichtbare Figuren der Souveränität." *Lettre International* 105:88–95.

Hennis, Wilhelm. 1987. *Max Webers Fragestellung*. Tübingen: Mohr Siebeck.

Horkheimer, Max. 1937. "Philosophie und Kritische Theorie." *Zeitschrift für Sozialforschung* 6:625–631.

Jentges, Erik. 2010. *Die soziale Magie politischer Repräsentation*. Transcript. Bielefeld.

Kamper, Dietmar. 1986. *Zur Soziologie der Imagination*. München: Hanser.

Kohler-Koch, Beate. 2010. "Civil Society and EU Democracy: 'Astroturf' Representation?" *Journal of European Public Policy* 17:100–116.

Koschorke, Albrecht. 2002. "Macht und Fiktion." In *Des Kaisers neue Kleider. Über das Imaginäre politischer Herrschaft. Texte Bilder Lektüren*, edited by Thomas Frank, Albrecht Koschorke, Susanne Lüdemann and Ethel Matala de Mazza, 73–84. Frankfurt am Main: Fischer.

Koselleck, Reinhart. 1979. *Vergangene Zukunft. Zur Semantik geschichtlicher Zeiten*. Frankfurt am Main: Suhrkamp Verlag.

Krämer, Sybille, and Horst Bredekamp. 2003. "Kultur, Technik, Kulturtechnik." In *Bild Schrift Zahl*, edited by Sybille Krämer and Horst Bredekamp, 10–23. München: Fink.

Kruse, Christiane. 2010. "Imagination, Illusion, Repräsentation. Bildbetrachtung als Kulturtechnik." In *Imagination und Repräsentation*, edited by Horst Bredekamp, Christiane Kruse and Paul Schneider, 195–218. München: Fink.

Latour, Bruno. 2008. *Wir sind nie modern gewesen*. Frankfurt am Main: Suhrkamp Verlag.

Leibholz, Gerhard. 1965. "Verfassungsrecht und Verfassungswirklichkeit." In *Die Repräsentation in der Demokratie*, edited by Gerhard Leibholz, 249–271. Berlin: De Gruyter.

———. 1973. *Das Wesen der Repräsentation und der Gestaltwandel der Demokratie*. Berlin: De Gruyter.

Lietzmann, Hans J. 2012. "Kontingenz der Repräsentation: Bürgerbeteiligung." In *Zur kritischen Theorie der politischen Gesellschaft*, edited by Olaf Asbach, Reinhard Schäfer, Volker Selk and Alexander Weiß, 165–188. Wiesbaden: VS.

———. 2014. "Repräsentation und Bürgerbeteiligung. Eine 'neue Gewaltenteilung'?" In *Die Qualität von Bürgerbeteiligungsverfahren. Evaluation und Sicherung von Standards*, edited by Hans J. Lietzmann, Ludger Dienel and Raban B. Fuhrmann, 87–102. Berlin: Oekom.

Linden, Markus, and Winfried Thaa. 2011. "Krise der Repräsentation." In *Krise und Reform der politischen Repräsentation*, edited by Markus Linden and Winfried Thaa, 305–324. Baden-Baden: Nomos.

Manow, Philip. 2006. "Die politische Anatomie demokratischer Repräsentation." *Leviathan* 34:149–181.

———. 2008. *Im Schatten des Königs*. Frankfurt am Main: Fischer.

Mansbridge, Jane. 2003. "Rethinking Representation." *American Political Science Review* 97:512–528.

———. 2011. "Clarifying the Concept of Representation." *American Political Science Review* 105:621–630.

Citizenship, Democracy 69

Mitchell, William J. 2009. "Bildwissenschaft." In *Ikonologie der Gegenwart*, edited by Gottfried Boehm and Horst Bredekamp, 99–114. München: Fink.

Nassehi, Armin. 2002. "Politik des Staates oder Politik der Gesellschaft?" In *Theorie der Politik*, edited by Kai-Uwe Hellmann and Reiner Schmalz-Bruns, 38–59. Frankfurt am Main: Suhrkamp.

Palonen, Kari. 1998. *Das "Webersche Moment."* Wiesbaden: Westdeutscher Verlag.

Panofsky, Erwin. 1927. "Die Perspektive als symbolische Form." In *Aufsätze zu Grundfragen der Kunstwissenschaft*, edited by H. Oberer and E. Verheyen, 99–153. Berlin: Volker Spiess.

Pitkin, Hannah Fenichel. 1967. *The Concept of Representation*. Berkeley, CA: University of California Press.

Pocock, J. G. A. 1975. *The Machiavellian Moment: Florentine Political Thought and the Atlantic Republican Tradition*. Princeton, NJ: Princeton University Press.

Pollak, Johannes. 2007. *Repräsentation ohne Demokratie*. Wien: Springer.

Rancière, Jacques. 2009. *Die Politik der Bilder*. Zürich/ Berlin: diaphanes.

Rohe, Karl. 1990. "Politische Kultur und ihre Analyse. Probleme und Perspektiven der politischen Kulturforschung." *Historische Zeitschrift* 250:321–346.

———. 1996. "Politische Kultur: Zum Verständnis eines theoretischen Konzeptes." In *Politische Kultur in Ost- und Westdeutschland*, edited by O. Niedermayer and K. von Beyme, 1–21. Opladen: Leske+Budrich.

Rosanvallon, Pierre. 2010. *Demokratische Legitimität*. Hamburg: Hamburg Edition.

Sartre, Jean-Paul. 1971. *Das Imaginäre. Phänomenologische Psychologie der Einbildungskraft*. Hamburg: Rowohlt.

Saward, Michael. 2010. *The Representative Claim*. Oxford & New York: Oxford University Press.

———. 2011. "Slow Theory: Taking Time over Transnational Democratic Representation." *Ethics and Global Politics* 4:1–18.

Schmitt, Carl. 1928. *Verfassungslehre*. München & Leipzig: Duncker+Humblodt.

Stephan, Mark. 2004. "Citizens as Representatives: Bridging the Democratic Theory Divides." *Politics & Policy* 32:118–134.

Thaa, Winfried. 2008. "Krise und Neubewertung politischer Repräsentation: vom Hindernis zur Möglichkeit politischer Freiheit." *Politische Vierteljahresschrift* 49:618–640.

———. 2013. "'Stuttgart 21' – Krise oder Repolitisierung der repräsentativen Demokratie?" *Politische Vierteljahresschrift* 54(1):1–20.

Thompson, Simon. 2012. "Making Representations." *Contemporary Political Theory* 11:111–114.

Tisseron, Serge. 2007. "Unser Umgang mit Bildern. Ein psychoanalytischer Zugang." In *Bilderfragen. Die Bildwissenschaft im Aufbruch*, edited by Hans Belting, 307–316. München: Fink.

Urbinati, Nadia. 2006a. *Representative Democracy: Principals and Genealogy*. Chicago, IL: University of Chicago Press.

———. 2006b. "Political Representations as a Democratic Process." *Redescriptions* 10:18–40.

70   *Hans J. Lietzmann*

Urbinati, Nadia and Mark E. Warren. 2008. "The Concept of Representation in Contemporary Democratic Theory." *Annual Review of Political Science* 11:387–412.

Voegelin, Eric. 1959. *Die neue Wissenschaft von der Politik.* München: Anton Pustet. [1952. *The New Science of Politics: An Introduction.* Chicago, IL: University of Chicago Press.]

Warren, Mark. 2008. "Citizen Representatives." In *Designing Deliberative Democracy: The British Columbia Citizens' Assembly,* edited by Mark E. Warren and Hilary Pearse, 50–69. Cambridge, UK: Cambridge University Press.

Weber, Max. 1972. *Wirtschaft und Gesellschaft.* Tübingen: J.C.B. Mohr.

———. 1988. "Die drei reinen Typen der legitimen Herrschaft." In *Gesammelte Aufsätze zur Wissenschaftslehre,* edited by Johannes Winkelmann, 475–488. Tübingen: Mohr.

4 Abstaining Citizenship

Deliberative and Epistocratic Understandings of Refraining from Voting

Francisco Javier Gil Martín

Electoral voting as a fair procedure holds a central place in legitimizing democratic governments and continues to be a benchmark for citizenship entitlements and responsibilities. As a consequence of being a socially constructed and historically contingent political concept, voting is a breeding ground for interpretations and controversies. In this chapter I will not be concerned with issues such as the accountability of elected officials to voters, but with the meanings of voting and not voting as both a citizen right and a moral issue.[1] Nor will I examine the arguments for and against compulsory voting, even though they involve discussions about the political value of abstentions. Rather, I will pay attention to recent views about practising citizenship through voting that assume that universal turnout has become a dispensable principle whereas abstentions, no matter how qualified they may be, should be discounted as irrelevant.

Despite being a major structural phenomenon of most democratic societies and a genuine option for their citizens, abstention remains for many political agents and political theorists alike a functional and beneficial feature of well-established democracies and even a depoliticizing activity to be imposed as far as possible. I will specifically focus on Jason Brennan's epistocratic proposals that—taking seriously the evidence of widespread citizen incompetence—assert that citizens have no moral obligation to vote, but rather duties to vote well and to abstain from wrongful voting, and that even argue for restricting suffrage when voters are likely to be irresponsibly ignorant, irrational, or immoral, and are likely thereby to facilitate harmful decision-making.[2] Interestingly, these proposals owe obvious debts to John Stuart Mill's ethics of voting, although they are not exactly fair to it. Conceptual history provides inspiring insights to make some comparisons in that regard, to critically consider the modulations of abstention that Brennan's arguments prioritize, and to show that the concept of abstention is itself an object of ongoing definitional and political debates.

I will maintain that Brennan's alternatives to mass voting and electoral democracy depreciate the fact that refraining from voting involves, under

72 *Francisco Javier Gil Martín*

certain circumstances, a deliberative commitment as a realization of the rights of political participation, and that citizens could abstain as a way of implementing democratic conditions and institutions. Many deliberative democrats are also far from acknowledging the epistemic value of abstention or neglect the relevance of discriminating between qualified and unqualified forms of it. In the final part of this chapter I will suggest that other 'anti-voting theorists' (Malkopoulou 2014, 85) among the advocates of the 'mini-publics approach' declare themselves agnostic about mass participation while approving a vast majority of citizens as abstainers who blindly transfer their authorization to a few representative ones.

Brennan on Duties to Abstain from Wrongful Voting

Jason Brennan has presented some provocative arguments for voting ethics, restricted suffrage and voting lotteries. Firstly, he asserted that citizens have no obligation to vote, but moral duties to vote in a qualified way and to refrain from wrongful voting, because their choices at the polls have consequences for others (Brennan 2009 and 2011a). Shortly afterwards, he advocated for a 'competence principle' against the democratic principle that citizens should have equal political influence, and argued that they have instead the right that any political power held over them should be exercised by competent people in a competent way (Brennan 2011b). All these arguments work with a three-track concept of abstention as a discretionary action derived from the legally protected right to vote, as a strict moral obligation correlative to the duty to vote with good epistemic credentials, and as a legal obligation under the right to a competent electorate. More recently, Brennan has reformulated his preferences for restricting suffrage by appealing to voter lotteries as an alternative to general elections (Brennan 2014), which implies introducing a sort of abstention by lot.

The target of his 2011 book *The Ethics of Voting* are some entrenched common-sense beliefs, captured in these three statements: "each citizen has a civic duty to vote", "it is better to vote than to abstain" and any good faith vote is morally acceptable, and "it is inherently wrong to buy or sell one's vote" (Brennan 2011a, 3). In refuting this 'folk theory of voting ethics', Brennan draws copiously on illustrations that collect common-sense intuitions, such as those concerning what we used to understand by a responsible parent or a responsible driver. A similar scheme applies to these and many other options and practices: you are not under the obligation of doing something, but if you eventually do it, then you should do it well or otherwise it is better to refrain from that activity. The same goes for voting: "Citizens generally have no standing obligation to vote. They can abstain if they prefer. However, they do have strict duties regarding voting: they must vote well or must abstain". Brennan concludes that, "so long as these duties are not violated, vote

Abstaining Citizenship 73

buying, selling, and trading are not wrong" (ibid., 4). In what follows, I will put aside this last statement and focus on the duties and permissions on which such a commodification of voting would be prefaced.

In most countries with voluntary voting systems, adult people enjoy the political right to vote by default. But this entitlement does not imply *eo ipso* that it is morally correct to honour it at any time. Brennan's first thesis against folk theory argues that our ethical obligations as voters do not include a genuine duty to vote, it being understood as mandatory and not merely as optional or as supererogatory. Accordingly, he rebuts the main arguments that try to justify the supposed duty of voting because of its instrumental value or by appeal to civic virtue (ibid., 15–67). Being, as it is, an individual act whose impact is insignificant while taking time and effort, no prudential reasons can override the fact that voting has a vanishingly small instrumental value. And being, as it is, an entitlement and a free choice, voting cannot be the civic duty so often claimed in the Republican traditions or by most supporters of compulsory voting.

Brennan's first thesis against folk theory also says that voters can abstain if they prefer. Once they are entitled to an equal right to vote, choosing not to vote is likewise legally protected and can be a reasonable and autonomous action. The view that not voting is a conduct above reproach (and that voting is a choice and occasionally even a praise-worthy one) fits into the liberal tradition. It is not only the doctrine of "everything which is not forbidden is allowed" that applies here. It is also that legal permission does not imply a moral obligation and rather favours a moral discharge.

A second and stronger thesis links the voter's moral burdens to the epistemic justification for their votes. Citizens who vote must do it not for the sake of their narrow self-interest, but on the basis of sound evidence for what they justifiably believe to promote the common good. Conversely, citizens whose reasons for voting are not morally and epistemically justified should abstain from voting, as is the case if they vote out of ignorance, in an irrational or biased manner, or driven by immoral beliefs. Hence Brennan's favourite analogy compares the voter's duties to the professional practice of physicians and, in particular, to the responsibility of the surgeons that operate on a patient. Nobody is obligated to become a surgeon and not everyone is qualified to become one. But if someone who has acquired the necessary skills practices as a surgeon, then she ought to be a responsible one or at least should strive to be a good one. She is expected to act professionally in the best interest of the patients and owes them a duty of care to choose the best possible course. Undoubtedly, surgeons make excusable mistakes, but they must not be negligent or careless. Under no circumstances can they afford or should they be allowed to make incompetent decisions that can hurt innocent people.

A similar combination of the beneficence and non-maleficence principles applies to adult citizens as eligible voters. When one of them casts

74 *Francisco Javier Gil Martín*

her ballot, she does not merely express a personal choice that affects no one but herself. As Mill said, she does exercise power over others or, as Brennan prefers to say, imposes externalities upon others. Citizens who "take on the office of voter" do thereby "acquire additional responsibilities" (ibid., 128–129), namely they ought to seek the common good and not to contribute to collective harms. On the one hand, citizens owe it to each other "to be adequately rational, unbiased, just, and informed about their political beliefs" and to "vote for policies or candidates who they are justified in believing will promote the common good" (ibid. 69, 70). Therefore, Brennan endorses a public-spirit view of voting instead of the egoistic view that holds that citizens try to choose programs and governments favourable to themselves and to take advantage of their fellow citizens (ibid., 112–134). On the other hand, citizens who are largely uninformed—or are unwilling to find out—about the consequences that a party or a candidate will cause if elected ought to abstain rather than register harmful votes. Analogously, a person without medical skills or with an unsteady hand, if allowed to perform surgery, would likely hurt others and cause them to suffer. Certainly, surgery and voting are not completely analogous. While the surgeon's malpractice on a patient could be individually harmful, voting, like air pollution, becomes harmful when many people engage in it. Consequently, the duty not to vote badly rests on "the more general duty not to engage in collectively harmful activities" and satisfies a proviso clause of the so-called Clean Hands Principle, pursuant to which the duty remains in force provided that the individual does not incur significant personal costs from his restraint (ibid., 72–73). Because refraining from harmful voting incurs little personal costs, it may well be possible that abstention is ethically mandatory for a high proportion of eligible voters.

Indeed, Brennan repeatedly brings up evidence of low levels of citizen competence when confronted by complex issues. Moreover, he accepts Bryan Caplan's argument from voter's rational irrationality, according to which average voters not only are systematically biased and have systematically wrong beliefs about which policies will promote the common good, but they tend to be satisfied with their less accurate beliefs as long as they pay little cost for holding them (ibid., 28, 171–175). Furthermore, like Caplan (2007, 198), he estimates that the efforts to increase voter turnout will further damage the epistemic qualities of democracy: "Given the extent of bad voting and its effects on policy, some constitutional democracies might function better with even less participation than is now seen" (Brennan 2009, 543).

Turning the Epistocratic Analogy Around

If only competent citizens who decided to vote could vote, while those who pollute the polls must abstain, then the former would enjoy greater

Abstaining Citizenship 75

capacity for political influence. Brennan tries initially to attenuate the anti-democratic impact of this view by underlining its moral character as a claim about voter's responsibilities for the sake of their fellow citizens. However, it is not a coincidence that—since Plato first used it as support for knowledge-based rule—the analogy of the doctor-patient relationship has been a commonplace for epistocrats. Brennan also puts the analogy at the service of a mild variant of epistocratic democracy. John Stuart Mill, the main forerunner of the ethics of voting, is the reference in this regard. Brennan's combination of the anti-paternalist defence of voluntary voting and the endorsement of duties concerning voting cannot hide the Millian's trails. Famously, Mill is regarded as a predecessor of the current deliberative democrats, among other things, because of his conception of powers and responsibilities behind the exercise of voting and because of his demand to protect the common good from voters ignorance and "sinister interests and discreditable feelings". As illustrated by his comparisons of voters with figures who are required to be impartial (the juryman, the parliamentarian and the sole voter), voting is not a right, but a trust or public duty whose moral and epistemic qualities make it equivalent to a well-considered judgement on the common good. That being so, voting should be performed publicly (Mill 1977, vol. 19, 441, 489–503).

Mill's application of the doctor-patient analogy to the function of voting points to central aspects of representative government by highlighting the blending between the authority derived from the epistemic superiority of the physician and the non-delegable authorization by the patient (see ibid., vol. 18, 39–41; vol. 19, 623, 651). Rather than emphasizing the incommensurability between the few wise and the ignorant masses and the hand-over of power to the former, it does invert the Platonic relationship between ruler and ruled by turning citizens into masters that make proper use of the parliamentarians for the sake of their collective goals. A patient's capacity for not transferring her authorizing power and for choosing and employing servants more skilful than herself (without needing in turn to directly control their expert knowledge) is analogous to the democratic idea that the power comes from the people (ibid., vol. 18, 71–72). Competence should be the specificity of parliament, having both a deliberative and a representative function, because voters retain their democratic "power of selection and dismissal [as] the most effectual means of securing the best services of those whom they choose" (ibid., 40).

Interestingly, some epistemic conceptions of deliberative democracy reconsider the moment of authorization through a renewal of the medical–political analogy that assumes the requirements of 'informed consent' as an expression of the autonomy of the patient and as a condition of legitimacy for medical interventions (Gil 2015, 214–217). In contrast to traditional medical paternalism, these requirements import into an asymmetric relationship a less hierarchical kind of interaction.

76 Francisco Javier Gil Martín

David Estlund's use of the analogy stresses this point—the indispensable, uncoerced, and informed authorization of the patient who consents while recognizing the doctor's expertise—in order to defuse the 'expert/boss fallacy' and to remove the threat of epistocracy (Estlund 2008, 3, 117). Estlund's response to the fallacy of moving directly from expertise to political power, namely that no political expertise would be undisputed and beyond the reasonable objections of other citizens, foregrounds the epistemic qualities of the deliberation process that any democratic authority should pursue, but without privileging the positions of the presumed experts. Instead of exclusively basing the democratic legitimacy on political equality and procedural fairness, as other deliberativists do, Estlund's epistemic proceduralism claims that "democratically produced laws are legitimate and authoritative because they are produced by a procedure with a tendency to make correct decisions" (ibid., 8). James Fishkin, for his part, considers deliberative democracy a form of collective informed consent (Fishkin 2009, 34–43, 83, 90, 195–196). Because the patients who wish to receive the benefits from a medical intervention must take their own risks, informed consent imposes upon the health professionals the moral and even legal requirement to disclose all relevant information and to verify that it is understood. The statistically representative microcosms embodying both political equality and deliberation play an equivalent function regarding the citizen's considered judgements about questions of collective political will. These mini-publics are designed and implemented to arrive at what all citizens would accept on reflection if they were fully informed and weighed the reasons for and against the relevant political issues.

Let us now advance to Brennan's shift from abstention as a moral duty to abstention as a legal sanction. In the article "The Right to a Competent Electorate" he claims that "just as it would be wrong to force me to go under the knife of an incompetent surgeon, or to sail with an incompetent ship's captain, it is wrong to force me to submit to the decisions of incompetent voters", and that "as a matter of justice, they ought to be excluded from holding political power, including the power to vote" (Brennan 2011b, 700). It is no more the purely moral complaint against the wrongful voting that is at stake here, but the claim that people engaged in wrongful voting (and hence in collectively harmful activities) should be legally prevented from such political participation. Now, the right to a competent electorate leads to the defence of restricted suffrage by requiring that masses of people be forced not to vote. That is highlighted by the analogy, which internalizes a patient-centred model of the doctor–patient relationship and assumes the enforceable regulation of the informed consent (Caplan 2013, 15). Brennan shares both Estlund's emphasis on the autonomous authorization of the capacitated patient to proceed with a medical intervention and Fishkin's emphasis on the respect due to this patient as an epistemic subject who bears the burdens and pays the costs. However, the autonomous and qualified authorization is now readjusted not only with an epistocratic intent, but in libertarian terms. It is noteworthy that there are no masses in the medical arena consenting or disallowing surgeons' interventions by way of an informed consent. On the contrary, any patient retains her veto power even against the decisions of many physicians. Indeed, Brennan's comparisons focus on duties and rights in the horizontal relationships among citizens, especially on obligations upon the bad voters towards single innocent citizens who do not have to tolerate their abuses. Brennan's reconsideration of the informed consent analogy reshapes the ongoing control over the untrained masses that the patient's veto power favours. In other words, the power authorized by the right to a competent electorate does not merely recommend bad voters to abstain, but should put into effect a widely abstaining citizenship.

Compulsory Abstention and Restricted Suffrage

Brennan's epistocracy at times reminds us more of Plato's forebear than of Mill's modern and democratic variant. Certainly Mill asserted that "men, as well as women, do not need political rights in order that they may govern, but in order that they may not be misgoverned" (Mill 1977, vol. 19, 480). However, Brennan's comparisons of voters and surgeons (or ships' captains) seemingly share a deeper concern with Plato's guardianship doctrine. As Hannah Arendt wrote, citing *The Republic* 347 b–d, "the wish of the philosopher to become a ruler of men can spring only from the fear of being ruled by those who are worse" (Arendt 1958, 229). No doubt, Brennan contends that his epistocracy does not commit the expert/boss fallacy, not even in the Millian variation thereof. Nevertheless, the reasons given in this regard revealingly distort the way in which Mill's demands for universal suffrage and universal education tightly linked competence to participation.

Indeed, Brennan initially declared that his theory of voting bore more democratic credentials than Mill's plural voting scheme by echoing Estlund's discussion of "the epistocracy of the educated thesis" (Estlund 2008, 206–222). Facing the proposal that every citizen should have the right to vote but the better educated deserve more votes, Brennan claimed to advocate a better elitism, one that held both that all adult citizens have an equal political right to vote, and that some citizens should not exercise their right (Brennan 2009 and 2011a, 95–96, 107–109).

However, Brennan reveals himself to be a post-democratic thinker that does not even appreciate the genuine democratic tenets defended by Mill when, in "The Right to a Competent Electorate", he discusses Estlund's objection to the Millian proposal of qualification exam. As it is suggested by the way his reshaping of the medical–political analogy departs from the expert/layperson axis, Brennan's advocacy of the competence

78 *Francisco Javier Gil Martín*

principle does not fall prey to the expert/boss fallacy insofar as it does not necessarily imply that the experts are the best qualified for holding power, but only that "incompetent and unreasonable people should not be imposed upon others as bosses" (Brennan 2011b, 713). Nevertheless, as Estlund states, epistocracies violate the liberal principle of justice that any basis for distributing political power has to be acceptable to all reasonable points of view. Although Brennan's competence principle does not deliver more political influence to those who know best (for instance, having more than one vote), but urges a restriction of suffrage by disenfranchising those citizens without sufficient political competence, it remains unjust according to liberal principles. Nonetheless, Brennan contends that the competence principle, in addition to probably producing better policies, is less intrinsically unjust than the practice of universal suffrage because the latter is potentially more harmful and does not honour the normative requirement that any political power held over the citizens should be exercised competently by competent people. On that point, Brennan appeals to the innocent defendant's entitlements to competent juries as a basis to be forced to comply with their decisions. This differs substantially from Mill's comparison of voters and jurymen. Far from underlining the judgemental and representative, impartiality-oriented aspects of voting, the juryman analogy is adduced to justify that any unreasonable majoritarian electorate is more unjust and dangerous than a selected one. For this reason, even though Brennan harbours reservations about voting exams as a non-distorting measure to enforce the competence principle by filtering the 'restricted electorate', he points out that "a properly administered voting examination system would be approximately as unjust as these voting age laws" that currently "draw an artificial bright red line between the competent and incompetent in a way reasonable people could object to" (ibid., 715–716, 719).

Certainly, Mill's epistocratic proposals concerning voters' requisites and influence should counteract the trend to "declare ignorance to be entitled to as much political power as knowledge" (Mill 1977, vol. 19, 478). Among the qualifications any citizen should meet in order to earn the right to vote Mill considered the literary test, the application of which meant excluding a significant proportion of the population from political participation. However, Mill endorsed the democratic commitment that disenfranchising the illiterate could only be implemented provided that universal education had previously been ensured by the state. Similarly, Mill's reasons for plural voting as an ameliorative measure were linked to his support for extending the franchise to everyone, including women and the labouring class, at a time when the default rule was limited suffrage. Plural voting was not an elitist arrangement for weighting votes that could be carried out without the institutionalization of universal suffrage (ibid., vol. 1, 288–289; vol. 19, 324–327, 474–479, 632).

Abstaining Citizenship 79

In sum, Brennan misreads Mill's support for plural voting as solely endorsing competence, and he ends up making an ever more selective move with his proposal of a restricted electorate. Mill understands the competence principle as complementary to the egalitarian principle and in an enriching and productive tension that encompasses the episto-cratic arrangements in a wider democratic framework. On the contrary, Brennan disengages the epistemic demand of the best outcomes from political equality and applies his competence principle with an exclusion-ary purpose.

Moreover, Brennan's commitment to the model of bounded rationality determines his renouncement of ameliorative collective measures that can make us trust that widespread rational ignorance could be remedied by getting voters to become more knowledgeable. Mill famously trusted the transforming power of education and the educative function of political participation. For him, public voting should presumably realize some-thing of the deliberative style of politics remodelled by parliamentary representation, such as moving ordinary citizens closer to the practice of arguing *in utramque partem*. More generally, electoral and non-electoral modes of political involvement (including jury duty, participation in voluntary associations, at the place of work, and in the local govern-ment) should have an educative and developmental role for the moral, intellectual, and active capacities of the persons concerned. In contrast, Brennan is unenthusiastic about the favourable impact of better educa-tion on citizens' beliefs and behaviours, because the amount, diversity and sophistication of the required knowledge for training truly compe-tent citizens would exceed the current epistemic division of labour in any complex society (Brennan 2011a, 110–111; 2011b, 722–723; 2014, 89–91). As detailed in his writings, anybody might do her best as a virtu-ous citizen by withdrawing from political participation altogether and by engaging in nonpolitical activities that promote the common good in very different ways. On the other hand, Brennan is deeply wary of the alleged educational and ameliorative benefits of political engagement, let alone when they are expected from compulsory voting (2011a, 102–103; 2014, passim). Although the search for enlightened preferences and the increase in political knowledge could improve some voters' qualifica-tions, Brennan seems to think that any attempt to lead error-prone voters to develop their judgemental and argumentative capabilities will become even worse under real-world circumstances. At best, he does not take seriously that the involvement in voting and political activities could enhance the very competence of citizens.

Similarly, abstentions may well be morally and epistemically justified, and deliberation might favour such qualified abstentions, but the question of whether and how the reasonable citizens should be qualified abstain-ers for the sake of their fellow citizens is a minor issue overshadowed by

80 *Francisco Javier Gil Martín*

the evidence that politically active citizens tend to lack the deliberative virtues, and to be biased and polarized as extremists (2011a, 175–176). Maybe the unreliability of the electoral process at large forces you to vote badly and you must abstain after deliberation as a way of contesting the prevailing electoral conditions that inadequately support the legitimacy of local, national and regional democratic orders (Hanna 2009). Such considerations are not restricted to considering, as Brennan does, abstention as a personal choice, a moral sanction and an enforceable duty. But, for him, they lend little more than a testimonial value in contrast to the less unjust and more consequential demand on voters and non-voters alike to oppose the grim and stubborn evidence that a very high percentage of "voters in democracy do worse than random in selecting leaders and politics" (Brennan 2011b, 722; see also 2014, 92–94).

In "The Right to a Competent Electorate", Brennan concluded that "voters examinations systems are less intrinsically unjust" and are likely to "produce better results than democracies with universal suffrage", provided that they be subject to careful experimentation and wary improvements, "starting small, and moving successes upwards in scale" (ibid., 723, 724). More recently, he inquires into a less punitive and more deferential variant of mandatory abstention and advises another way of restricting the electorate that also calls for experimentation. Instead of delimiting the portion of the populace that can pass the voter exams, he recommends institutionalizing consultations of a representative random sample of the population (Brennan 2014). In the remaining section I will suggest that these alternative procedures to universal voting in elections bear striking family resemblances to some of the experimental innovations of deliberative mini-publics. Similar to these mechanisms of random selection and rational deliberation, voting lotteries also prioritize representativeness by relying on a sample of incentivized citizens and by discounting the political valence of abstention.

Deliberative Constraints on Democratic Abstention

Among deliberative democrats, the engagement of citizens and representatives in processes of having to give reasons for their claims is seen as overcoming voting mechanisms and bargaining deals, not in the sense of abolishing them, but rather as framing and re-signifying them. Drawing in part on Mill's views, deliberative theorists initially characterized voting as expressing a cognitive judgement on the common good against the aggregative conceptions defended by Schumpeterian, pluralist and economic theories of democracy. For instance, according to Joshua Cohen, voting does not express personal interests or preferences for policies, but "beliefs about what the correct policies are according to . . . an account of justice or of the common good that is independent of current consensus and the outcome of votes" (Cohen 1986, 34). Rawls, for his part, asserted that, unlike common views of voting as guided by interests and preferences or by comprehensive convictions, voting according to public reason and its duty of civility should proceed "as ideally expressing our opinion as to which of the alternatives best advances the common good" (Rawls 1993, 219–220).

Most deliberative theorists resist considering public discussions for justifying binding decisions as a mere complement of the electoral consultations. Rather, deliberativists that don't see electoral turnouts as simply a convenient mechanism among others widely argue the other way around: whereas well informed voting requires the openness of deliberation, the deliberative outcomes will not be effective without the temporary completion provided by the elections.

It is less usual to find similar considerations concerning abstention as a form of citizens' political judgement and as part of broader deliberative processes. No doubt, given the increasingly low turnout rates in democratic societies, the number of quiescent, apathetic and uncommitted citizens is growing all over the world. However, there may also be a burgeoning proportion of people who feel morally and epistemically justified in opting out of voting on any occasion. Citizens have duties to vote, but not always and at every election. Abstentions are sometimes morally and epistemically required and some are presumed to be a consequence of transformed beliefs and preferences that have been reached on reflection, even through a process of giving and asking for reasons, and that achieve better epistemic results than those offered by the pre-deliberative ones.

Taking this for granted, the concern remains that "abstention only gives you abstention and an ambiguous silence" (Hill 2002, 93). Whereas votes give the deliberative citizens an opportunity to make their voices heard, are abstentions a valuable political act for these very talking citizens? There is no unambiguous meaning of the intentions and behaviour of the nonvoters in any particular election. Conscientious abstainers may be sending the message that they tacitly consent to the existing order or simply displaying their political satiety or lack of interest. They may be choosing to express dissatisfaction towards specific policies or with an incumbent government. Not voting could be their nonconformist reaction to the available menu of parties, reveal their lack of trust in political institutions or even exhibit a perpetual opt-out of electoral participation altogether. The variety of meanings turns the thunderous silence of abstention into something hard to discern. Of course, there can also be numerous reasons and motivations spurring people to vote as they do, but reasonable abstention is far more ambiguous than voting as a way of channelling and launching political messages. In the absence of adequate mechanisms for voicing what they mean, well-considered abstentions are definitely an ineffective strategy of political communication and an easy target for misinterpretation. Due to this vagueness, abstention as a whole seems doomed to become a sort of emblem or empty signifier.

82 Francisco Javier Gil Martín

In addition, although individual votes have a negligible impact on electoral outcomes and voters barely have control over the way their votes will be interpreted and used in post-electoral contexts, well-considered abstentions and conscientious abstainers are comparatively powerless. By choosing not to vote, abstainers refuse to exert power over others and are far from being free-riders of voters' contributions to the common good. Whereas voters actually benefit from their own votes and from the refraining of others to vote, the aforementioned ambiguity leaves the latter unprotected against the institutional silencing and the partisan exploitation of their political opinions. When political and media agents ignore or manipulate this situation it seems to rest on the assumption that abstention is to be discounted as 'missing data' in our well-established, but self-complacent democracies.[3] From a deliberative point of view, however, the question must be raised whether something really valuable is being overlooked when we don't differentiate among the epistemic credentials of abstainers. Further, we can question whether they are not being treated unfairly when their claims are systematically neglected or left unattended.

However, many deliberative democrats tend to disdain the significance of the qualified abstention and agree to a certain extent with rival models of democracy on the desirability and convenience of voting abstention, even when they appeal to the diversity of participation and the promotion of dissent. As I will suggest, this could be the case with some proponents of mini-publics as institutional designs that promise to renew traditional democracies. It also applies to Brennan's episto-cratic constraints on the established electoral processes. His reservations towards the "quasi-religious reverence for democracy and for the act of voting" (Brennan 2014, 24) or his libertarian fears towards the incompetents turn out to be unduly paternalistic. The highly controversial reforms for restricting suffrage should be effectively addressed to a large degree by state interventions, and not without violence to the many. The freedom from polluted polls would be achieved at the expense of depoliticizing them, because it should neutralize the unavoidable moral disagreements in response to which we have learned to use the unrestricted right to vote to make binding political decisions (González-Ricoy 2012). This depoliticization in the name of the right to a competent electorate means, in practice, disregarding the political opinions of the many (Brennan 2014, 45). Consequently, the widening of compulsory abstention as a 'blessing in disguise' would only be enforced by the means of a disguised epistocratic paternalism that, by omitting the persistence of deep moral and political disagreements, silences the voices of the abstainers and does not explicitly discriminate among them. In the case of voting lotteries, prescribed as a therapy less expensive and less time-demanding than standard elections, the political equality moves from equal voting to equal eligibility to vote, and representativeness is

Abstaining Citizenship 83

ensured by a well-remunerated "subset of the population [as] a mirror image of all eligible voters" (ibid., 32–39). However, the moral and epistemic credentials of the conscientious abstainers remain indiscriminately mixed with other motivations and attitudes and subsumed under statistical aggregations of sociologically relevant groups.

As mechanisms that randomly select a subset of citizens as representative of the general electorate, deliberative mini-publics can be democratic in a further sense: along with the treatment of all the eligible candidates as a priori equal, the tutored citizens discuss public policy issues under conditions of equality and impartiality. These small-scale deliberative venues can be simply informative for public debates, adopt an advisory role for public opinion, or be supportive of entrenched democratic processes. In addition to contributing to social learning and opinion formation, they can provide deliberative citizens with more direct access to formal decision making. Unlike Brennan, authors like James Fishkin, Michael MacKenzie and Mark Warren don't claim that mini-publics have to be fully and exclusively adopted as a superior alternative to voting in elections or that their outcomes should substitute the ordinary elections outcomes. However, they recommend mini-publics as providing an authoritative procedure for exerting influence on the decision-making process or even for exerting power to make decisions, because it guarantees political equality and representativeness even though sacrificing mass electoral participation. Objections have been raised against the presumed preservation of a not merely nominal political equality and the alleged representative virtues that micro-publics are said to honour. One of these objections foregrounds the blind deference by nonparticipants to a few deliberative citizens that results from eschewing mass participation (Lafont 2015). Moreover, if nonparticipants are asked "to remain passive [and] to hand over powers of decision to others and to forgo monitoring" (MacKenzie and Warren 2012, 99), the deliberative "agnosticism about participation" (Fishkin 2009, 191) brings with it another agnosticism about abstention, which is procedurally compelled and substantially subsumed under the micro-representative functions of the relevant sample. In sum, removing universal political inclusion combines again with a disdainful disregard for abstention.

Conclusion

The proposals for dismantling electoral democracy by epistocrats and defenders of selective deliberation not only affect universal voting, but urge a depoliticization of the abstaining citizenship as well. Both sides share the view that a well-functioning democracy deserves citizens' efforts beyond voting by default, and aspire to counteract the widespread condoning of citizens' political ignorance and misuse of voting. Even if this is the right diagnosis in response to the democratic malaise, it

84 *Francisco Javier Gil Martín*

remains a questionable form of therapy to prioritize representativeness at the cost of both excluding in practice the majority of citizens from the decision-making process and ignoring the political valence of abstention as a legitimate opposition to be forced to vote wrongly.

Conceptual history shows us the inherent ambiguity and contestability of political concepts. Abstention currently has a shifting and controversial meaning and the aforementioned anti-voting theorists provide attempts to re-signify it. I have claimed alternatively that reasonable and conscientious abstainers might be loyal citizens that decide to be heard or to exit. As a consequence, instead of praising the trends to misrecognize, exploit and detract from the abstentions, our well-established, but self-complacent democracies would do better to deal with the stream of warning signals these citizens are sending.

Notes

1 This chapter is part of the project Civic Constellation II (Spain's National Research Fund, FFI2014-52703-P).
2 By epistocracy I mean not only the rule of those who know, the wise or the experts, but also the implementation of institutional designs that give 'more power' (and not 'the power') to an instructed minority or that disempower a significant portion of citizens because of their alleged incompetence.
3 I am grateful to Sebastián Linares for this point.

References

Arendt, Hannah. 1958. *The Human Condition*. Chicago, IL: University of Chicago Press.
Brennan, Jason. 2009. "Polluting the Polls: When Citizens Should Not Vote." *Australasian Journal of Philosophy* 87(4):535–549.
———. 2011a. *The Ethics of Voting*. Princeton, NJ: Princeton University Press.
———. 2011b. "The Right to a Competent Electorate." *Philosophical Quarterly* 61:700–724.
———. 2014. "Medicine Worse than the Disease? Against Compulsory Voting". In *Compulsory Voting: For and Against*, edited by Jason Brennan and Lisa Hill, 1–107. New York: Cambridge University Press.
Caplan, Bryan. 2007. *The Myth of the Rational Voter*. Princeton, NJ: Princeton University Press.
———. 2013. "Thoughts on Jason Brennan's The Ethics of Voting." *Reason Papers* 35(1):11–16.
Cohen, Joshua. 1986. "An Epistemic Conception of Democracy." *Ethics* 97(1):26–38.
Estlund, David. 2008. *Democratic Authority*. Princeton, NJ: Princeton University Press.
Fishkin, James S. 2009. *When the People Speak*. Oxford: Oxford University Press.
Gil, Javier. 2015. "Democratic Authority and Informed Consent." In *Parliamentarism and Democratic Theory*, edited by Kari Palonen and José María Rosales, 207–227. Leverkusen & London: Budrich.

González-Ricoy. 2012. "Depoliticising the Polls: Voting Abstention and Moral Disagreement." *Politics* 32(1):46–51.

Hanna, Nathan. 2009. "An Argument for Voting Abstention." *Public Affairs Quarterly* 23(4):279–286.

Hill, Lisa. 2002. "On the Reasonableness of Compelling Citizens to 'Vote': The Australian Case." *Political Studies* 50(1):80–101.

Lafont, Cristina. 2015. "Deliberation, Participation, and Democratic Legitimacy: Should Deliberative Mini-Publics Shape Public Policy?" *The Journal of Political Philosophy* 23(1):40–63.

MacKenzie, Michael, and Mark Warren. 2012. "Two Trust-Based Uses of Minipublics in Democratic Systems." In *Deliberative Systems*, edited by Jane Mansbridge and John Parkison, 95–124. Cambridge: Cambridge University Press.

Malkopoulou, Anthoula. 2014. "Does Voting Matter? The Devaluation of Elections in Contemporary Democratic Theory." In *The Politics of Dissensus*, edited by Kari Palonen, Jose Maria Rosales, and Tapani Turkka, 81–99. Santander & Madrid: Cantabria University Press & McGraw Hill.

Mill, John Stuart. 1977. *The Collected Works of John Stuart Mill*. Toronto & London: University of Toronto Press & Routledge and Kegan Paul.

Rawls, John. 1993. *Political Liberalism*. New York: Columbia University Press.

Part II
Debating Citizenship

Hanna-Mari Kivistö, Anna Björk, Katja Mäkinen and Claudia Wiesner

The chapters in the following part, *Debating Citizenship*, bring concrete empirical political debates on citizenship explicitly to the fore. They examine discussions and political struggles over the concept of citizenship with regard to access, rights and political activity that take place in parliaments and related arenas. The four chapters of *Debating Citizenship* examine topical themes demarcating citizenship, including territorial and, above all, political and conceptual demarcations. Each is considered to have important implications for the concept of citizenship, each posing new questions and demands for analysis. While investigating how citizenship is interpreted, negotiated and struggled over, the chapters show how new questions are emerging and become the foci of debate. As the history of the concept of citizenship is about inclusions and exclusions, common to all of the chapters in this part is precisely the inclusive and, in particular, the exclusive politics of citizenship.

The chapters in *Debating Citizenship* apply the reflexive and constructivist approach to concepts in different ways. The authors analyse debates taking place in different national and international fora, including national parliamentary settings. These arenas are considered sites for politics and loci of conceptual debates: here citizenship is politicised, interpreted and revised, new conceptualisations are introduced, and different categorisations and conditions for access are made up. As each of the chapters demonstrates, isolated definitions and singular end results are less interesting for our analysis of citizenship than the debates and struggles that take place over the concept in particular contexts and arenas involving political actors.

The debates analysed refer to different dimensions of the relation between citizens and political communities: access to citizenship (Björk), migrants' rights as well as debates around the recognition of particular rights (Kivistö; Nielsen), and the tension between the state, international law and non-state citizenship in connection to the struggle for indigenous citizenship of the Sámi people (Valkonen and Valkonen).

All chapters refer to the complex relation between citizenship and nationality and the multitude of ways in which it is problematised. They

88 Hanna-Mari Kivistö et al.

all focus on the margins of citizenship and on the persons who live in these margins: migrants, asylum seekers and refugees as categories of non-citizens in the chapters by Björk, Kivistö and Nielsen, and the Indigenous Sámi people in the chapter by Valkonen and Valkonen, as examples of people for whom nation state–based citizenship has not guaranteed full political membership. As the margins are considered crucial in shaping and contesting citizenship (see also Clarke et al. 2014), in *Debating Citizenship* they are brought explicitly to the centre of the analysis.

A particular demarcation is the one between citizens and non-citizens. The latter is an analytical and political category that refers to persons who do not have legal membership to a particular polity granted by citizenship. Full citizenship status has manifold dimensions on conceptual, legal, practical and symbolic levels, all of which are discussed throughout this volume. Non-citizens—e.g., asylum seekers, refugees, migrants, posted workers, permanent residents and foreign students— lack the legal and political status of membership while being subjected to national legislation. Non-citizens' access to rights and possible forms of agency are regulated and constituted by the state in which they reside. Whereas it is within their own power to either strive for, or refrain from seeking full citizenship, the state nonetheless defines the rules for access and membership.

Björk's chapter focuses on this problematic, in particular, and on the construction of the rules and conditions for access to citizenship— their definitions and explications in the political debates analysed. The chapter shows how different statuses for immigration imply different possibilities and limitations for active participation for future residents and citizens. The analysis of the UK case is connected to the broader framework by European states of introducing new requirements and procedures for naturalisation and immigration, and for applying for permanent residence since the early 2000s, and its implications for the politics of citizenship. Here, as well as in other chapters in *Debating Citizenship*, citizenship is conceptualised from the point of view of its borders. Hence the question of who citizens are and what the conditions are for citizenship constitute the concept of citizenship: when the limits and rules for accessing the status of citizenship or even partial rights are being debated, the norms and values of the polity are also being problematised (see Björk 2011 and 2014).

The variety of concepts, categories, labels and (legal) definitions related to the non-citizenry, and the ways in which non-citizens are "classified, labelled, problematized and constituted" (Isin 2002, 263), require careful conceptual and political analysis. As has been said in the Introduction, we understand categorisation as never innocent and as a political act in itself. Moreover, each category, definition and label, even those that might be normative, is historically contingent and socially constructed. Both citizenship and immigration bring forth formal statuses and status

Debating Citizenship 89

categories of different kinds. In regard to citizens as well as non-citizens, the respective status—e.g., "legal" or "illegal" status—has considerable practical significance in relation to, for instance, the legal rights one is entitled to (see Gündoğdu 2015; McNevin 2011). Defining and/or the granting of a status, such as the status of citizen, or of a refugee, or the non-status of an undocumented, or irregular migrant, therefore is a decisive act of defining power relation and individual life chances. Addressing the conceptual divisions—and how they are used for different political purposes—is vital for the analysis of the inclusive and exclusive politics of citizenship and the uses of citizenship as a tool for political exclusion.

The chapters by Björk, Kivistö and Nielsen all examine the sovereign practices by states related to non-citizens in the context of political and legislative changes. Kivistö's chapter focuses on debates related to the right of asylum in the context of Germany and the UN in the immediate postwar period; Nielsen's chapter explores the debate related to extending the right to medical care to irregular migrants in Sweden, whereas Björk addresses the conditions of access for immigrants by analysing a debate from the UK. These debates and different empirical case studies not only resonate well in contemporary political and scholarly discussions in Europe related to migration and the challenges it poses to nation state citizenship, but they also demonstrate how the state practices connected to claims of entry and access, recognition and exercise of rights depend on the status (or non-status) of the person. Kivistö's chapter highlights the historical particularity of refugees and asylum seekers as a specific category of migrants in terms of admission, whereas irregular migrants are persons in exceptional situations in present-day Europe without official status or legal residence, as Nielsen's chapter shows. The conceptual hierarchical demarcations of non-citizenry and, in particular, the temporalities related to accessing different categories of non-citizens are discussed in the chapter by Björk.

In addition to the boundaries between the citizens and non-citizens, the chapters address demarcations related to rights. Kivistö's and Nielsen's chapters both manifest the idea of citizenship as a "right to have rights" as formulated by Hannah Arendt ([1951] 1994), which has not only historical but also present-day relevance for the political struggles related to migrants (see, e.g., Gündoğdu 2015). In the chapter by Kivistö, Arendt's notion is used to approach and rethink the problematic connection of citizenship and rights in the analysis of both historical and present-day debates. The chapter investigates political and conceptual struggles related to the right of asylum as a particular right of non-citizens. Whereas asylum is a contested right in Europe and a central question on political agendas, the theme also has historical significance in terms of analysing a state's obligations and responses towards the rights claims presented for the protection of non-citizens. In the chapter by Nielsen, the relationship between citizenship rights and human rights is discussed

90 *Hanna-Mari Kivistö et al.*

by analysing struggles over the right to medical care with reference to irregular migrants. Whereas social rights are rights that have been closely connected to citizenship in the Marshallian model (see Marshall 1950), by investigating the Swedish case example Nielsen challenges this notion and argues for a discursive and conceptual shift in the understanding of access to medical care as a right that can be seen as a right regardless of the legal status of the resident. Nielsen's chapter shows how the language of human rights is used to mobilise the discussion concerning the right to medical care that has previously been seen as a right of membership.

Each of the chapters in *Debating Citizenship* examines political boundaries related to memberships and political communities. Whereas the movement of people across borders challenges old political boundaries, the contested notions of membership are also evident in the chapter by Valkonen and Valkonen, who discuss the political struggle related to the Indigenous Sámi people in Northern Finland. By addressing questions related to belonging and struggles related to the claims of recognition, the chapter contests the idea of nation state membership of citizenship. The authors investigate conceptual and political disputes involved in the notion of indigenous citizenship as a form of non-state citizenship. Indigenous citizenship is also an example of the internal diversification of citizenship: the Sámi in Finland, Norway, Russia and Sweden have national citizenship in their states but also a distinct status "beyond" the state. This status is both intrastate and transnational, and involves divisions both at the intrastate and transnational levels. The chapter explores the intersection of citizenship with ethnicity and identity, and sheds light on many similar situations from different contexts. The politics of the concept of Indigenous people, therefore, resonates well with the contestedness of citizenship analysed in the various contributions of this volume.

Citizenship, finally, can be understood as a formal legal status, but it also can be conceptualised as "being political" (Isin 2002), which is not based on the status of the citizen. Therefore, non-citizens, when claiming their rights just like citizens would do, or the Indigenous Sámi people when struggling for political recognition, develop new forms of political agency, new ideals and diversifications of citizenship. Whether related to the claiming of rights or requests for entry and access, these conceptual readings help us to understand the politics of citizenship and the demarcations created by the exclusiveness of citizenship. The exclusiveness constitutes strangers and outsiders (see Isin 2002), but the outsiders, non-members, persons at the margins of citizenship also constitute citizens and citizenship; politicise new questions; challenge old self-evident conceptions, categories and power relations; and require new theorising. Citizenship is, therefore, shaped in each of the political debates, the conceptual contestations, the struggles over recognition and the articulation of rights analysed in *Debating Citizenship*.

References

Arendt, Hannah. [1951]1994. *The Origins of Totalitarianism*. New York: Harcourt.

Björk, Anna. 2011. "The Politics of Citizenship Tests: Time, Integration and the Contingent Polity." PhD dissertation. University of Jyväskylä.

———. 2014. "Accessing Citizenship: The Conceptual and Political Changes of the German Naturalization Policy, 1999–2006." *Contributions to the History of Concepts* 9(1):74–87.

Clarke, John, Kathleen Coll, Evelina Dagnino, and Catherine Neveu. 2014. *Disputing Citizenship*. Bristol: Policy Press.

Gündoğdu, Ayten. 2015. *Rightlessness in an Age of Rights: Hannah Arendt and the Contemporary Struggles of Migrants*. Oxford: Oxford University Press.

Isin, Engin F. 2002. *Being Political: Genealogies of Citizenship*. Minneapolis: University of Minnesota Press.

Marshall, T. H. 1950. *Citizenship and Social Class, and Other Essays*. Cambridge: Cambridge University Press.

McNevin, Anne. 2011. *Contesting Citizenship: Irregular Migrants and the New Frontiers of the Political*. New York: Columbia University Press.

5 Right of the Politically Persecuted Non-Citizen or Right of the State?

Conceptual Debates on Asylum

Hanna-Mari Kivistö[1]

In the context of recent political crisis related to migration, questions of asylum have come to play a focal role on the agendas of European politics. Although not for the first time, the right of asylum has caused political tensions in Europe, ethical concerns and administrative problems. This chapter examines debates on asylum in a more historical framework by looking at the recognition of asylum as a right in an international and a national setting during the late 1940s. These debates took place after the displacement of an estimated 60 million people as a result of the Second World War (see Frank and Reinisch 2014, 478). Even if the immediate postwar debates on asylum were carried out under quite different circumstances, institutional setting and politico–historical context than those today, the themes nevertheless have strong resonance in the present-day framework in which the right of asylum continues to be a matter of controversy and political, as well as real life, struggle. The political questions in Europe currently include the contested notion of burden-sharing of asylum seekers and refugees, the question of state responsibility towards asylum seekers arriving, the practices of admission and non-admission by states, as well as the questions connected to the protection of the human rights of persons seeking asylum.

Asylum seekers and refugees are closely connected to the history of European nation states (cf. Frank and Reinisch 2014), and the right of asylum is linked to the ideals and traditions of liberal democracies (Price 2009). Gibney (2004, 2) has noted how asylum as a principle—and as a principle of state in particular, as this chapter will demonstrate—is often endorsed, whereas the receiving, and presently also accessing, protection has been made exceedingly difficult for refugees. Furthermore, Seyla Benhabib (2004, 2), among others, has spoken about the evident contradiction between practices of states and the protection of the human rights of asylum seekers. Even if a contested right in political practice, asylum today has both constitutional and international law importance; it is codified in different regional documents, including the European Charter of Fundamental Rights (see Gil-Bazo 2008). In European states, the right

94   *Hanna-Mari Kivistö*

is included in domestic legislations in most countries, and few countries, such as Germany, France and Italy still have constitutional guarantees for asylum, although these provisions have been argued to be almost obsolete at present (see Lambert et al. 2008).

Scholars have examined right of asylum in the framework of international law and in various national contexts (e.g., Frank and Reinisch 2014; Gil-Bazo 2015; Grahl-Madsen 1972; Kimminich 1968; Noiriel 1991). This chapter contributes to the discussion by providing an analysis of empirical political debates from a conceptual perspective. Disputes on asylum are examined by looking into two contexts and political constellations in which the right of asylum has been a focus of conceptual contestations: in the creation of the Universal Declaration of Human Rights (UDHR) (United Nations, 1948) and in the drafting of the postwar Basic Law ("Grundgesetz", 1949) in the Federal Republic of Germany. These debates resulted in different legal conceptions and codifications which continue to resonate in the understandings of asylum, its scope and limits, today. The first formulates asylum as a state prerogative, as a right of the state, whereas the latter recognises it as a fundamental constitutional human right of the individual (of this conceptual distinction, see also Lambert et al. 2008). This chapter looks at the arguments and conceptual controversies behind the creation of these two rights, including the disagreement over their meaning and content, and over the corresponding duties of the states. Furthermore, in this reading, the status that is given to asylum as a right, or how states respond or non-respond to refugees claiming protection, is understood to be, above all, a political question.

Whereas in pre-1945 international law, sovereignty was "nowhere more absolute than in matters of 'emigration, naturalization, nationality and expulsion'" (Arendt 1951/1994, 278), the debates analysed for this chapter are connected to the momentum of human rights in the immediate postwar context in which the contemporary international regime for the protection of refugees was also created. In terms of refugees and asylum seekers, the period resulted in several documents of importance, including national constitutions in which the right of asylum was recognised, the UDHR, and the Convention Relating to the Status of Refugees (United Nations, 1951). These were located in the framework of which the individual became a subject of international law, and the universalistic language of human rights placed the 'human', instead of the 'citizen', at the centre of rights.

The right of asylum is understood in this chapter as a particular right of politically persecuted non-citizens. The concept of 'non-citizen', although not explicitly used in the empirical material analysed, is applied as an analytical tool to bring to the fore the problematic connected to rights recognition of persons without the legal status of citizenship. Asylum is in this chapter connected to questions of citizenship, human rights and state sovereignty. As will be demonstrated, asylum as a right is, on the one hand, connected to the lack of, or escape from, protection of citizenship in the state of origin, and, on the other hand, to the questions of admittance, access and recognition of rights in the country of refuge. In terms of citizenship, the right of asylum raises also questions about belonging and the boundaries of political memberships: in the context of nation state citizenship asylum is a right that provides remedy for persons not having the protection of citizenship, and as Price (2009, 13) emphasises, for persons forced out from their political communities. In the late 1940s there were particularly acute historical experiences of the practices of nation states in relation to refugees, who had been "a product of the fluidity and mutability of states' definitions of who was deemed to be a citizen and who was not" (see Frank and Reinisch 2014, 480).

I will proceed to, firstly, give an outline of the conceptual starting points of the reading, then discussing conceptual demarcations related to asylum seekers and refugees, with emphasis on the particularity of these categories of non-citizens in terms of admission. The conceptions of asylum as a right of the state and of the individual are introduced in the part that follows. When placing asylum in the framework of human rights, the connection between asylum, human rights and citizenship are problematised with reference to Hannah Arendt's notion of citizenship as "right to have rights". Finally, the empirical part analyses how the two conceptions of asylum—right of the state and right of the individual—are put forward in the political debates of the late 1940s.

Conceptual Historical Starting Points

The right of asylum is connected in this chapter to a larger framework of interrelated changes, not only conceptual but also political, legal and constitutional. On historical occasions, such as the drafting of a constitution, concepts are object of changes (Ball and Pocock 1988), with particular definitions and meanings given to them by political actors. Texts such as constitutions and declarations can further be read as 'speech acts' taking part in a particular debate in their specific politico–historical contexts. The asylum paragraphs of both the UDHR and the West German Basic Law represent conceptual changes. In the Basic Law, the right of asylum was a constitutional innovation, being recognised as a right of the individual for the first time in German constitutional history. In terms of international law, the UDHR was the first time asylum was introduced in an international document declaring rights of individuals, even if the conception as such did not bring about a change in how asylum has been traditionally understood in international law, i.e., as a right of the state.

What is common to the conceptual disputes analysed in this chapter is that they take place in deliberative arenas of different kinds, particularly

96 Hanna-Mari Kivistö

in quasi-parliamentary assemblies. The notion of a 'quasi-parliamentary assembly' refers in this reading to fora that follow some, but not all, parliamentary procedural rules, and exhibit certain parliamentary characteristics. Examples of such assemblies referred to in this chapter are the West German constitutional assembly (Parlamentarischer Rat) of 1948–1949 and the UN Commission on Human Rights in the drafting the Universal Declaration of Human Rights 1947–1948 (see Kivistö 2013). The deliberative arenas are understood as particular loci of debate and for conceptual and political struggles and changes (see Ihalainen and Palonen 2009). This is in turn connected to the idea of political deliberation in the form of arguing for and against and the weighing of different alternatives. When turning attention to the analysis of deliberation, politics is understood as linguistically constructed activity connected to the formulation and voicing of differing and alternative courses of action. This means that there are no self-evident answers to political questions, but that every matter can and should be viewed as potentially controversial, contingent and contested (see Martin 2009).

The conceptual historical approach fosters an understanding that key concepts of political life and language are neither unhistorical nor unpolitical. Hence the political concepts significant for this chapter—asylum, refugee, human rights, citizenship—are understood as socially and historically constructed, and historically contingent. The chapter puts forward a situational analysis emphasising that the recognition and codification of a particular right, and the content and status given to it, is a result of political struggles at a particular time, and related to certain political constellations (see Palonen 2002 for situational analysis on concepts). Furthermore, as there has been historically changing conceptions of who the full citizen is, human rights also "owe their origins, guarantees, and reinvention to political practices of declaring and enacting rights in ways that are not fully authorized by the prevailing institutional and normative frameworks" (Gündoğdu 2015, 188). This means to claim rights, to struggle for rights recognition and the politicisation of new questions on behalf of those who are not yet the subject of rights.

Asylum Seekers and Refugees: Conceptual Demarcations

For the purposes of this chapter, the conceptual distinction—and the close connection—between asylum seekers and refugees is important. Refugees are understood as forced migrants with internationally recognised legal status (Haddad 2008, 23). The idea that refugees are acknowledged as a particular group of migrants to which the international community has to respond was established in the early twentieth century under the League of Nations, relating to the lack of state protection (Gil-Bazo 2015, 12).

Asylum means protection from political persecution, a shelter that, most often, a sovereign state grants. In international law asylum is an

Right of Non-Citizen or Right of the State? 97

institution of protection, whereas refugees are those to whom asylum is granted (Gil-Bazo 2015, 3–4). This means that even if granting asylum has largely been understood as a question concerning the sovereignty of states, the status of refugees has been established in international law. The normative description and admission criterion of 'refugee' dates back to the 1951 Geneva Refugee Convention and its 1967 protocol.[2] The status of political refugee gives access to the set of rights included in the Convention (see Hathaway and Foster 2014). 'Refugee' is thus a recognised status under international law, whereas asylum seeker is someone making a claim for protection and asking to be recognised as a refugee. It is therefore an uncertain category, someone who stands in the margins of state discretion: "the procedure of eligibility determination is in the sovereign hands of the authorities of the country of asylum" (Tabori 1972, 29). In the postwar international law, asylum seekers are protected by the non-refoulement principle (e.g., Art. 33 Refugee Convention), meaning the prohibition on returning a person to an area where there is a risk of persecution, or where her life or freedom would be in danger.

The movement of migrants and refugees between states is connected to exclusive jurisdiction of the state over its territory (see Goodwin-Gill 2014), the regulation of movements being seen as elementary to state sovereignty (Soysal 1994, 120). Whereas states have the right to control the entry of migrants, allowing them to stay as well as refuse admission, asylum seekers and refugees seeking protection are particular categories of migrants towards which states have accepted some responsibilities under international law (see also Kukathas 2016).

The concept of 'refugee' is a political one, as it is normative and descriptive (Haddad 2008, 23). The concept is also essentially contested, as is the question of who fits the definition: in different times there have been different ways of defining and conceptualising what kind of claims for asylum are legitimate in terms of accessing protection, and who is excluded from this. Whereas the concept also carries different meanings in its use in the works of scholars, Haddad's (2008) definition stresses the severing of the normal bond between citizen and the state. To Soguk (1999, 10), a refugee is similarly someone "who lacks the citizen's unproblematic grounding within a territorial space and, so, lacks the effective representation and protection of a state". Thus, in this account refugees represent exception, disruption; they are "uprooted, dislocated, displaced, forced out or self-displaced from the community of citizens" (ibid.). The idea links citizenship with a territorial belonging to a state, presupposing that everyone should belong to a state and that, on the other hand, states define the rules of the membership. From this perspective, asylum seekers and refugees are "between sovereigns" (Haddad 2008), 'in between' categories when moving across different jurisdictions: anomalies in the nation states system when not being protected by their state of origin and when asking for shelter and the restoration of protection in another state.

98 Hanna-Mari Kivistö

Asylum, Human Rights and Citizenship as "Right to Have Rights"

Asylum has been mentioned as the oldest of rights, its history relating to churches and sanctuaries (Kimminich 1968). In terms of states, asylum has traditionally been understood as "a right of the state in its sovereignty to decide whom it shall admit to its territory" (Weis 1966, 471); asylum is a right that is a state's authority to grant (Morgenstern 1949, 327), "a privilege freely granted or refused" (Kirchheimer 1959, 989). As a principle, asylum has been thus closely linked with the expression of state sovereignty, implying that the granting of asylum is something that other states should respect and not see as a hostile act (Gil-Bazo 2015, 3). The meaning of asylum as a right of the individual has, on the contrary, been more contested (cf. Grahl-Madsen 1972), although the idea was expressed in the postwar framework, for instance, by García-Mora, who claimed that "states should be under the legal obligation to grant asylum to those fleeing from persecution and oppression", and by granting asylum a state is merely "enforcing an already existing human right" (García-Mora 1956, 2). Conceptions of asylum as a human right were put forward also in the making of the UDHR and they were realised in constitutional asylum provisions, as will be shown in this chapter. Furthermore, many present-day scholars have emphasised the causal link between human rights violations and refugee movements (e.g., Loescher 1999), as well as the connection between asylum as an institution of protection and the enforcement of human rights: For Gil-Bazo, for instance, "the right to be granted asylum, [is] an essential premise for the enjoyment of other rights" (2015, 12).

The connection between human rights and asylum was articulated also by Hannah Arendt, who saw asylum as "the only right that ever figured as a symbol of the Rights of Man in the sphere of international relationships" (Arendt 1994, 280). Refugees, lacking the protection of their government were for Arendt "the most symptomatic group in contemporary politics", revealing the perplexities of human rights. The plight of the stateless persons, in particular, persons living "outside the pale of the law" (ibid., 277), showed how closely the 'inalienable rights'—rights that by definition were not dependent upon nationality or membership to a political community—were, in practice, rights of citizens (ibid., 291–292). Belonging to an organised political community, having "a place in the world which makes opinions significant and actions effective" entailed "the right to have rights" (ibid., 296–297). In terms of refugees and stateless persons, this notion was connected to the idea that human rights failed to protect persons deprived of their citizenship: rights became unenforceable to those who were no longer citizens of sovereign states, who had lost their homes and for whom it become impossible to find a new one. The loss of protection of their own government meant the loss of legal status in all countries when no authority or institution was guaranteeing and protecting the rights (ibid., 292–294).

Arendt's theorising does not take into account the postwar institutional responses on asylum seekers and refugees, but it sheds light on the historical experiences behind their creation. It also illustrates the evident connection of asylum and refugees, human rights and citizenship to nation states. When rights are protected and enforced in nation states contexts and there is a lack of legal protection provided by citizenship, the question of whether there is any territory that would admit and grant protection for a refugee becomes crucial. The protection of asylum seekers and refugees raises questions of admittance, state responsibility and human rights enforcement. Whereas asylum operates on both national and international levels, the question of state obligations has remained a very contested issue in relation to international protection in political practice (see, e.g., Marx 2001). The chapter demonstrates this controversy by looking at two responses to territorial protection of asylum seekers in the form of different meanings given to the right of asylum.

(Re)making Asylum as a Right of the State

Conceptual interpretations and institutional locations of asylum will be discussed here by making remarks on asylum debates in the fora of the United Nations when drafting the Universal Declaration of Human Rights (1946–1948) as well as in the West German Parliamentary Council when creating the asylum paragraph of the Basic Law (1948–1949). The political contexts and constellations are different in these two cases: those deliberating and negotiating on the UDHR were state representatives and diplomats creating an international 'bill of rights', whereas in the writing of the Basic Law the politicians were drafting a Basic Law for the divided Germany as authorised by the Western Allied states (see Kivistö 2013; for the UDHR see also Morsink 1999).

The deliberations resulted in different (legal) conceptions of asylum as a right. The two ways of talking about asylum are politically and conceptually significant as each gives the right a different meaning as well as political and legal implication. The UDHR acknowledged the human right for the politically persecuted to seek and enjoy asylum, whereas not posing states any (moral) duties with regard to the granting of asylum. The contemporary Basic Law listed asylum among fundamental rights and thus linked it to the constitutional values of the state: politically persecuted have the human right to asylum and the state a corresponding duty to protect these persons. From conceptual perspective what is interesting in terms of the two rights is not only the end result, but, above all, the alternative ways to interpret and conceptualise the right and the definitional dispute and contestation that takes place.

100   *Hanna-Mari Kivistö*

The Article 14(1) of the UDHR proclaims how: "Everyone has the right to seek and enjoy in other countries asylum from persecution". Although the article has been criticised for lacking substance (e.g., Lauterpacht 1950, 422), the political history of the asylum paragraph in the UDHR was neither clear-cut nor self-evident: during its drafting, the wording went through several changes and the article was rewritten multiple times to find a formulation that could accommodate the conflicting views and be acceptable for the majority of the delegates. Whereas the document acknowledges the right to seek asylum from persecution in other countries, the 'seek and be granted' formulation— which would have posed the refugee a human right to receive asylum and the states a (moral) duty to grant asylum to political refugees— was put forward, debated and accepted several times during the drafting stages. Importantly, the Commission on Human Rights chaired by Eleanor Roosevelt—which made important decisions regarding the UN rights framework and in regard to "which ideas to accept, which rights to recognize, and which instruments to draft" (Norman and Zaidi 2008, 23–24)—also supported it in the form of "Everyone has the right to seek and be granted asylum in other counties from persecution" (E/CN.4/ SR.57, 11).[3] This wording was, however, voted down by the majority of state representatives in the last phase of the drafting process in the Third Committee deliberations in the autumn of 1948.

In the negotiations related to the creation of the UDHR, some of the most vocal voices speaking and advocating for the 'be granted' conception came from the non-governmental organisations taking part in the negotiations as consultants and observers. In these arguments, asylum was linked explicitly to the protection and recognition of other human rights listed in the draft text of the document, such as, for instance, "right to hold or change ones beliefs" (Tony Sender, American Federation of Labor, E/CN.4/SR.56, 7), and to the right to life (A.L. Easterman, World Jewish Congress, E/CN.4/A/C.2/SR.5, 4), as denying the right from Germans "had resulted in the deaths of thousands" (ibid.).

In the Third Committee debates the distinction between the interests of the states and the interests of the refugees became particularly evident. Garcia-Mora (1956, 151) criticised the Third Committee debates by noting that the drafters were concerned more about safeguarding the powers of the state than with the rights of the individuals. The asylum debates demonstrate how, quite paradoxically, when creating the UDHR as a document that sets standards and aspirations as regards to state policies, and when setting principles upon themselves in the form of declaring a list of rights, a central principle protected is that of state sovereignty. As the representative of the United Kingdom, Geoffrey Wilson, saw during the drafting, "one of the most jealously guarded rights of a State was the right to prevent foreigners from crossing its border" (E/CN.4/SR.56, 10). When debating human rights in the loci of asylum

Right of Non-Citizen or Right of the State? 101

and admission, a clear line of demarcation was thus drawn between members and non-members.

Although the question of implementation was seen as particularly problematic among the delegates with reference to asylum, there were also advocates for the right to be granted asylum conception in the Third Committee. In these accounts, asylum was emphasised as a right "inherent in the human person", meaning that it "should be established, even if for accidental reasons, it did not seem impossible to ensure immediate implementation", in the argumentation of Karim Azkoul from Lebanon (A/C.3/SR.121, 335). The representative of Pakistan, Agha Shahi, spoke for including right to asylum among fundamental human rights, emphasising that the "recognition of the right of everyone to seek and be granted asylum was a welcome step forward" in international law (A/C.3/SR.121, 336). He connected asylum with the freedom of thought and expression, and argued that the right of asylum should be included among the fundamental rights of man, arguing that "if everyone had the right of freedom of thought and expression, a person could obviously preserve his intellectual and moral integrity only by seeking refuge abroad, should his own country deny him the enjoyment of those essential liberties" (A/C.3/SR.121, 337). The particularity of asylum in terms of admission and migrants was underlined by the representative of Uruguay, Eduardo Jiménez de Aréchaga, who criticised the delegates for confusing asylum and immigration, which "were two quite different things" (A/C.3/SR.121, 333). Rene Cassin, the French delegate, spoke of asylum aptly as a right with "essentially international character", meaning that in distinction from most articles of the UDHR, ensuring the right went beyond "the national society in which the individual was living". Therefore, it was "necessary to specify who was to ensure the enjoyment of the right" (A/C.3/SR.121, 328). The French delegation advocated for the UN as representative of the international community to have a central role in ensuring the right, to benefit both the victims of persecution as well as the states so that disproportional burdens of refugees would not fall upon states (ibid.). This idea was, however, rejected by the clear majority of the delegates.

An interesting argument regarding asylum in connection to human rights was presented by Margery Corbet, the delegate of the UK, to whom the asylum article "revealed certain defeatism" and was "out of place in the Declaration". She regarded it as a contradiction that the declaration "envisaged an ideal life for all members of society", and in spite of this, the asylum article "admitted the existence of persecution within that society" (A/C.3/SR.121, 329). Whereas Corbet argued that asylum's place is not in a declaration that promotes "ideal life", it also demonstrates the idea of asylum as a right needed in situations where there is a lack of protection of one's human rights.

The Third Committee accepted the wording suggested by the UK delegation. The meaning of the "to enjoy asylum" expression was that

102   Hanna-Mari Kivistö

"no foreigner could claim the right of entry into any State unless that right were granted by treaty". Right of asylum was "the right of every State to offer refuge and to resist all demands for extradition" (Corbet, UK, A/C.3/SR.121, 330). Thus, asylum remained "a right to admit any particular person" (ibid.). People asking refuge would be "treated with sympathy" (ibid.), but the right to decide on admission and non-admission was left to the sovereignty of each state, with asylum remaining as a state prerogative, as a right of the state to grant, without any assurance on how to enforce or where to receive the right.

Redefining Asylum as a Human Right

Whereas the UDHR is silent in regard to states' obligations towards asylum seekers, in the West German Basic Law, the state was presented with the duty to protect politically persecuted refugees by granting asylum. In the Basic Law, asylum was codified as a right of the individual with the short wording "Politically persecuted enjoy the right to asylum" [Politisch Verfolgte genießen Asylrecht, Art. 16(2) 2] (see Kivistö 2013). Although constitutional asylum rights are well known, the West German asylum right came to be unique in international comparison in its scope. This right was amended in 1993 with added references to safe third countries and safe countries of origin, changing considerably the conditions under which the right could be accessed to be claimed (e.g., Lambert et al. 2008).

There were acute historical and personal experiences behind the creation of the constitutional asylum provision. Several of the authors of the Basic Law had made use of the right to asylum when they had escaped Germany during the Third Reich to live in political exile, having thus first-hand "experience of such rights" (Main Committee, 44th Meeting, Friedrich Wilhelm Wagner, Social Democratic Party, 69). The meaning of the right was connected to the experience of persecution of political opponents as well as to the experiences of past expulsions, arbitrary decisions made by border authorities, and the closing of borders by states to refugees seeking shelter. It was also closely related to the political context of the divided Germany (see Kivistö 2013).

The constitutional asylum was emphasised in relation to granting access: access to the asylum procedures as opposed to decisions made at the borders by the police or by the border authorities as had happened in the past and as had denied the protection from persons seeking shelter. As Hermann von Mangoldt (Christian Democratic Union) stated:

> We have a special reason for being cautious [. . .] We have experiences from the last war, especially from Switzerland. The right to asylum can be kept if the clause establishes it simply and plainly: politically persecuted enjoy the right to asylum.
>
> (Committee on Basic Questions, 23rd Meeting, 14)

Right of Non-Citizen or Right of the State? 103

The right of asylum that Hannah Arendt described as an "unofficial practice destined for exceptional cases" (Arendt 1994, 294) lost its purpose during the Second World War when those seeking shelter from political persecution became too numerous. Furthermore, the old assumption of asylum seeker presupposing political convictions could not be used to describe the new groups of refugees "persecuted not because what they had done, or thought, but because of what they unchangeably were" (ibid.). Above all, asylum lost its practical meaning when states refused to grant protection to refugees escaping (e.g., Kukathas 2016, 260). In the debates of the Parliamentary Council, the experiences of the non-admission policies were connected, in particular, to Switzerland, as a destination for many refugees from Germany. As Ludi's (2010) research depicts, instead of being allowed access and admission, the unwanted refugees were sent back from the Swiss borders, and Jewish refugees, particularly, became seen in Switzerland as 'undesirable foreigners'. To prevent the arrival of Jewish refugees, the Swiss government introduced measures such as the so-called J-stamps in the passports to identify and spot the refugees directly at the border, before eventually closing the borders for Jewish refugees in 1942 as a response to the growing numbers of arrivals seeking refuge (Ludi 2010, 82, 93–94).

Dorothy Thompson wrote in the late 1930s about the acute refugee plight between and without jurisdictions by describing how "[i]t became a common experience for a refugee to find himself on a frontier, trapped between a country that had spat him out and a country that would not let him in" (Thompson 1938, 39). This historical experience was of importance in the Council when justifying the constitutional asylum right. Von Mangoldt described the cruel "game" that had been related to refugees trying to access protection at the borders: "the person is sent back, or sent to another border from where it goes further again" (Main Committee, 18th Meeting, 14).

In the postwar documents, political persecution in the state of origin continued to be the criteria for eligible asylum seeking. As the wording of public documents are politically significant, the authors of the Basic Law very knowingly chose not to create any definitions that constitute 'political persecution' or conditions for the access of asylum seekers. This was different from other constitutional asylum provisions, such as in France (see Burgess 2014). Instead, the idea was to create a right to asylum that was written ambiguously enough to be claimed in the various situations arising, taking into account the German geopolitical setting, in particular. Although offering asylum has been closely linked with the promoting of political values (Price 2009), the asylum article and granting of asylum was emphasised in the Parliamentary Council not to be dependent upon the political convictions of the applicant as regards to the receiving state. It is noteworthy that the intent and dignity of the act of granting of asylum was linked, instead, to ideas of unconditionality and generosity:

104   *Hanna-Mari Kivistö*

> Granting of asylum is always a question of generosity, and if one is generous, then there is a risk of being mistaken about the person. That's the other side and perhaps also the dignity of such an act. If one makes a restriction, something along the lines of: right of asylum but as long as the person is politically close or sympathic, then too much is taken away.
>
> (Main Committee, 18th Meeting, Carlo Schmid,
> Social Democratic Party, 13)

The generosity of asylum was, nevertheless, not to be practised unconditionally, but "according to the provisions of international law" (ibid., 14).

The asylum provision was not accepted without objections with reference to security concerns in particular: politicians proposing stricter conditions for accessing the right argued that the right could lead to a situation where Germany would become "an oasis and shelter for persons who had acted undemocratically in their state of origin and allowing them access would harm the political order of the new state" (Main Committee, 44th Meeting, Heinrich von Brentano, Christian Democratic Union, 66–67). The clear majority of politicians on the Council, nonetheless, supported the idea that if asylum as a right was included in the Basic Law then it should be from the perspective of the individual and not the state: restrictions and conditions were seen as "the beginning of the end of the ancient legal principle of asylum" (Main Committee, 44th Meeting, Friedrich Wilhelm Wagner, Social Democratic Party, 68).

Concluding Remarks

This chapter has examined conceptual debates related to the recognition of asylum as a right of political refugees. These postwar debates have present-day relevance not only in placing the topical debates in a historical perspective, but also in terms of the current contestedness of the right of asylum in political practice. Furthermore, the immediate postwar asylum debates resonate in the questions of how the human rights of persons without the legal and political status of citizen are actualised, practiced and enforced, most often in the frameworks of nation states (see also Nielsen in this volume).

The disputes on the interpretation and content of the right of asylum illustrate particularly the controversial notion of asylum as a human right of the individual: whereas the drafters of the West German Basic Law quite uniquely granted protection to political refugees, the state delegates creating the UDHR held on to the right to admit and non-admit persons asking for protection, reaffirming asylum thus as a right of the state.

Right of Non-Citizen or Right of the State?   105

As this chapter has demonstrated, the right of asylum raises questions about admission and conditions of access (see Björk in this volume), enforcement and recognition of rights, boundaries of membership and practices of state sovereignty. Moreover, as asylum is a right located "in the crossroads of state sovereignty and human rights" (Benhabib 2004, 2), asylum seekers and refugees seeking protection at the borders, moving between international and national jurisdictions, acutely challenge to rethink political and conceptual demarcations connected to access, rights and memberships.

Notes

1 This chapter is based on research project "The Politics of Human Rights: Conceptual and Rhetorical Reading of the Postwar Debates", funded by Kone Foundation.
2 According to the Article 1 of Convention Relating to the Status of Refugees, a 'refugee' is someone, who "owing to well-founded fear of being persecuted for reasons of race, religion, nationality, membership of a particular social group or political opinion, is outside the country of his nationality and is unable or, owing to such fear, is unwilling to avail himself of the protection of that country; or who, not having a nationality and being outside the country of his former habitual residence as a result of such events, is unable or, owing to such fear, is unwilling to return to it".
3 Full reference information for citations in this format may be found under 'Other Sources' listed after the main references.

References

Arendt, Hannah. [1951]1994. *The Origins of Totalitarianism*. New York: Harcourt.

Ball, Terence, and John Pocock, ed. 1988. *Conceptual Change and the Constitution*. Lawrence: University Press of Kansas.

Benhabib, Seyla. 2004. *The Rights of Others: Aliens, Residents and Citizens*. Cambridge: Cambridge University Press.

Burgess, Greg. 2014. "Remaking Asylum in the Post-War France." *Journal of Contemporary History* 49(3):556–576.

Frank, Matthew, and Jessica Reinisch. 2014. "Refugees and Nation-States in Europe." *Journal of Contemporary History* 49(3):477–490.

García-Mora, Manuel. 1956. *International Law and Asylum as a Human Right*. Washington, DC: Public Affairs Press.

Gibney, Matthew J. 2004. *The Ethics and Politics of Asylum: Liberal Democracy and the Response to Refugees*. Cambridge: Cambridge University Press.

Gil-Bazo, María-Teresa. 2008. "The Charter of Fundamental Rights of the European Union and the Right to be Granted Asylum in the Union's Law." *Refugee Survey Quarterly* 27(3):33–52.

———. 2015. "Asylum as a General Principle of International Law." *International Journal of Refugee Law* 27(1):3–28.

106 *Hanna-Mari Kivistö*

Goodwin-Gill, Guy S. 2014. "The International Law of Refugee Protection." In *The Oxford Handbook of Refugee and Forced Migration Studies*, edited by Elena Fiddian-Qasmiyeh, Gil Loescher, Katy Long and Nando Sigona, 1–16. Oxford Handbooks Online. Accessed December 13, 2016. doi:10.1093/oxfordhb/9780199652433.013.0021

Grahl-Madsen, Atle. 1972. *The Status of Refugees in International Law: Asylum, Entry and Sojourn*. Leyden: A.W. Sijthoff.

———. 1980. *Territorial Asylum*. Stockholm: Almstedt & Wiksell.

"Grundgesetz für die Bundesrepublik Deutschland." 23.5.1949.

Gündoğdu, Ayten. 2015. *Rightlessness in an Age of Rights: Hannah Arendt and the Contemporary Struggles of Migrants*. Oxford: Oxford University Press.

Haddad, Emma. 2008. *Refugee in International Society: Between Sovereigns*. Cambridge: Cambridge University Press.

Hathaway, James, and Michelle Foster. 2014. *The Law of Refugee Status*. Cambridge: Cambridge University Press.

Ihalainen, Pasi, and Kari Palonen. 2009. "Parliamentary Sources in the Comparative Study of Conceptual History: Methodological Aspects and Illustrations of a Research Proposal." *Parliaments, Estates & Representation* 29:17–43.

Kimminich, Otto. 1968. *Asylrecht*. Berlin: Luchterhand.

Kirchheimer, Otto. 1959. "Asylum." *The American Political Science Review* 53(4):985–1016.

Kivistö, Hanna-Mari. 2013. *Debating Right to Asylum: A Conceptual and Rhetorical Reading of the German Post-War Deliberations*. PhD Dissertation. University of Jyväskylä.

Kukathas, Chandran. 2016. "Are Refugees Special?" In *Migration in Political Theory: The Ethics of Movement and Membership*, edited by Sarah Fine and Lea Ypi, 249–268. Oxford: Oxford University Press.

Lambert, Hélène, Francesco Messineo and Paul Tindemann. 2008. "Comparative Perspectives of Constitutional Asylum in France, Italy, and Germany: *Requiescat in Pace?*" *Refugee Survey Quarterly* 27(3):16–32.

Lauterpacht, Hersch. 1950. *International Law and Human Rights*. London: Stevens.

Loescher, Gil. 1999. "Refugees: A Global Human Rights and Security Crisis." In *Human Rights in Global Politics*, edited by Tim Dunne and Nicholas J. Wheeler, 233–258. Cambridge: Cambridge University Press.

Ludi, Regula. 2010. "Dwindling Options: Seeking Asylum in Switzerland 1933–39." In *Refugees from Nazi Germany and the Liberal European States*, edited by Frank Caerstecker and Bob Moore, 82–102. New York: Berghahn Books.

Martin, James. 2009. *Politics and Rhetoric: A Critical Introduction*. Abingdon: Routledge.

Marx, Reinhart. 2001. "Adjusting the Dublin Convention: New Approaches to Member State Responsibility for Asylum Applications." *European Journal of Migration and Law* 3:7–22.

Morgenstern, Felice. 1949. "The Right of Asylum." *British Yearbook of International Law* 26:327–357.

Morsink, Johannes. 1999. *The Universal Declaration of Human Rights: Origins, Drafting and Intent*. Philadelphia: University of Pennsylvania Press.

Right of Non-Citizen or Right of the State? 107

Noiriel, Gérard. 1991. *La tyrannie du national: le droit d'asile en Europe (1793–1993)*. Paris: Calmann-Lévy.

Norman, Roger, and Sarah Zaidi. 2008. *Human Rights at the UN: The Political History of Universal Justice*. Bloomington: Indiana University Press.

Palonen, Kari. 2002. "The History of Concepts as a Style of Political Theorizing: Quentin Skinner's and Reinhart Koselleck's Subversion of Normative Political Theory." *European Journal of Political Theory* 1(1):91–106.

Price, Matthew E. 2009. *Rethinking Asylum: History, Purpose and Limits*. Cambridge: Cambridge University Press.

Soguk, Nevzat. 1999. *States and Strangers: Refugees and Displacements of Statecraft*. Minneapolis: University of Minnesota Press.

Soysal, Yasemin Nuhoğlu. 1994. *Limits of Citizenship. Migrants and Postnational Membership in Europe*. Chicago: University of Chicago Press.

Tabori, Paul. 1972. *The Anatomy of Exile: A Semantic and Historical Study*. Harrap: London.

Thompson, Dorothy. 1938. *Refugees: Anarchy or Organization?* New York: Random House.

United Nations. 1948. The Universal Declaration of Human Rights.

———. 1951. The Convention Relating to the Status of Refugees.

Weis, Paul. 1966. "The Right of Asylum in the Context of the Protection of Human Rights in Regional and Municipal Law." *International Review of the Red Cross* 6(66): 470–477.

Other Sources

Drafting of the Universal Declaration of Human Rights

Commission on Human Rights, 2nd Session, Working Group on the Declaration of Human Rights, 08/12/1947, E.CN.4/AC.2/SR.5

———, 3rd Session, 56th Meeting, 02/6/1948, E/CN.4/SR.56.

———, 3rd Session, 57th Meeting, 07/06/1948, E/CN.4/SR.57.

General Assembly, 3rd Session, Third Committee, 121st Meeting, 03/11/1948, A/C.3/SR.121.

Parliamentary Council, Stenographical Records

Committee on Basic Questions, 23rd Meeting, 19/11/1948.

Main Committee, 18th Meeting, 4/12/1948.

———, 44th Meeting, 19/1/1949.

6 Temporality at the Borders of Citizenship

Conditioning Access in the Case of the United Kingdom

Anna Björk

Access to citizenship is one of the most important loci for debating the concept of citizenship. As a question of legal status, access has been tied to the nation state development of the concept of citizenship since it concerns the state's right to define the limits of citizenship and regulate the tension between inclusion and exclusion. The tension of internal inclusion and external exclusion, which according to Brubaker (1992, 72) characterises citizenship, implies that the points of access for overcoming external exclusion are important sites of politics, both for the agent and the legislator. There are at least three possible steps of access for the externally excluded individual: first, access in the sense of entry to the country through immigration; second, access to a recognised status and limited rights within its scope; and finally third, access to full citizenship status. In this chapter, I focus on the *conditions* of access.

Generally speaking, the steps of access aim at producing well-integrated new citizens capable of realising their full citizenship status through participation in the polity (Björk 2014b), which has discursively linked access to citizenship with integration (for a critical discussion of admission criteria and integration policies, see Kostakopoulou 2010). Since the late 1990s and early 2000s there has been a tendency in continental Europe of shifting the responsibility for active integration from the accommodating polity to the immigrants themselves (Kostakopoulou 2010, 7), and here I discuss the case of the United Kingdom, where legislation on immigration and citizenship has been revised along those lines. Whereas, as Mantu (2015, 181) notes, nationality and immigration have been linked throughout the history of UK citizenship legislation, the Nationality, Immigration and Asylum Act 2002 further emphasised this link in the government's discourse (ibid., 180). As discussed below, the emphasis on citizenship as a privilege and the new naturalisation measures emphasising the applicant's integration and commitment to the UK not only make the Nationality, Immigration and Asylum Act 2002 important for the conceptualisation of citizenship, but also resonate with developments in countries of continental Europe at that time. The discourse, which Kostakopolou (2010, 7) has referred to as the

Temporality at the Borders of Citizenship 109

"new civic integration paradigm", means a crucial shift in European politics of recent decades from the point of view of conceptualising citizenship. An important key to this paradigm is active participation, which has two dimensions: on one hand, the immigrant is expected to actively engage in the polity's practices, and on the other hand, the policies aimed at fostering integration also need to be facilitative enough to enable active engagement. Van Oers et al. (2010) have shown that, at raise of the new civic integration paradigm, this relationship has become "unidirectional, mandatory and sanction-based" (Kostakopoulou 2010, 11).

As an endeavour in conceptual history, I turn toward the temporal dimension of conceptual history, where it is recognised that time has a pivotal role in politics and political concepts, although it is frequently not thematised explicitly. In practical terms for this chapter it means that temporal components central to the conditioning of steps of access are explicated within the context of the UK's Nationality, Immigration and Asylum Act 2002, and I will give brief examples of how these, and the spaces they are tied to, both limit and enable individual agency. The concept of citizenship renders temporality explicitly through the political use of the concept: national histories, historical events and turning points, the future expectations for the polity and the individuals striving for the status, are being turned into an inherent part of citizenship in political debates (on the German case, see Björk 2011 and 2014a). However, this perspective also makes visible the spatial indexes, as the contexts in which citizenship and its counterpoints are debated remain in the framework of national borders—even when such novelties as EU citizenship are discussed—linking different groups of noncitizens and citizens in a novel way. Yet, whereas the first aim of this chapter is to explicate conditions of access for differentiated groups of individuals, an equally important aim is to introduce the relationship between time and conceptual history as a fruitful means of analysis.

Whereas the question of access has been at the heart of citizenship debates and legislation throughout the Western history of the concept (see Introduction in this volume), the turn of the millennium meant a turn toward a revision of the conditions for access to citizenship in many European countries. These debates mostly concerned access to citizenship through naturalisation—as opposed to the debates in former centuries on primary acquisition of citizenship through birth (the principles of *jus sanguinis* and *jus soli*; see Introduction in this volume). Since then, a general European direction has been to introduce new procedures for naturalisation, immigration, and application for permanent residence.

One of the central features of the new requirements is added emphasis on the activity of future residents and citizens: it has become a commonplace to presume and stress the requirement of active participation in courses on language or civic education among naturalisation candidates or those applying for permanent residence. Also, sets of tests have

110 *Anna Björk*

been introduced in various European countries for different stages of immigration and naturalisation. In the academic field, these political developments have prompted interest ranging from discussing the contents of the tests to broader questions of citizenship and immigration (Björk 2014a and 2015; Van Oers et al. 2010; Joppke 2010).

The Nationality, Immigration and Asylum Bill 2002 was based on the Labour Government's White Paper "Secure Borders, Safe Haven" (Home Office 2002). The White Paper has aroused critical commentaries from various angles: Yuval-Davis (Yuval-Davis 2007, 568–570) argues that putting responsibility for social cohesion onto immigrants rather than on the British legislators and policy makers, or citizens, is problematic. Further issues have been raised from the perspectives of gender and intersectionality (Yuval-Davis, Anthias and Kofman 2005), of increasing exclusion instead of inclusion (Sales 2006), and of promoting tighter border control and security discourse as means of increasing social cohesion (Yuval-Davis 2007). The UK case has also been analysed as part of the wider European framework, especially regarding the integration and naturalisation practices in the bill (Van Oers et al. 2010; especially Van Oers in that volume).

A central element in the processes for revising naturalisation practices was the celebration of citizenship as a distinctive status, which should have been esteemed and celebrated (on the German case, see Björk 2011 and 2014b). In the case of the United Kingdom, this development, which was catalysed in the Nationality, Immigration and Asylum Act 2002 produced the concept of 'earned citizenship' (White 2008; Van Oers 2010, 68–69). Considering that one of the debated points in the UK and also in other countries (such as Denmark, the Netherlands and Germany) was active immigrant integration before and through naturalisation, earned citizenship highlights a citizen's personal engagement with the polity through active participation.

Hence, like in other European countries (Björk 2011; Van Oers et al. 2010; Joppke 2010), celebration of citizenship in the UK was not only debated in relation to naturalisation, but linked with the question of immigration. In these cases, then, it was not merely about revising the access to citizenship, but also to other rights through immigration. Thus, I argue that the conceptual nexus of earned citizenship, integration and citizenship conceptually link citizens and non-citizens, who in time may have the chance and desire to be granted full citizenship status. After outlining the conceptual point of this chapter, I proceed to introducing the UK case study and finally give examples of temporal demarcation.

A Conceptual Perspective for Temporality

In the field of conceptual history, temporality is an important aspect of analysis and debate. For Koselleck, concepts bore a temporal element

Temporality at the Borders of Citizenship   111

and he wrote about the relationship between time, concepts and history in several publications (see, e.g., Koselleck 1979; 2000; 2006. For overview on Koselleck's ideas on temporality, see Jordheim 2011 and 2012). Time applied to analysing politics and political theory with a conceptual historical perspective has been extensively performed by Kari Palonen, whose analyses not only explicitly thematise time as key element of doing politics, but further focuses his discussion to the level of parliamentary politics (Palonen 2008; 2014a; 2014b).

In general, a useful division for describing the relationship between time and politics is to differentiate between "time of politics" (which refers to politicking with time, e.g., playing with time-related elements such as calendar, or temporal routines) and "politics of time" (which means politicising temporal categories, such as continuums, breakages, cycles or accelerations) (Lindroos and Palonen 2000, 12–15; Björk 2011). For my analytical purposes, this division should be understood as an idea of how time can be analysed on multiple levels and situations. Here, this generally means two levels. On one, there are dates, timeframes, and deadlines, which are written into laws and policies. On the other, there is the conceptual and rhetorical level, where national histories, events, experiences or future expectations can be used as components for building narratives and arguments. The former kind are, in this chapter, examples of demarcation between citizens and groups of non-citizens in relation to the conditions of access; the latter in turn is visible in the language for citizenship in the material.

Demarcation is manifold in its expressions. They can be conceptual and as such employed and produced by political and legal discourses, e.g., in which case their concreteness becomes realised by those subjected to the implications. Territorial demarcations which are more visible, general and every-day are, of course, also political products in the form of controlled state borders or larger territories, such as the borders of the European Union (on the variety of symbolic, legal, conceptual and territorial borders in Europe and migration, see Rigo 2009 [2007]).

The combination of spatial and temporal demarcations, in my analysis, is political and legal, and focuses mainly on the borders demarcated within the legal territory of a sovereign state. The conceptualisation in this case takes place on the parliamentary level of politics. Laws, their drafts and the debates that concern them are potentially situations where concepts are revised, updated or introduced to meet the requirements of the prevailing political situation. The concepts are then used in further situations, e.g., when the law is commentated on, implemented in specific conditions, or debated outside the parliament. Thus, the interrelations of social, political and institutional changes, which were referred to in the Introduction to this volume, are potentially well represented in situations for legislative action.

Cohen (2010 and 2011) has called the impact of temporal signifiers for citizenship the principle of *jus tempus*, referring to the temporal

112 Anna Björk

conditions for accessing citizenship alongside the principles of *jus sanguinis* and *jus soli*. Examples of how the temporal elements formulated in citizenship law and embedded in the policies affect a person's chance of acquiring citizenship are the ways historical dates and events are used as watersheds for who is entitled to naturalisation or the right to permanent settlement, and how these affect an individual's political agency (on the German post WWII situation, see Björk 2015). Hence Cohen's analysis serves as an inspiration for my investigation of temporal demarcations for non-citizens and citizens, the conditions of access, and the regulation of agency in this chapter.

Nationality, Immigration and Asylum Act 2002: Examples of Content

The political developments behind the introduction of the white paper and the bill included strived for civic education (Kiwan 2008), institutional reforms and political unrest, which resonated with debates on "multiculturalism, integration and the meaning of Britishness" (Mantu 2015, 179). The devolution reform, completed by the Blair government in 1997, accompanied by the Northern Ireland peace process, had already intensified the debate on 'Britishness' and British citizenship, both on the public and academic levels. Furthermore, the riots in 2001, taking place in Oldham, Burnley and Bradford, provoked the debate on integration and citizenship, especially in relation to permanent residents and second-generation immigrants, i.e., established immigration communities, with an emphasis on strengthening the idea of British citizenship (McGhee 2009, 44–45). This was also acknowledged in the white paper explicitly as it was argued that the riots were a symptom of a lack of "a sense of common values or shared civic identity to unite around" (Home Office 2002, 10; quoted in Van Oers 2010, 65). Thus, citizenship was explicitly debated together with the issues of immigration and asylum seeking. As the Home Secretary David Blunkett stated, the Nationality, Immigration and Asylum Act was to offer "an holistic and comprehensive approach to nationality, managed immigration and asylum that *recognises the inter-relationship of each element in the system*" (Home Secretary David Blunkett, HoC Deb 7 February 2002, Col 1027; emphasis added).

A specific feature of the Nationality, Immigration and Asylum Act 2002 was that it connected citizenship and immigration explicitly with the question of counterterrorism, thus framing the debate with the issue of security and emphasising citizenship as a privilege and a contract between the individual and the polity (Mantu 2015, 179–181). Tying together counterterrorism with immigration control and citizenship was, then, brought about only after the international developments of the early twenty-first century, even though the history of Irish terrorism had gone on for many years before without having a corresponding effect on the

Temporality at the Borders of Citizenship 113

legal discourse (ibid., 181). Thus, the UK was amongst the states where the War on Terror strongly influenced the so-called 'refugee-migration nexus'—the differentiation made in international law that there is a distinction between 'refugees', i.e., involuntary or forced migration, and 'migrants' who choose to leave their homes for a variety of reasons—by intensifying the search for any signs of terrorist activity within and outside the borders (Loescher et al. 2008).

As primary sources, I am using the material preceding the Nationality, Immigration and Asylum Act 2002, including: the statement of the Home Secretary for the Labour Government, at that time David Blunkett, on 29 October 2001, about the issues of "Asylum, Migration and Citizenship" (HoC Deb, 29 October 2001, Col 628); the original white paper "Secure Borders, Safe Haven" (Home Office 2001); and the parliamentary debates around the topic (between 29 October 2001 and 12 June 2002). A wide consensus prevailed that, firstly, the issue of immigration needed to be dealt with and the reform was welcomed by opposing parties, and secondly, that the debate needed to be "rational" in order to take the force away from the far right parties and their representatives. In introducing the white paper, the Home Secretary expressed his hopes to "find solutions that balance the needs of this country and those who seek asylum and those of the British people and the confidence and security that they demand" (HoC Deb, 7 February 2002, Col 1031).

In the Ministerial Statement from 29 October 2001, the title of the proposal was still "Asylum, Migration and Citizenship" (HoC Deb, 29 October 2001, Col 627). The white paper, however, put the concept of nationality in the lead. According to David Blunkett, the aim was not to "tinker with the existing system, but to introduce radical and fundamental reform" (HoC Deb, 7 February 2002, Col 627). This, he stated, was to be a piece of legislation "which will provide a comprehensive approach to asylum, nationality and immigration" (ibid.).

Introducing the white paper, the Home Secretary stated that Britain's "future social cohesion, economic prosperity and integrity depend on how well we rise to the global challenge of mass migration, communication and flight from persecution" (HoC Deb, 7 February 2002, Col 1029). The "challenges", as was explained in "Secure Borders, Safe Haven", "are cultural, economic and social" (Secure Borders, 9). This meant that the cultural challenge was one posed to the idea of nationality and citizenship, i.e., the way "migration has increased the diversity of advanced democracies, leading to changes in national culture and identity" (ibid.).

Affirming Citizenship

One of the features of the proposed bill was the quest for raising the appreciation of citizenship. For this purpose, the government was looking to reform the naturalisation process and introduce new measures

114 *Anna Björk*

for soon to-be citizens. Among the novelties were a citizenship pledge and a test, along with new set of language requirements with courses (Secure Borders, 29–33). MP Oliver Letwin (Conservative) commented on the plans for making citizenship more significant than what Britain needed was "to be able to accommodate wholesale diversity with a lack of friction, by having at its centre a set of institutions, understandings and acceptances that all of us share" (HoC Deb, 24 April 2002, Col 357).

A further step in the goal of affirming citizenship was to make sure that naturalisation would be seen as a desirable option for immigrants. Increasing the conditions for accessing citizenship raise the questions of the impacts of increasing naturalisation requirements and at which point of the integration process the potential candidate should be granted the possibility to apply for citizenship status. The debate on whether or not naturalisation should be used as a tool for integration or a 'prize' for the well-integrated is a debate familiar in other European countries (on Germany, see, e.g., Björk 2011 and 2014; on the Netherlands see Van Oers 2010). Is it beneficial for active integration to be included into the citizenry at a relatively early stage after one's access to residency, or should citizenship be something which then only is reachable when the candidates are far into their cultural and social integration with steady ties to the polity?

In the light of the new naturalisation requirements, Home Secretary Blunkett appointed an Advisory Group for consultation. The group was, according to the opening words of its final report "The New and the Old" (Home Office 2003),

> to advise the Home Secretary on the method, conduct and implementation of a "Life in the United Kingdom naturalisation test", which implied defining what should be meant by "sufficient" in both the cases of ability in language and knowledge of society and civic institutions.
>
> ("The New and the Old", 3)

The report ended up with recommendations for the preparatory material and the content for the naturalisation test, which was implemented in 2005 (on the work of the Advisory Group, see Kiwan 2008). The material, published as a book by the Home Office (2004 and 2007) came to be known as "Life in the United Kingdom".

One of the main ideas was that recognising the significance of citizenship meant that whoever wished to make that step also understood the common values that strengthened the "wider community", which referred to the British citizenry (see, e.g., HoC Deb, 7 February 2002). Some reservations were expressed toward the citizenship classes and the proposed language test, which was planned for the spouses of British citizens: MP Jim Marshall (Labour) expressed concerns for using citizenship

Temporality at the Borders of Citizenship 115

classes for promoting cultural uniformity, and posing language tests to spouses as intervening with people's freedom of choice in partner without hindrances (HoC Deb, 24 April 2002, Col 366).

The need for the civic education of already existing citizens was also raised. There was indeed a need for "affirming citizenship [. . .] by a sensitive method of assimilating them", but also "an equal need for that to apply also to young people growing up in this country" instead of focusing only on

> people coming from other countries, who often display much better behaviour and respect for other people than, sadly, do some of the people who were born in this country and who have grown up in our community.
>
> (MP Simon Hughes, Liberal Democratic Party,
> HoC Deb, 24 April 2002, Col 371)

This reflected the turn in the policy for civic education, which had already taken place in the UK, introducing this subject to the curricula at schools. It also bluntly displayed the exclusion embedded in the concept of citizenship as well as the idealisation of that status by referring to the "sensitive assimilation" of "them".

Outside the Borders of Full Citizenship: Asylum Seekers, Refugees and Economic Migrants

Because the case at hand explicitly links the forms of immigration with the question of citizenship, a number of policies concerning groups of non-citizenry are incorporated into the legislative texts. In relation to the group of family members, e.g., the question of access is extended to the conditions of the persons connected to the primary subject. The law also includes the British overseas citizens, who are in practice regarded as full citizens, albeit differentiated from British nationals for historical reasons.

The importance of the case of the Nationality, Immigration and Asylum Act 2002 lies in the way counterterrorism was linked with citizenship. The conceptually interrelated groups of asylum seekers, refugees and economic migrants form a central triad in the debates for the bill (on the debates for the right to asylum, see Kivistö in this volume). In general, the grounds for granting the status of a refugee are far from straightforward and are constantly debated in international law (for a recent contribution see Burson and Cantor 2016), and the status of economic rights as the basis for an asylum claim is certainly a controversial one (Foster 2016). The figure of economic migrant has no legal bearing but refers to a differentiation between grounds of migration on the axis of voluntary–involuntary migration. Hence economic migrant as a rhetorical tool indicates someone who is looking for a better life without facing

116　*Anna Björk*

persecution and who should not be granted a refugee status; yet, as Foster notes, socio–economic rights seem to be gaining in importance when it comes to defining the conditions for granting asylum (ibid.). Also in the case of the Nationality, Immigration and Asylum Act 2002, the concept of economic migrant (or economic migration) serves only as a concept of rhetoric in the debates and the additional material, and is missing from the act itself. Below, these three groups—asylum seekers, refugees and economic migrants—are brought into focus in terms of explicating temporal conditioning of access.

New Immigration Policies

The policies aimed at facilitating asylum seekers meant that "from the moment people present themselves, they will be tracked as well as supported" (David Blunkett, HoC Deb, 29 October 2001, Col 627). The asylum seekers were channelled through a system of reformulated centres: induction, accommodation, and removal centres. The induction and accommodation system combined with the removal centres were claimed to add efficiency to the system. The Home Secretary's vision for such a process was that integration procedures are improved for those who are granted asylum, whereas the process for removal was to be, in his words, "streamlined" and "those who have no right to stay must leave the country immediately" (HoC Deb, 29 October 2001, Col 629). On the issue of sending illegally residing migrants back to France, the Home Secretary stated that it seemed Britain returned "just under 6,000 people to France every year—speedily and often before they manage to cry asylum" (HoC Deb, 29 October 2001, Col 638).

The 'tracking and supporting' meant that the centres were put into place in order to ensure that there was a "seamless approach from induction through to integration or removal" (HoC Deb, 7 February 2002, Col 1027), as the white paper states. The induction centres were the first welcome to those seeking asylum, before being relocated to an accommodation centre. There, the immigrants were provided with legal aid, educational opportunities, accommodation and an allowance which could be used with a smart card. The accommodation centres would ideally be hosting the migrant for six months at the most, after which the asylum seeker was either granted refugee status or was once more relocated to a removal centre and subsequently to leave the country. Those with the new refugee status were then to be quickly integrated into British society (Secure Borders, 49–60). Integration into the labour market was, however, only available to those who had already been accepted as refugees. The Home Secretary's explanation of this was that "it would be even more difficult to remove them if they turned out to be an economic migrant rather than a refugee" if they had a permanent job (HoC Deb, 29 October 2001, Col 634).

As for the question of economic migrants, the main issues were the granting of work permits and the question of how to improve the appeal of the UK for high-skilled migrants. Concerns were expressed for appealing to those 'high-skills' migrants and how to make Britain accessible enough for them and for whom a new programme was launched. "The ultimate message", according to the Home Secretary, was that "if you want to be in our country and have something to offer, but know in your heart that you are not a refugee from persecution, the new economic migration proposals will enable you to achieve that goal" (HoC Deb, 29 October 2001, Col 632). The new measures in regard to economic migrants were also positively received by the Conservatives, because

> the British economy and British society have much to gain from a controlled inflow of talented and energetic people who seek to better their circumstances by setting to work and engaging as entrepreneurs in our society. [. . .] All those entering the country as migrants should be proficient in English and should acquire an early understanding of our constitutional arrangements.
>
> (MP Oliver Letwin, HoC Deb,
> 29 October 2001, Col 1030)

Temporalities

The three groups of non-citizens—economic migrants, asylum seekers and refugees—thus face different procedures to which the individuals in these groups are subjected. The procedures define expectations in terms of responsibilities to which the individuals as categorised are to fulfil. They also define rights to which the individuals are entitled. Obviously, it matters both to the individual immigrant and state how the conditions for the individual's immigration status are defined and what kind of possibilities and limitations for active participation the status implies.

The 'streamlining' of integration and migration processes that the government wanted to attain meant combining citizenship, immigration and refugee policy as intertwined concepts in the debate. To integrate, to educate oneself, to contribute through work and participate locally were promoted as keys to integration. For those who have a case for refugee status, learning the language and taking courses on civic society as well as volunteering were presented as choices for self-education (e.g., HoC Deb, 7 February 2002; Secure Borders, 14). Thus, with the emphasis on obtaining citizenship and engaging with the procedures for naturalisation, which ensure that one had some level of civic education, the intention was that active integration into society would occur from the start, even if the individual had no ultimate desire to achieve formal citizenship status. Those entering straight into the labour market

118   *Anna Björk*

were not required to undertake these civic elements of education or citizenship procedures—which was logical, because they presumably were not looking for citizenship status or even permanent residence. Those applying for refugee status, on the other hand, were considered potential citizens from the beginning—hence the need to bring the applicants into the realm of education policy.

Distinctive temporal categories to which the groups of immigrants were subjected included, e.g., waiting periods of varying length or timetables for fulfilling their integrative duties. The right of employment also clearly distinguished the asylum seekers from refugees and economic migrants, which produced further differentiation of temporalities as well. All three categories, but especially asylum seeker and refugee, bore the temporal index of temporariness as opposed to the permanent status of citizen, which was emphasised in the way the bill included the whole process from entering the country to finally applying for citizenship.

The parliamentary debates around the bill dealt mostly with the issue of asylum (Yuval-Davis et al. 2007; Van Oers 2010, 74). Thus, the question here is how this dominance of asylum, refugee and, in a wider sense, immigration policy impacts the concept of citizenship. On the obvious level, the emphasis on citizenship is a corollary of the focus on noncitizens, hence gaining in weight as a political tool. One can only think of the broader issues linked with citizenship through diverse forms of legislation: education, border controls, rhetorical demarcations, political agency and subjectivity, legislation on families, taxation, political rights, freedom of movement or discrimination, to name a few examples.

In terms of temporality, the length of the stay, the temporary sense of the status, and the waiting periods become parts of how participation and agency are constituted in these groups. Further, the way the past and the future are played together in arguing for immigration or citizenship policy in parliament and the media construct temporal horizons for the concept of citizenship. National history and its contemporary interpretation is also detectable quite concretely in any state's citizenship and immigration legislation where different policies are applied to individuals from different backgrounds, as is the case of British overseas citizens in the UK context, or EU nationals within the borders of the European Union.

As for sites for performing these temporalities, the possibility of employment means the possibility for opening to new spaces and communities in which one can perform their agency. But the fundamental sites for becoming incorporated into times of routines, duties, deadlines and social hierarchies are the induction, accommodation and removal centres. These are places where the individual is subjected to policies which deal directly with immediate needs, such as shelter and food, but also financial and legal aid, as well as practical assistance for coping with daily necessities, although the educational element of the accommodation centre expands its purpose in the direction of civic integration.

The government's plan was not to force anyone to stay in an accommodation centre, but it tied the provision of financial aid to a smart card linked with staying in the centre. Hence the policy of "tracking and supporting" meant that people were entitled to cash in addition to accommodation and food, if they so chose, but were left without the aid if they chose not to enter the process as recommended. In terms of naturalisation for full citizenship, the temporal elements of the national past, the contemporary interpretation of the political and cultural situation, are embedded into the plan for the new naturalisation process, including the preparatory material for the citizenship test and the test itself. In the debates and documentation, this image of contemporary UK is presented as inherently multicultural: the idea is that the culturally diverse reality is recognised, whereas there are to be central values which are shared by all—at least in principle. This also resonates with the Home Secretary's aims of increasing social cohesion, which presumes strong communities and sense of belonging (for an analysis of the politics of belonging in this context, see Yuval-Davis 2007).

Conclusion

The revision of the nationality laws in the UK included the recognition of cultural differences which also played a significant rhetorical role in constituting the image of the UK as a diverse and accommodating polity. This was very different from other European countries such as Germany, e.g., where the official policy line has only recently changed from being dismissive of the realities of immigration to now recognising the historical status of certain cultural communities or the increased movement of both European and non-European citizens (e.g., Björk 2014). On the other hand, launching the "Life in the UK" citizenship test for naturalisation and the related material with the aim of integrating the new citizens more efficiently before earning citizenship, and stressing the importance of controlled immigration, actually moved into a direction which has more in common with European countries such as Denmark, the Netherlands and Germany. Home Secretary Blunkett, e.g., emphasises the need for the "trust and support from the wider community", where the wider community refers to the British citizenry, and stresses that in order to have this support, the British citizenry needs a reassurance of the fairness and transparency of the system. This resonates with the shift in emphasis from the openness of the receiving society to the active role of the immigrant; the introduction of new measures for immigration, integration, and naturalisation procedures; and the increased enthusiasm for testing practices (see Van Oers et al. 2010 for a discussion on continental European cases).

The temporal elements—established in the debates on the policies regarding the centres, waiting periods or visas—constitute the temporality

120 *Anna Björk*

of non-citizens. As such, they become temporal indexes for the concepts employed—asylum seekers, refugees or economic migrants. Citizenship, as a legal status and a political concept, follows these and opens up new horizons of agency. The agency of these three groups is regulated and defined through a variety of administrative directives. Hence, the tension between expecting participation in the presumably integrative activities and the regulation of participation by closely monitoring the subjects is embedded in the revised policy.

The various steps of access are at the heart of the Nationality, Immigration and Asylum Bill 2002: There is access in the sense of entering the country (economic migrants and asylum seekers alike), and access to residence through either asylum claims or other immigration routes. There is the question of access to the labour market too, because this also includes different options of working permits and the high-skill programme. Considering that there is a strong point made for 'tracking and supporting' and, following this, integrating the immigrants into communities, initial access to the country and the labour market becomes the most significant step for gaining access to the entire process leading ultimately to permanent residence or full citizenship. In this sense, the emphasis on asylum in the parliamentary debates links the legal status of full citizenship with the initial conditions for entry.

The language of 'shared values', 'belonging' and 'active citizenship', familiar from other European examples, appear in the documents and debates on the British case as well. These ideals then apply to both citizenry and the constructed non-citizenry, which, judging from the documents and debates in the British case are all potential members of the citizenry. The hierarchical arrangement of statuses regarding immigration means that full citizenship is dependent on the candidate's ability to respond to the requirements.

References

House of Commons, Debates. October 29, 2001. www.publications.parliament. uk/pa/cm200102/cmhansrd/vo011029/debtext/11029-04.htm. Accessed February 19, 2017.
———. February 7, 2002. www.publications.parliament.uk/pa/cm200102/ cmhansrd/vo020207/debtext/20207-06.htm. Accessed February 19, 2017.
———. April 24, 2002. www.publications.parliament.uk/pa/cm200102/cmhan srd/vo020424/debtext/20424-05.htm. Accessed February 19, 2017.
———. June 12, 2002. www.publications.parliament.uk/pa/cm200102/cmhan srd/vo020612/debtext/20612-29.htm. Accessed February 19, 2017.
"Secure Borders, Safe Haven." 2001. Home Office. www.gov.uk/government/ uploads/system/uploads/attachment_data/file/250926/cm5387.pdf. Accessed February 19, 2017.
"The New and the Old." 2003. The report of the "Life in the United Kingdom" Advisory Group. Home Office.

Temporality at the Borders of Citizenship   121

Literature

Björk, Anna. 2011. *The Politics of Citizenship Tests: Time, Integration and the Contingent Polity.* PhD dissertation. University of Jyväskylä.

———. 2014a. "Accessing Citizenship: The Conceptual and Political Changes of the German Naturalization Policy, 1999–2006." *Contributions to the History of Concepts* 9(1):74–87. DOI: 10.3167/choc.2014.090103. ISSN 1807-9326.

———. 2014b. "Dissensus and the Contingent Polity: Parliamentary Debates on Citizenship Tests in Germany." In *The Politics of Dissensus: Parliament in Debate,* edited by Kari Palonen, José Maria Rosales, and Tapani Turkka, 475–494. Santander & Madrid: Cantabria University Press & McGraw-Hill.

———. 2015. "Parliamentary Politics and Migration: Reinterpreting Citizenry in Germany." In *Challenges to Parliamentary Politics: On Rhetoric, Representation and Reform,* edited by Suvi Soininen and Tuula Vaarakallio, 79–98. Baden-Baden: Nomos.

Brubaker, Rogers. 1992. *Citizenship and Nationhood in France and Germany.* Cambridge, MA: Harvard University Press.

Burson, Bruce, and David James Cantor, ed. 2016. *Human Rights and the Refugee Definition: Comparative Legal Practice and Theory.* Leiden & Boston: Brill & Nijhoff.

Cohen, Elizabeth F. 2010. "*Jus Tempus* in the Magna Charta: The Sovereignty of Time in Modern Politics and Citizenship." *Political Science and Politics* 463–466. https://ssrn.com/abstract=1599943. Accessed February 19, 2017.

———. 2011. "Reconsidering US Immigration Reform: The Temporal Principle of Citizenship." *Reflections* 9(3):575–583. DOI: https://doi.org/10.1017/S1537592711002787. Accessed February 19, 2017.

Foster, Michelle. 2016. "Economic Migrant or Person in Need of Protection? Socio-Economic Rights and Persecution in International Refugee Law." In *Human Rights and the Refugee Definition: Comparative Legal Practice and Theory,* edited by Bruce Burson and David James Cantor, 229–252. Leiden & Boston: Brill & Nijhoff.

Joppke, Christian. 2010. *Citizenship and Immigration.* Cambridge: Polity.

Jordheim, Helge. 2011. "Does Conceptual History Really Need a Theory of Historical Times?" *Contributions to the History of Concepts* 6(2):21–41. DOI: 10.3167/choc.2011.060202 ISSN 1807-9326. Accessed February 19, 2017.

———. 2012. "Against Periodization: Koselleck's Theory of Multiple Temporalities." *History and Theory* 51:151–171. DOI: 10.1111/j.1468-2303.2012.00619.x. Accessed February 19, 2017.

Kiwan, Dina. 2008. "A Journey to Citizenship in the United Kingdom." *International Journal on Multicultural Societies* 10(1):60–75. www.unesco.org/shs/ijms/vol10/issue1/art4. Accessed February 19, 2017.

Koselleck, Reinhart. 1979. *Vergangene Zukunft: Zur Semantik geschichtlicher Zeiten.* Frankfurt am Main: Suhrkamp.

———. 2000. *Zeitschichten.* Frankfurt am Main: Suhrkamp.

———. 2006. *Begriffsgeschichten: Studien zur Semantik und Pragmatik der politischen und sozialen Sprache.* Frankfurt am Main: Suhrkamp.

Kostakopoulou, Dora. 2010. "Introduction." In *A Re-Definition of Belonging? Language and Integration Tests in Europe,* edited by Ricky van Oers, Eva Ersbøll, and Dora Kostakopoulou, 1–24. Leiden & Boston: Martinus Nijhoff Publishers.

122 Anna Björk

Lindroos, Kia, and Kari Palonen. 2000. "Aika Politiikan Kohteena." In *Politiikan Aikakirja: Ajan Politiikan ja Politiikan Ajan Teoretisointia*, edited by Kia Lindroos and Kari Palonen, 7–24. Tampere: Vastapaino.

Loescher, Gil, Alexander Betts, and James Milner. 2008. *The United Nations High Commisioner for Refugees (UNHCR): The Politics and Practice of Refugee Protection into the Twenty-First Century*. Oxon & New York: Routledge.

McGhee, Derek. 2009. "The Paths to Citizenship: A Critical Examination of Immigration Policy in Britain since 2001." *Patterns of Prejudice* 43(1):41–64. DOI: 10.1080/00313220802636064. Accessed February 19, 2017.

Mantu, Sandra. 2015. *Contingent Citizenship: The Law and Practice of Citizenship Deprivation in International, European and National Perspectives*. Leiden & Boston: Martinus Nijhoff Publishers.

Palonen, Kari. 2008. *The Politics of Limited Times: The Rhetoric of Temporal Judgement in Parliamentary Democracies*. Baden-Baden: Nomos.

———. 2014a. *Politics and Conceptual Histories: Rhetorical and Temporal Perspectives*. Baden-Baden: Nomos.

———. 2014b. *The Struggle with Time: A Conceptual History of "Politics" as an Activity*. Berlin: LIT Verlag.

Rigo, Enrica. 2009. *Rajojen Eurooppa*. Helsinki: Polemos. [2007. *Europa di confine: Trasformazioni della cittadinanza nell'Unione allargata*. Meltemi editore.]

Sales, Rosemary. 2005. "'Secure Borders, Safe Haven': A Contradiction in Terms?" *Ethnic and Racial Studies* 28(3):445–462. DOI: 10.1080/0141987042000337830. Accessed February 19, 2017.

Van Oers, Ricky. 2010. "Citizenship Tests in the Netherlands, Germany and the UK." In *A Re-Definition of Belonging? Language and Integration Tests in Europe*, edited by Ricky van Oers, Eva Ersbøll, and Dora Kostakopoulou, 51–106. Leiden & Boston: Martinus Nijhoff Publishers.

Van Oers, Ricky, Eva Ersbøll, and Dora Kostakopoulou, ed. 2010. *A Re-Definition of Belonging? Language and Integration Tests in Europe*. Leiden & Boston: Martinus Nijhoff Publishers.

White, Patricia. "Immigrants into Citizens." *The Political Quarterly* 79(2):221–231. DOI: 10.1111/j.1467-923X.2008.00929.x. Accessed February 19, 2017.

Yuval-Davis, Nira. 2007. "Intersectionality, Citizenship and Contemporary Politics of Belonging." *Critical Review of International Social and Political Philosophy* 10(4):561–574. DOI: 10.1080/13698230701660220. Accessed February 19, 2017.

Yuval-Davis, Nira, Anthias Floya, and Eleonore Kofman. 2005. "Secure Borders and Safe Haven and the Gendered Politics of Belonging: Beyond Social Cohesion." *Ethnic and Racial Studies* 28(3):513–535. DOI: 10.1080/0141987042000337867. Accessed February 19, 2017.

7 Access to Medical Care: A Citizenship Right or a Human Right?

On Struggles over Rights, Entitlement and Membership in Contemporary Sweden

Amanda Nielsen

> Are you primarily a human being or are you primarily a citizen? Are human rights supposed to be rights of citizenship, something you earn because you are born in a certain country [. . .] or do you have them from birth [. . .] just because you are a human being? My answer to that question is: human rights are for all humans.
>
> (Addr. 2, Kalle Larsson, Left Party, 2007/08:115)

> It should not be made based on where one happens to be born or what citizenship one happens to hold. All people should have the right to health—and medical care as a part of the human rights. Health is a human right.
>
> (Addr. 37, Gunvor G. Ericson, Green Party, 2007/08:115)

In the early 2000s, the circumstances of a group of former asylum seekers staying in Sweden without residence permits began receiving increased attention from media and politicians. From the beginning, their precarious living circumstances were the focal point of representations concerning the group. Their predicament ruptured the dominant understanding of Sweden as an inclusive welfare state and spurred a series of debates in both the parliament and in society at large. From the outset, the lack of access to medical care[1] was singled out as one of the most severe consequences of staying in Sweden without requisite permits, and a campaign for policy revision was initiated. In this campaign, notions of human rights were mobilized, and the key argument was that affordable, and hence subsidized, medical care is a human right and that it should be provided to all residents regardless of their legal status. This argument, in turn, challenged not only the policy in question, but also the underpinning assumptions about entitlement to social rights. Access to health and medical care, and other social rights, has customarily been conceived of as

124 *Amanda Nielsen*

a component of citizenship. Certainly, the linkage between citizenship, as a formal legal status, and access to social rights has diminished over time as immigrants with residence permits have been granted access to rights. Yet, even if social rights have been detached from formal citizenship status, they remain dependent on legal status and consequently limited to a demarcated group of people. It was this continual linkage of social rights and citizenship that came under scrutiny in the 2000s.

This chapter explores political debates on access to subsidized medical care for irregular migrants[2] that has taken place in the Swedish parliament[3] through the overarching lens of conceptual history. In general terms, conceptual history is concerned with the emergence, successive change and possible disappearance of concepts and terms. According to this paradigm, conceptual and terminological change is intimately linked to political change and political struggles (cf. Farr 1989, 24–25). Moreover, it is assumed that conceptual change is often initiated in response to perceived tensions and contradictions. In the words of James Farr:

> Conceptual change is one imaginative consequence of political actors criticizing and attempting to resolve the contradictions which they discover or generate in the complex web of their beliefs, actions, and practices as they try to understand and change the world around them.
>
> (Farr 1989, 25)

Farr thus argues that conceptual change tends to be an outcome of attempts by political actors to make sense of inconsistencies. My analysis, here, begins from the assumption that the recent debates in Sweden were brought about by the appearance of irregular migrants who—as rightless subjects in the welfare state—shed light on the exclusions generated by the current citizenship regime and the denial of basic rights, of some considered to be human rights, to non-citizens. The focal point of my analysis is the conceptual struggles—which is consistent with the overarching framework of this book. Fundamentally, these struggles entail attempts to determine the meaning of citizenship rights and human rights. The focus will thus be on how the meaning of citizenship rights and human rights are articulated in the debates. The conceptual debates were, however, spurred by a very particular and delimited problem—namely the exclusion of irregular migrants from certain basic rights—that political actors took a stance on. The interpretations of human rights, and the demarcation between human rights and citizenship rights, that were advanced in the debates should accordingly be understood as responses to this particular problem.

The debates studied in this chapter constitute one instance among many where the presence of irregular migrants has paved the way for contestation of prevailing notions of citizenship and its relationship to rights.

Access to Medical Care   125

To some degree, these debates are distinct as they take place against the backdrop of a citizenship regime and discourses that are particular for Sweden. This said, I argue that the basic theme of the analysis—the challenge that notions of human rights pose to citizenship as a concept and practice—have parallels in debates that have taken place elsewhere in Europe. These include but are not limited to debates on irregular migration. The (lack of) fulfilment of the human rights of non-citizens is, as shown in Kivistö's chapter of this volume, also actualized in other contexts.

This chapter begins with two sections that put the contemporary debates in Sweden into context. This entails, firstly, a discussion about how the debates can be understood as a response to inherent contradictions in citizenship and, secondly, an outline of the two concepts that form the focal point of the debates studied—citizenship and human rights—and the relationship between them. Thereafter, follows the empirical analysis.

Irregular Migrants and the Exposure of a Paradox of Citizenship

Citizenship is, both conceptually and practically, marked by an unresolved tension between inclusion and exclusion. The appearance of the irregular migrants and their precarious circumstances drew attention to this tension. In Sweden, there has been a recurring tendency to hold out the presence of the group, and its predicament in particular, as an anomaly. The blatant exclusion of irregular migrants has been considered paradoxical given Sweden's reputation as a universal welfare state and a pioneer when it comes to the recognition of immigrant rights. However, although the precariousness and rightlessness the group suffers from is incongruent with these inclusive ambitions, it is, I contend, a result of fundamental principles of the Swedish citizenship regime.

This regime has been described as a denizenship model (cf. Hammar 1990). Denizenship, here, is the label for the status of non-citizens that are permanent residents and enjoy equal access to most rights. The hallmark of this approach is the so-called principle of equality. This principle was adopted in 1968, in the wake of the first wave of postwar labour migration, when it was decided that the overall principle of the universal welfare state—equal social rights—would apply to immigrants on the same terms as for citizens (Borevi 2010, 59). The principle gives immigrants with a residence permit the threshold to denizenship status—access to an almost similar set of rights as citizens. However, it leaves immigrants without a permit with no access to any rights or social services. Accordingly, the Swedish framework for rights distribution can best be described in terms of an all-or-nothing approach. Those who are included—citizens and immigrants with a permanent residence permit—are entitled to a broad

126 *Amanda Nielsen*

range of rights and services without discrimination, whereas those who are excluded are left completely outside the system. Concordant with this, I argue that the precariousness that irregular migrants suffer from is a direct effect of the principles that underpin the citizenship regime.

Moreover, from a broader perspective, the predicament of irregular migrants is indicative of the inherent duality in citizenship. A number of scholars have drawn attention to the fact that the concept of citizenship is characterized by a basic ambiguity. Internally, it is connected to ideals of the welfare state and widely considered to be "an inherently egalitarian ideal", in the sense that it "implies full legal and political equality among citizens" (Brubaker 1989, 17). However, as has been pointed out by Linda Bosniak, whereas the idea of citizenship is often "invoked to convey a state of democratic belonging or inclusion", the inclusion envisioned presumes a bounded and exclusive community (Bosniak 2006, 1). Consequently, she argues, it is also characterized by a "basic ethical ambiguity". This means that whereas the ideal of citizenship can be mobilized against subordination, it also represents an axis of subordination itself (ibid.).

The concept of citizenship can, accordingly, be used to shed light on a constitutive tension between inclusion and exclusion that marks the (national) welfare state. The tensions arise from the fact that whereas citizenship signifies a normative ambition to guarantee all citizens an equal status, these inclusive objectives tend to bring about the exclusion of those regarded as 'alien' to the community because these objectives have, so far, been framed in bounded communities. The Swedish approach to migration and integration can be read as a manifestation of this tension between an inclusive and exclusive logic. On the one hand, there is an inclusive ambition whereas, on the other hand, it is limited in scope and only applies to residents whose presence is sanctioned by the state. Moreover, the inclusive ambition is explicitly linked to a policy of regulated migration.[4]

Thus, ultimately the predicament of irregular migrants can be ascribed to the exclusionary logic of citizenship. In accordance with this logic, rights are reserved for citizens—and, in the Swedish case, immigrants with a residence permit—whereas other categories of residents are excluded. This order is, however, potentially challenged by the mobilization of notions of human rights.

The Relationship Between Citizenship and Human Rights

The meaning of human rights, and its relationship to citizenship rights, is far from uncontested. The dominant contemporary understanding of human rights is based on a distinction between citizenship rights and human rights. The latter are understood to be universal and inherent, whereas the former are rights that are tied to membership in bounded communities.

Access to Medical Care 127

This fundamental difference is captured by Bryan Turner and Engin Isin, who argue that the basis for the forms of rights differ as "human rights are regarded as innate and inalienable, [whereas] the rights of citizens are created by states" (Isin and Turner 2008, 12).

The dominant contemporary understanding thus holds human rights to be inherently different from citizenship rights, with the fundamental difference being that the former are enjoyed in the capacity of being human whereas the latter are enjoyed in the capacity of being a member of a particular political community. This sharp distinction is, however, of more recent origin, and the two concepts have a partially overlapping genealogy as both concepts can be traced back to a discourse of universal rights that emerged in conjunction with the American and French revolutions. At these moments, declarative assertions were made that "asserted the equality of all men, the sovereignty of the people, and the inalienable rights of the individual as universal principles" (Jacobson 1997, 1). Initially, however, it was assumed that these rights were to be realized within a national framework (ibid.). Consequently, as argued by Yasemin Soysal, these revolutions "codified individual rights and freedoms as attributes of national citizenship, thus linking the individual and the nation-state" (Soysal 1994, 17). Thus, historically there was no sharp distinction between human rights and citizenship rights. Human rights, on the contrary, were articulated as rights that were to be realized through citizenship. This stands in sharp contrast to the contemporary understanding of human rights, which rests, as argued by historian Samuel Moyn, on a "recasting of rights as entitlements that might contradict the sovereign nation-state from above and outside rather than serve as its foundation" (Moyn 2010, 13). Historically, he argues, there was a universal agreement that human rights should be secured through the construction of "spaces of citizenship" in which rights should be accorded and protected. Accordingly, he highlights the novelty of understanding human rights as individual rights within the framework of international law (ibid.).

Moyn's argument, that the contemporary notion of human rights constitute a significant break in the way we comprehend rights, is far from undisputed and has been challenged by other scholars who highlight the continuity of the universalist basis of human rights. However, leaving this controversy over genealogy aside, I argue that any attempt to disentangle the relationship between the two sets of rights is bound to be challenging. As argued by Alison Kesby, attempts to "fix the line separating 'citizens' rights' and 'human rights'" definitively will always be unsuccessful, as this relationship is "contingent, constantly shifting, and contested" (Kesby 2012, 111). From the perspective of conceptual history, the shifts in meaning that both citizenship and human rights have undergone throughout the last decades are part of a constant process of change that takes place in response to new problems and contradictions and attempts to solve these.

128   *Amanda Nielsen*

Furthermore, from this perspective, it makes sense to study this conceptual change in tandem. One of the key assumptions of conceptual history is that studies of conceptual change need to take account of the fact that "concepts are never held or used in isolation, but in constellations which make up entire schemes or belief systems" (Farr 1989, 33). Concepts, that is, must be put into context and studied as components of larger systems of thought. This is especially relevant with regard to the case at hand, as it is evident that the meaning of each concept, i.e., citizenship rights and human rights, are determined in relation to each other.

The Campaign for Policy Revision

Up until the turn of the millennium, the criteria for eligibility for provision of health and medical care in Sweden—permanent residency—was not a contested issue. This changed in the early 2000s when provision of medical care to irregular migrants became a policy issue in conjunction with the implementation of the UN Convention on the Rights of the Child. In the wake of this process, former asylum-seeking children in hiding were granted access to subsidized medical care. This paved the way for further demands for subsidized care for other categories of irregular migrants.[5]

The early demands for subsidized medical care were restricted to children and rested on two main arguments. First, the right of the child and the UN Convention, which prescribes a right to medical care for all children, was mobilized as an argument for policy revision. Second, notions of innocence and non-responsibility were mobilized and it was argued that children, in contrast to adults, should be granted access to basic rights because they lack responsibility for the situation they are in. The initial claims made on behalf of irregular migrants thus rested on, and reproduced, a distinction between children and adults that was drawn on the basis of responsibility for the situation at hand. Gradually, however, adults were incorporated into the demands for policy reform. This process was also accompanied by an important shift in claim making.

The early demands for medical care for undocumented adults were primarily justified with reference to humanitarian arguments. This was consistent with the understanding that adults, in contrast to children, could not claim entitlement to medical care as a right. However, this changed in the wake of the publication of a UN report in 2007. The report, issued by Paul Hunt, the UN Special Rapporteur on the right of everyone to the enjoyment of the highest attainable standard of physical and mental health, contained sharp criticism of Swedish policy. Hunt argued that Swedish legislation that denied unauthorized residents access to subsidized care was in violation of international law—more precisely, because medical care as a human right should "be enjoyed by all without

Access to Medical Care 129

discrimination" (Hunt 2007). Accordingly, he pleaded that in order to bring legislation into line with international law, undocumented migrants, as well as asylum seekers, should be given access to care on the same basis as other residents (ibid.). The report had a considerable impact and was widely referenced in the debate during the consequent years. First and foremost, the report was significant as it contributed to establishing an understanding that access to medical care is a human right and, as such, something that all residents, irregular migrants included, are entitled to.

In 2008, shortly after the publication of Hunt's report, the government presented a bill regarding provision of health, medical and dental care to asylum seekers.[6] The proposed legislation, which entailed continual exclusion of irregular migrants from subsidized medical care, was controversial and led to intense debates and campaigning. The presentation of the bill resulted in extra-parliamentary mobilization and a broad coalition, called the Right to Health Care initiative (*Rätt till vård-initiativet*), was formed to lobby against its adoption.[7] The consequent parliamentary debates form the focal point of the analysis in this chapter. This analysis will not account for all aspects and complexities present in these debates (for a more detailed account see Nielsen 2016). Rather, it will focus on one particular aspect, namely, the competing interpretations of the relationship between citizenship rights and human rights that are articulated in these debates. Before I proceed, however, I will briefly summarize the key arguments in the debates.

The proponents of reform justified their position with reference to the norms stipulated by medical ethics and human rights law. In accordance with these norms, they argued, it is unjustified to exclude residents without legal status from access to subsidized medical care. With regard to ethics, it was argued that any kind of distinction, or discrimination, between patients due to factors other than medical need is incompatible with medical ethics. With regard to human rights, there were differing opinions on whether human rights law permits any kind of distinction. These differences aside, there was a shared belief that the implication of health being a human right is that everyone should be able to afford medical care and that it consequently should be subsidized. Another key argument, linked to the above, was that the provision of medical care should be exempted from consideration as a legitimate policy instrument. The advocates of reform rejected the idea that there needs to be consistency between social policy and migration policy, and that the former must work to reinforce the principled commitment to a regulated immigration. Opponents of this view also put forward a number of arguments. Among the most prominent was the argument that it would be inconsistent of the state to grant rights to people whose applications to stay in the country had been rejected. Such a measure, it was recurrently argued, would undermine respect for the authority decisions and obstruct their enforcement. Another frequently invoked argument was that provision

130 *Amanda Nielsen*

of subsidized medical care would create an incentive for people to stay in the country irregularly and lead to the establishment of a permanent parallel structure in society.

The positions of political parties in these debates shifted over time. From the start, support for reform was expressed by parties across the political spectrum. The initial calls came from the smaller parties in parliament whereas the two biggest parties, the Social Democrats and the Moderates, were hesitant or remained silent on the issue. The Moderates long remained opponents of reform, and it was their reversal that paved the way for the 2013 bill. This was eventually supported by all parties except for the Sweden Democrats (for a more detailed account see Nielsen 2016).

The Meaning and Scope of Human Rights

The debates and political struggles studied in this chapter originate in a fundamental controversy over article 12 of the UN Covenant on Economic, Social and Cultural Rights. This states that everyone has a right to "the enjoyment of the highest attainable standard of physical and mental health" and that this right should be exercised without any form of discrimination. It was the meaning and implications of this article with regard to the state's obligations towards non-citizens that formed the focal point in the Swedish debate (for a further discussion on human rights and non-citizens, see Kivistö's chapter in this book). The discussions, to be more precise, revolved around two issues: first, whether the state has a duty to provide subsidized medical care to irregular migrants and, second, whether the state is allowed to discriminate—in the sense of providing more or less comprehensive medical care—between different categories of residents. These issues, which were bound up with efforts to draw a boundary between citizenship rights and human rights, formed the focal points of the debates that took place in the Swedish parliament in the early 2000s. In these debates it is possible to discern three different interpretations of the meaning of human rights and its relationship to citizenship rights.

A first interpretation is that the implication of the article is that health and medical care should be provided to all residents on equal terms. The following quote reflects this understanding:

> The right to health care is universal and individual. It applies to all and must never become a migration policy instrument. All asylum seekers and undocumented migrants, not only children but also adults, should be given the same right to health and medical care as everyone else in Sweden. Everything else is a violation of human rights.
>
> (Addr. 16, Christina Höj Larsen,
> Left Party, 2010/11:79)

Access to Medical Care 131

This reading of human rights rests on the understanding that any kind of discrimination in this matter between residents with a basis in legal status is in violation with human rights law. This is the interpretation that was advanced by Paul Hunt in the UN report cited above.

A second interpretation is that irregular migrants should be given access to subsidized care, but that the scope of care provided should be less extensive than that offered to residents with legal status. This reading thus rests on a recognition that there are basic rights, that medical care is among those, and that all people residing in a country are entitled to it irrespective of legal status. These rights—human rights—are, however, distinguished from the more extensive set of rights enjoyed by citizens and residents with a permanent residence permit. This understanding is exemplified in the following quote:

> The principle that people who are not resident in Sweden, and not included in the Swedish health insurance, should pay for themselves is reasonable. At the same time, through international conventions Sweden has committed to ensure that all people are assured the best possible health through medical care in case of illness. We therefore believe that it is reasonable to grant undocumented migrants access to care under the same conditions as asylum seekers.
>
> (Addr. 1, Eva-Lena Jansson, Social Democrats, 2012/13:109)

This understanding of human rights thus leaves room for preferential treatment of some residents as long as everybody, including irregular migrants, is guaranteed basic level access.

The interpretations discussed thus far are alike in that they both hold access to subsidized care to be a human right. This is not the case with the third interpretation that rests on the understanding that subsidized medical care should be considered a citizenship right. The quote below, which makes explicit use of the two concepts, is illustrative of this line of reasoning:

> It is about distinguishing between what are human rights—care should be open for all—and what are citizenship rights. Equal care is about citizenship rights.
>
> (Addr. 61, Tobias Billström, Moderates, 2009/10:48)

According to this more restrictive reading, one must thus distinguish between being given the possibility to access medical care, which is a human right, and being given access to *subsidized* medical care, which is taken to be a privilege reserved for people with an authorized right to stay in the country. This leaves the state with more limited obligations towards

132   *Amanda Nielsen*

irregular migrants compared to the previously discussed interpretations. Accordingly, the advocates of this view also expressed scepticism towards those interpretations of human rights that stress a more comprehensive responsibility for non-citizens. It is, they argued, "no human right to get access to state subsidised medical care in a country that you reside in illegally" (Addr. 41, Björn Söder, Sweden Democrats, 2012/13:109). To make such a claim, moreover, was argued to be contrary to the intent of the drafters of the convention. The third interpretation, that is to say, maintains that social rights are a privilege that people qualify for through membership rather than rights that everybody is entitled to.

The three interpretations thus reflect three different understandings of entitlement and its dependency on membership. The first interpretation suggests that status is of no relevance whatsoever when it comes to the provision of this particular social right. The second interpretation, on the other hand, maintains that there should be a difference between those who are recognized members of the community and those who are not, but that the difference should be less pronounced. The third interpretation, finally, affirms that membership should be a criteria for eligibility. These interpretations, and the distinctions and demarcations they entail, are often made with explicit use of the concepts of human rights and citizenship rights; conceptual struggles accordingly moved to the forefront in the debates.

Towards a Re-Demarcation of the Welfare State

The debates during the 2000s eventually resulted in a shift in policy. The first step towards new legislation was taken in 2010 when the government appointed a commission to investigate the provision of medical care to irregular migrants. Its primary conclusion, published in a report in 2011, was that irregular migrants, as well as asylum seekers, should have access to medical care on equal terms with other permanent residents regardless of age (SOU 2011, 23, 48). This recommendation was motivated with reference to all forms of distinction between different categories of residents being incompatible with the principle of non-discrimination that underpins human rights law. That is to say, the commission report confirmed the recommendations that were advanced by Paul Hunt in the 2007 UN report. Two years later, in spring 2013, the government presented a bill that proposed that irregular migrants should be granted access to subsidized medical care. The bill, in contrast to the recommendation from the commission, proposed that irregular migrants' access to care should be less extensive compared to other residents. More precisely, the government proposed that adults residing in the country without permission should be granted access to subsidized health and medical care under the same terms as adult asylum seekers, whereas children should be granted the same access as permanent legal residents. The same terms as

Access to Medical Care 133

asylum seekers means, more precisely, access to medical care that "can't be deferred"[8] (Prop. 2012/13, 109). The proposal was consistent with a new majority view that had crystallized during the 2000s. This view rested on the understanding that the state is obliged to provide subsidized medical care to all residents regardless of legal status. However, differentiated treatment, i.e., to give some residents access to more extensive care, was understood to be compatible with human rights law as long as all residents are granted access to some form of affordable care. This interpretation was dismissed by a parliamentary minority that maintained that human rights law require that all residents are granted equal access to medical care. The 2013 bill was thus far from uncontroversial, and it was criticized both on the grounds of being too far-reaching and insufficient. However, this controversy aside, the bill was eventually accepted by an almost unanimous[9] parliament, and on July 1, 2013, the new legislation came into force (Nielsen 2016, 159–163).

The adoption of the bill meant that Swedish policy, previously singled out as one of the most restrictive in Europe,[10] was revised in a more inclusive direction. The reform, moreover, implies a step towards a new way of conceiving the relationship between rights and status. At the beginning of this chapter, I discussed how Sweden moved from a model that distributed rights and privileges in accordance with a citizenship logic to a model based on a denizenship logic in the late 1960s. Concordant with this approach—where the residence permit make up the threshold to most rights—people who resided in the country without authorization were denied access to any social rights. Consequently, I contend that the new legislation, although the rights granted are limited in scope, could be interpreted as a first step to a revision of this logic as it recognizes undocumented migrants as right-bearers.

Furthermore, I argue that the adoption of the bill is indicative of a significant shift in understanding. At the turn of the millennium, the third interpretation sketched above, that access to subsidized medical care is a citizenship right rather than a human right, seemed a common-sense and unproblematic assumption. This view is, for instance, reflected in the quote below:

> This is about aliens who have applied for asylum or a residence permit in Sweden, whose applications have been assessed, and who have not been found to be in need of protection from persecution or to have other grounds to stay in Sweden. He or she should consequently urgently leave the country. In my view, it would be an inconsistent and unclear order if the state should compensate the regions for health- and medical care to people who do not have the right to reside in Sweden according to the same regulations as asylum seekers.
> (Addr. 1, Maj-Inger Klingvall, Social Democrats, 2000/01:65)

134   *Amanda Nielsen*

This statement, presented by the Minister of Migration at the time, is representative of the dominant approach at the turn of the millennium. At this point, most leading politicians dismissed claims for medical care for irregular migrants as absurd, and it was regarded as inconsistent to grant rights to a category of people whose presence is unsanctioned by the state. I contend that the fact that a large majority supported the same measure a decade later was linked to the emergence of a new consensus.

The mobilization of notions of human rights was conducive in bringing about this consensus and, subsequently, policy revision. Firstly, because they rendered the discussion about responsibility, and the associated distinction between children and adults, redundant. I argue that the designation of some rights as human rights—distinguishable from citizenship rights—has been of momentous importance to attempts to establish undocumented adults as right-bearers. Secondly, notions of human rights have been central in limiting the legitimate scope of migration control. Historically, Swedish policy has been guided by an underpinning assumption about a need for consistency, and accordingly social policy has been considered subsidiary to migration policy. In the wake of the mobilization of human rights, the legitimacy of using social policy as a means to control migration has been called into question.

Concluding Remarks

This chapter has approached the politics of the concept of citizenship through an analysis of the parliamentary debate on the provision of health and medical care to irregular migrants in Sweden during the 2000s. This debate has focused primarily on whether this particular social right should be regarded a citizenship right, and hence be reserved for a demarcated community of people, or a human right, and hence provided to all without distinction. The debates, which were initiated in response to the exclusion suffered by irregular migrants and formed part of an attempt to establish these as right-bearers, thus had a clear conceptual component. Concordant with this, attempts to determine the meaning of the two concepts, and their relationship, formed a key component of the debates. In their aftermath, moreover, the conceptualization of citizenship has undergone a slight modification that is in agreement with a new understanding of the link between membership and entitlement to rights.

The analysis is thus illustrative of how conceptual change is brought about in interplay with contestation of circumstances in the world. This chapter is also exemplary of an instance where conceptual change goes hand in hand with policy change. As I have argued here, it was a change in the understanding of the meaning and implications of human rights that paved the way for the 2013 reform. This change, in turn, took place in the wake of intense political struggles where the concepts, and how they should be interpreted, was one of the focal points. The chapter is

Access to Medical Care 135

thus also illustrative of the importance of concepts, and how these are interpreted, in politics.

From a conceptual point of view, it is also important to highlight that political struggle over the demarcation between citizenship rights and human rights are likely to continue in the future. Fundamental concepts such as these are notorious for their disputed character. The new consensus, and its conceptual underpinnings, is thus more or less bound to be challenged in the future. I contend that there are already signs that suggest that such a process is taking place. Since 2015, in the wake of the sharp increase in asylum seekers across Europe, Swedish debates on the rights of non-citizens—a category to which both asylum seekers and irregular migrants belong—has undergone significant changes. This shift, moreover, has been accompanied by policy being drastically restricted. These entail changes in asylum policy as well as in policies that are oriented towards those asylum seekers whose applications have been rejected. Given this development, it remains to be seen whether the changes, conceptual and legislative, I have sketched in this chapter will be of a lasting character or, rather, a historical parenthesis.

Notes

1 Up until 2013, undocumented migrants, with the exception of one category of undocumented children, namely former asylum seekers, were formally denied access to subsidized health and medical care. This meant that care only was provided on a voluntary basis. However, some regions in Sweden provided medical care to irregular migrants already prior to 2013, in accordance with local decisions.
2 The term irregular migrant refers to non-citizens that have either crossed state borders or remained within state territory without sanction from the host state (McNevin 2011, 18). In this chapter I will use this term interchangeably with the term undocumented.
3 The analysis and conclusions in this chapter are based on a broader study that I have conducted during the course of my Ph.D. studies. This investigates the politicization of irregular migration in Sweden through an analysis of minutes from parliamentary debates during the 2000s. The basis for the analysis at hand has been those minutes in which irregular migrant's access to health and medical care appear as a theme.
4 Swedish policy has accordingly been described as an attempt to find a balance between generous policies on entry and comprehensive inclusion in society through various welfare institutions (Öberg 1994). This approach was established in conjunction with the adoption of the principle of equality in 1968. At the same time as the parliament embarked on a policy of equal treatment, it confirmed the overall need of migration control (Borevi 2010, 59).
5 The convention was ratified in 1990 and in the wake of this a parliamentary commission was appointed to investigate how the convention could be implemented in Swedish law. The commission's work resulted in a recommendation to grant former asylum-seeking children in hiding access to health and medical care (SOU 1997:116). This recommendation resulted in a government decision in 2000 that granted one subcategory of undocumented children, namely former asylum-seeking children in hiding, access to subsidized medical care.

136 *Amanda Nielsen*

6 The bill (Prop. 2007/08:105) was induced by an EU directive about the receiving conditions of asylum seekers in the member states. In response to the directive the government decided that it was necessary to pass legislation to regulate the regional responsibility to provide health, medical and dental care to asylum seekers. The bill—which meant that prevailing policy, enforced through agreements between the state and the regions, was confirmed by law—entailed no substantial shift in policy. However, in the wake of a burgeoning critique of prevailing policy the lack of change in itself was controversial.

7 The coalition consisted of a number of diverse organizations—ranging from NGOs and asylum rights groups to professional organizations within the health care sector, and foundations providing care to irregular migrants on a voluntary basis—that united around a demand for an expansion of the provision to health care.

8 The term is controversial. In the bill, it is defined as an expansion of immediate care, i.e., not only emergency care but also care that is provided when even a moderate delay would have severe consequences for the patient (Prop 2012/13:109:18–19).

9 Three hundred and three MPs voted yes, 20 MPs voted no (the Sweden Democrats) and 26 were absent (2013/14:109).

10 Sweden was, for instance, together with Austria, placed in the most restrictive category out of five possible in a PICUM (Platform for International Cooperation on Undocumented Migrants) report about irregular migrant's access to health and medical care in the EU (see PICUM 2007, 8).

References

Borevi, Karin. 2010. "Sverige: Mångkulturalismens flaggskepp i Norden." In *Velferdens grenser*, edited by Grete Brochmann and Anniken Hagelund, 41–130. Oslo: Universitetsforlaget.

Bosniak, Linda. 2006. *The Citizen and the Alien: Dilemmas of Contemporary Membership*. Princeton, NJ: Princeton University Press.

Brubaker, Rogers. 1989. "Introduction." In *Immigration and the Politics of Citizenship in Europe and North America*, edited by Rogers Brubaker, 1–27. Lanham, MD: University Press of America.

Farr, James. 1989. "Understanding Conceptual Change Politically." In *Political Innovation and Conceptual Change*, edited by Terence Ball, James Farr, and Russell L. Hanson, 24–49. Cambridge: Cambridge University Press.

Hammar, Tomas. 1990. *Democracy and the Nation State: Aliens, Denizens and Citizens in a World of International Migration*. Aldershot: Avebury.

Hunt, Paul. 2007. *Mission to Sweden. Report of the Special Rapporteur on the Right of Everyone to the Enjoyment of the Highest Attainable Standard of Physical and Mental Health*. United Nations General Assembly, Human Rights Council.

Isin, Engin F., and Bryan S. Turner. 2008. "Investigating Citizenship: An Agenda for Citizenship Studies." In *Citizenship Between Past and Future*, edited by Engin F. Isin, Peter Nyers, and Bryan S. Turner, 5–17. Abingdon: Routledge.

Jacobson, David. 1997. *Rights Across Borders: Immigration and the Decline of Citizenship*. Baltimore, MD: The John Hopkins University Press.

Kesby, Alison. 2012. *The Right to Have Rights: Citizenship, Humanity, and International Law*. Oxford: Oxford University Press.

Access to Medical Care 137

McNevin, Anne. 2011. *Contesting Citizenship: Irregular Migrants and New Frontiers of the Political*. New York: Columbia University Press.

Moyn, Samuel. 2010. *The Last Utopia: Human Rights in History*. Cambridge, MA: Harvard University Press.

Nielsen, Amanda. 2016. *Challenging Rightlessness: On Irregular Migrants and the Contestation of Welfare State Demarcation in Sweden*. Växjö: Linnaeus University Press.

Öberg, Nils. 1994. *Gränslös rättvisa eller rättvisa inom gränser? Om moraliska dilemman i välfärdsstaters invandrings- och invandrarpolitik*. Uppsala: Acta Universitatis Upsaliensis.

PICUM. 2007. *Access to Health Care for Undocumented Migrants in Europe*. Brussels: PICUM.

Soysal, Yasemin Nuhoğlu. 1994. *Limits of Citizenship: Migrants and Postnational Membership in Europe*. Chicago, IL: University of Chicago Press.

Other Sources

Minutes from parliamentary sessions: 2000/01:65; 2007/08:115; 2009/10:48; 2010/11:79; 2010/11:96; 2012/13:109; 2013/14:109.

Prop. 2007/08:105, Lag om hälso- och sjukvård åt asylsökande m. fl.

Prop. 2012/13:109, Hälso- och sjukvård till personer som vistas i Sverige utan tillstånd.

SOU 1997:116, Barnets bästa i främsta rummet – FN:s konvention om barnets rättigheter förverkligas i Sverige.

SOU 2011:48, Vård efter behov och på lika villkor – en mänsklig rättighet.

8 The Non-State Sámi

Struggle for Indigenous Citizenship in the European North

Sanna Valkonen and Jarno Valkonen

In this chapter, we approach the complexity of implementing a form of non-state citizenship in the European nation state-centric tradition of citizenship. We analyze the debate and political consequences of establishing an indigenous polity and citizenship in the context of the only Indigenous people in the European Union, the Sámi people. The category of Indigenous people is an excellent example of a political concept that has made visible (and given voice to) the dignity and political position of the people who are often the most marginalized groups in their home countries and who lack economic and political power. Considering their marginal position, Indigenous peoples have become increasingly significant political actors in contemporary international and national politics, and the concept itself has become politically significant. The concept of Indigenous people and the global political movement accompanying it has generated a form of non-state citizenship which challenges the legitimacy of nation states to govern their territories and citizens, dismantles the state-centered world order and questions its foundations and legitimacy (see e.g. Stewart-Harawira 2005, 56–66). What follows from this is that indigenous citizenship is an object of a specific kind of political struggle—a struggle that illustrates many burning contemporary questions of belonging to an ethnos and demarcation of a demos. Our task in this chapter is to analyze the politics of indigenous citizenship. The central point is that the concept of Indigenous people inherently includes an idea of political struggle: indigeneity is about politicizing self-evident power relations and structures and about creating political space and time from a subaltern position. Thus, it often encounters strong resistance from majority positions.

For the purposes of analyzing the politics of indigenous citizenship from a conceptual historical perspective, we regard "Indigenous people" or "indigeneity" as a political concept which has been formed by different (colonial and other) power relations, and which is defined and shaped by political actors through their political actions. This approach turns attention to the controversy and contingency of the concepts illustrating their deeply political nature. In the case of Indigenous people, the conceptual

The Non-State Sámi   139

history approach shows how the concept itself has been transformed during decades of close interaction with concrete changes in the international political system and ideologies. It also demonstrates how the concept of Indigenous people and its ambiguity has actually enabled and engendered the political conflict relating to Sámi citizenship in Finland. In addition, the concept of Indigenous people is itself an object of ongoing definitional debate; it also opens a space for political action.

The classical notion of citizenship refers to membership of a nation state that relates to special rights and duties (e.g. Marshall 1992). Historically, nation state citizenship has been an essential way to understand and govern the relationships between peoples. There are, however, millions of people for whom the nation state citizenship does not guarantee the full (or even any) membership in their respective home countries and thus rights it should. Nation state citizenship has been blind to differences (e.g. Kymlicka 1995; Yuval-Davis 2011).

The category of Indigenous people is a special form of non-state citizenship which by definition covers about 300 million people all over the world in more than 70 countries (Merlan 2009). The legal category of Indigenous people refers to distinct peoples who are particularly protected in international or national legislation as having a set of specific rights based on their historical ties to a particular territory, and their cultural or historical distinctiveness from other populations. Indigenous peoples also form non-dominant sectors of society. They are usually in a minority position and often marginalized culturally, politically, economically and socially in the states where they live (Martinez-Cobo 1986). Indigenous people are commonly regarded as being the first inhabitants of a given territory, or at least to have occupied it prior to successive waves of settlers (Gausset et al. 2011, 136). Among them are Indigenous peoples of the Americas, the Inuit and Aleutians of the circumpolar region, the Sámi of northern Europe, the Aborigines and Torres Strait Islanders of Australia and the Maori of New Zealand (see Merlan 2009).

A nation state citizenship is not enough to guarantee Indigenous peoples' full political participation in the states in which they live nor the construction of their own political communities in order to foster their culture, language and identity. As nation state citizenship treats everyone equally, it is blind to particular needs of Indigenous peoples whose cultural survival is strongly dependent on special protection. In many cases, Indigenous peoples are political minorities and, thus, unable to gain a political position and power within majority democracies so that their political agendas can become heard and taken into account. From this long-lasting minority position grows the importance of indigenous self-determination and self-governance. From the perspective of Indigenous peoples, nation state citizenship can actually be seen in many cases as a form of contemporary colonialism, as it reproduces the sovereignty of the majority over its minorities (see e.g. Alfred and Corntassel 2005).

140 *Sanna Valkonen and Jarno Valkonen*

At the same time, from the state citizen perspective, indigenous citizen ship can appear as a deeply political position that is open to strategic use for achieving extra rights in relation to other citizens from the same region. Positive discrimination is easily regarded as violation of the equal treatment of each citizen (see Lehtola 2015).

Yuval-Davis (2011, 201) argues that "citizenship should not be seen as limited to state citizenship alone but should be understood as the participatory dimension of membership in all political communities". Not all citizenships involve the same kind of participation and not all of them relate to citizenships in a state (Yuval-Davis 2011, 46). Indigenous citizenship has become political reality and practice through mechanisms of international law (for the role of European law in promoting a conceptual innovation and implementing the category of Union citizenship, see Wiesner in this volume). Indigenous peoples have an established position within the UN system with their own political bodies, such as the Permanent Forum on Indigenous Issues (Minde 2008). The rights of Indigenous peoples (for example rights to traditional lands, own language and culture and forms of society) are recognized in several international conventions and declarations such as the ILO Convention No. 169 (1989) and the United Nations Declaration on the Rights of Indigenous Peoples (2007). Indigenous citizenship can thus be regarded both as a membership to an international indigenous polity, and as membership of national or local indigenous polities. At the level of states, recognizing and securing indigenous rights has contributed different national solutions from autonomous indigenous areas (e.g. Nunavut) to establishing different indigenous political bodies (e.g. Sámi parliaments in Nordic countries) or to denying the existence of indigenous groups (e.g. Bangladesh; see Alfred and Corntassel 2005).

The Sámi are an Indigenous people who in their home countries of Finland, Sweden, Norway and Russia, belong to two populations and two overlapping civil societies within nation states (c.f. Selle and Strømsnes 2010). The Sámi of Finland are recognized as an Indigenous people in the Constitution of Finland (para 17) with the right to maintain and develop their language and culture. Consequently, the Sámi are subject to international regulations concerning Indigenous peoples. Most concretely this subjectivity is materialized as particular group rights to which the Sámi are entitled. Since 1996, The Sámi of Finland have enjoyed cultural autonomy in the Sámi home region governed by an elected and representative Sámi body, the Sámi Parliament. The Sámi Parliament has a certain amount of political power regarding Sámi cultural and language issues and it officially represents the Sámi of Finland. It can, however, be said to be lacking real political power and it is strongly dependent on state's financial support (see e.g. Valkonen 2009). The Act on the Sámi Parliament (1995/974) provides a definition of a legal Sámi subject who is entitled to vote and stand as a candidate in elections to the Sámi Parliament.

The Non-State Sámi   141

Based on the definition of the legal Sámi subject the Sámi electoral roll is constructed. In practical terms, the Sámi become members of their own polity with participatory rights, in other words, Sámi citizens, by fulfilling the criteria of the Sámi definition of the Act on the Sámi Parliament.[1]

We argue that creating an international indigenous polity has enabled international, national and local forms of indigenous citizenship which allows indigenous citizens to act as citizens and to participate in transnational forums. Indigenous citizenship can thus be regarded as a form of double citizenship—in the case of the article, the Indigenous Sámi people have full democratic rights both as Finnish state citizens and as indigenous Sámi citizens. This has led to a political debate which questions and politicizes both the contemporary Sámi group's existence as a distinct people and their indigenous status, and, thus, their special ties and rights to their home region.

We will first give an overview of how the concept of Indigenous people has been adopted and transformed within international legal and political framework. Secondly, we analyze the interplay of international norms, most importantly the ILO Convention No. 169 (1989), regulating indigenous citizenship, and the establishment of the indigenous Sámi polity in Finland. We illustrate how becoming part of the international indigenous movement, and thus introducing the concept of indigeneity into national politics, has come to mean a profound political and social change of position for Sámi people, and how it can be said to have contributed to the indigenous "citizenization" of the Sámi. Thirdly, we will take a closer look at a political struggle over Sámi and indigenous citizenship that institutionalizing the Sámi people's position in Finland as Indigenous people by legislative measures—i.e. establishing Sámi cultural autonomy governed by the Sámi parliament—has engendered. We point out how in this debate both the foundations and legitimacy of current Sámi polity and politics, as well as the indigeneity of the Sámi and boundary-making of the community, have been deeply questioned. In a final step, we will discuss what kind of citizenship non-state indigenous citizenship actually is.

The History of the Concept of "Indigenous People"

The use of the term "indigenous" in reference to a distinct human group or community with rights of self-determination is fairly recent. As Niezen writes:

> From its earliest use in the seventeenth century to about the mid-twentieth century the term did not even normally apply to people but, rather, was almost exclusively used to refer plants and livestock native to a particular region.
>
> (Niezen 2009, 27)

142 *Sanna Valkonen and Jarno Valkonen*

In the mid-twentieth century, the term began to be used to refer to human society. At that time, it was more a verb which was used to provide a hoped-for culturally sensitive approach to colonization. After that it became an adjective referring to human groups, and finally, a legal category of peoples with a distinct way of life on the margins of states (Niezen 2009, 27).

The concept and category of Indigenous People was adopted in international law to justify the control of these peoples by state powers (see Kenrick 2011; Rodríguez–Piñero 2005). The concept included a civilizing idea to make colonial politics acceptable. The concept of Indigenous people has also been described as a continuum for the need of majority societies to define their racialized "other"—sometimes primitive, sometimes noble (see Mathisen 2003; Sissons 2005). Also, the categorical opposition of indigenous and non-indigenous, conceived as descendants of natives and settlers, is itself a colonialist construction (Ingold 2000, 151).

The International Labour Organization (ILO), established in 1919, began inquiring into the working conditions of Indigenous peoples in Latin America. Based on four inquiries, the ILO proposed conventions for improving the position of indigenous workers. These propositions did not, however, lead to any specific action but generated discussion about indigeneity, defining "Indianness", and protecting these people both at national and international levels (Kingsbury 1995, 14, 17–19; Seurujärvi-Kari 2012, 79).

The first ILO Convention No. 107 concerning Indigenous peoples (1957) was—typically for the cultural and political atmosphere at that time—assimilative and paternalistic and did not recognize the Indigenous peoples as distinct peoples (Seurujärvi-Kari, 2012, 80–81). The initial goal was to include indigenous and tribal peoples more fully into the development projects of nation states in order to integrate them into the political culture of their nation states (see Niezen 2009, 9).

Rodríguez-Piñero (2005) describes the complexity and shifting use and meanings of the concept of indigeneity. There are important discontinuities regarding meanings, political contexts, normative assumptions and even actors with the ILO regime. According to Rodríguez-Piñero (2005, 3) "the very term 'indigenous' appears associated with shifting power/knowledge configurations, contingently connected to conflicting notions of 'civilization', 'development' and human rights." Often these discontinuities are related to broader, even dramatic, changes of the international law itself throughout the twentieth century, beginning from a time when it was a major instrument for legitimizing European colonial expansion and domination overseas, to a time when it turned into an important instrument for Indigenous peoples' struggle for survival and recognition as distinct cultural and political communities (Rodríguez-Piñero 2005, 3).

Despite its roots in the colonial world order, the Indigenous people have reclaimed the category of indigeneity through intense work in international forums since the 1960s. According to Merlan (2009, 303), internationalist indigeneity is also largely a product of Western liberal democracies: the stimuli for internationalization of the indigenous category originated principally from Anglo-American settler colonies and Scandinavia which are all cultures of liberal democracy and carry weight in international institutional affairs. The indigenous movement and growing recognition of indigenous rights are part of discourses of multiculturalism and pluralism, and a changed consciousness about the acceptance of difference. The new social movements, such as feminist, environmental, black power and red power movements, are all part of the same phenomenon (see e.g. Seurujärvi-Kari 2012, 52).

Minde (2008, 49) writes how the last decades of the twentieth century is a story of the international success of indigenous rights. From being marginalized socially, economically, and politically, with no possibility of being heard in international forums, Indigenous peoples have obtained direct access to existing UN bodies and have been directly involved in the development of new institutions in the United Nations system (such as Working Group on Indigenous Populations). The UN Declaration on the Rights of Indigenous Peoples (2007) strengthened their political and legal influence both locally and globally. According to Niezen:

> The leaders and organizations that represent indigenous peoples have thus in a remarkably short space of time constructed an international movement that takes the form of global network of those who share a consistent sense of self, a common sense on timelessness and fragility, and complementary aspirations of self-determination.
>
> (Niezen 2009, 9)

Concepts serve as strategic instruments for political action:

> They shape the horizon of the political possibilities in the situation, within which the agent has to form a policy, but can also be used in critical situations as a means of politicization, of revising the horizon of the possible and by this means revising the range of policy choices.
>
> (Palonen 1999, 47).

The concept of indigenous people has been reclaimed by Indigenous peoples for their political action for which it serves as a focus point, both internationally and within nation states. It has politicized the relation between states and these peoples as well as the relationship between indigenous people and other locals in their home regions. Conceptual history allows one to see the very essence of indigeneity as constructed and relational. When the concept goes global, it takes on radically different meanings according to the context (Hale 2009, 322). 'Indigenous' is thus an eminently political category and has no single a priori or fixed meaning. Neither is it a permanent condition "that is 'simply there'" but

144 *Sanna Valkonen and Jarno Valkonen*

is always context-related (Merlan 2009; Hale 2009). As Palonen (1997, 11) points out, concepts are not definitions that finish conversations but rather a bundle of questions which expect competing answers. Next, we will analyze the establishment of indigenous Sámi citizenship in Finland, the process we call indigenous citizenization.

You Know Brother, You Understand Sister: Indigenous Citizenization of the Sámi in Finland

The becoming of the Sámi as part of the international indigenous movement in the 1970s is crystallized in the lines, "You know brother, you understand sister", which are part of a poem written at the beginning of 1970s by a Sámi poet, musician, painter and activist, Nils-Aslak Valkeapää. In the poem, Valkeapää (1985) reflects the confusion the Sámi communities experienced when encountering Western legal order: "Law books that they have written themselves—This is the law and it applies to you too". Valkeapää also describes the shared feeling of loyalty, brotherhood and understanding which he found in the global community of Indigenous peoples when participating in the meetings of international indigenous movement: "You know brother, you understand sister".

Becoming part of the indigenous movement and introducing the concept of "Indigenous people" into national politics has promoted significant changes in Sámi people's political and social position in Norway, Sweden and Finland. It has contributed to the indigenous citizenization of the Sámi. In this process, the Sámi movement—the young and educated Sámi activists (artists, politicians, students), Valkeapää being one of the most influential—has played a significant role. Their interpretations and articulation of indigeneity, as well as concrete international and national political activism, have set the scene for concrete changes on the part of the state.

In Finland, there are currently about 10,000 Sámi. Until recently the Sámi have experienced strong assimilation politics as a result of the states' official policies. The assimilative policy of Norway and Finland has meant, for instance, the finlandization and norwegianization of the Sámi homeland area, prohibition of the Sámi language as a teaching language and the devaluing of Sámi culture (Lehtola 1997). The assimilation policy continued up until recently, although the cooperation of the Sámi started to strengthen after World War II and was followed by the re-estimation of the self-image of the Sámi and the reinvention of a new communality and cultural connection (Eidheim 1997).

In the late 1940s, several state-wide Sámi political organizations simultaneously emerged in Sweden, Norway, and Finland, and in 1953 was held a joint Nordic meeting of Sámi political organizations, which heralded the start of Nordic Sámi politics. In 1956, the Nordic Sámi Council was established, which dropped its prefix 'Nordic' when, after the collapse

The Non-State Sámi   145

of the Iron Curtain, the newly established Kola Sámi Association became a member of the Council (Eriksson 1997, 93, 105).

Becoming part of international indigenous movement in the beginning of 1970s opened a totally new horizon of political possibilities to the Sámi. Becoming defined as Indigenous people has meant both international and national recognition of the Sámi as a right-holding entity, and in the course of the 1980s and 1990s concrete political changes in the nation states where they live. The social consciousness of the Sámi has developed from the quest for interconnection, which was characteristic of the postwar period, to a fighting attitude which in some way culminated in the battle against damming the Alta-river in 1980–1981 (see Lehtola 1997). Merlan (2009, 308) concludes that "The Alta affair became defined as an indigenous peoples' issue and further stimulated Norway, also concerned with its reputation and relation between international and domestic norms, to develop new policies and ways of working with the Sami". This Sámi resistance can be said to have reconnected the Sámi from different states and created a transnational understanding of the Sámi as an Indigenous people strengthening Sámi nation building in the context of indigenousness (e.g. Lehtola 1997; Merlan 2009; Minde 2008).

The Alta affair led to several committee deliberations in Norway and finally, in 1989, to the establishment of the Sámi Parliament. The Alta case also strongly influenced Sámi policy in Finland. The Sámi of Finland had been incorporated into the Finnish welfare state citizenship following World War II as state citizens, which granted to the Sámi the same welfare state civil rights as the Finns. A type of legislative assimilation policy such as was adopted in Norway was never an official policy in Finland (Lehtola 2012; Nyyssönen 2008). Incorporating the Sámi into Finnish citizenship has, however, excluded alternative forms of citizenship and rights claims based on collective forms of social organization (Nyyssönen 2008, 87). Along with the new ILO Convention No. 169 on the Rights of Indigenous Peoples (1989), and several land right studies and reports, the state of Finland recognized the status of the Sámi as an Indigenous people with special rights in the Finnish Constitution. Legislative proposals were made for establishing local Sámi governance which finally materialized in 1996 as the cultural autonomy of the Sámi governed by a Sámi Parliament (The Act on the Sámi Parliament 1995).

The process that the Sámi have gone through in Finland and in other Nordic countries during past 50 years—for example, the Swedish Sámi Parliament was established in 1993—can be called the indigenous citizenization of the Sámi. Our interpretation of indigenous citizenization is based on our reading of Kymlicka (2012) and Tully (2001), and it refers to the historical process where formal citizenship is extended to the Sámi minority, but in a way that exceeds the formal status of citizenship. Citizenization goes beyond formal citizenship as it is founded on a commitment to build new relationships based on values of consent,

146 *Sanna Valkonen and Jarno Valkonen*

autonomy, self-determination and recognition. It therefore entails the willingness to consider challenges to the state's legitimacy and jurisdiction upon which formal citizenship is based. According to Tully (2001), the process of citizenization involves a commitment to allow all who are affected by common rules to participate in determining those rules.

In the Sámi case, establishing separate Sámi polity with indigenous citizen rights has meant the inclusion of the Sámi in the Finnish nation state but in a way that should better allow for their political participation and autonomy on issues that concern them, such as language and culture issues. Indigenous citizenization completes and fulfils the formal status of state citizenship. Considering indigenous citizenization as a process rather than a fixed list of traits or sites opens up space for thinking about new political possibilities.

However, indigenous citizenization, which has brought dignity and equality to the Sámi, has crashed into an idea of "double political citizenship" (c.f. Semb 2008; Selle and Strømsnes 2010, 87). Institutionalizing the Sámi people's position in Finland as Indigenous people via legislative measures has engendered a vigorous political struggle over Sámi and indigenous citizenship in Finland. In this debate, both the foundations and legitimacy of current Sámi polity and politics, as well as the indigeneity of the Sámi and boundary-making of the community, have been thoroughly questioned.

We Are You (Who Are We?): Struggle for Indigenous Citizenship in Postcolonial Finland

"Who are the Sámi?" is a question for which the majority have always had good answers, although the grounds have varied according to the prevalent social, political and scientific tendencies in the Nordic countries. The external definitions and descriptions of the Sámi (or earlier, the Lapps as the Sámi were called by majorities), have been based on racial, religious, cultural and/or linguistic differences. At the same time, both the authorities and other locals have been well aware of who is and who is not a Sámi at the local level—in other words, who are defined as Sámi in the social and ethnic dynamics of local communities (see Lehtola 2012). During the past 25 years the conception of a Sámi demos has started to change and broaden due to the establishment of the Sámi as an Indigenous people.

In 1989, the ILO concluded the only modern international convention on the human rights of Indigenous peoples, which is designed to allow Indigenous peoples to maintain their individual distinctive cultural features alongside the majority culture. However, only 22 countries (Norway as the only Sámi country) have ratified the convention, which illustrates the political and contested nature of indigenous citizenship in the context of a state-centered world system. The convention presupposes that states must undertake concrete measures to protect the rights of Indigenous peoples and, thus, deliver up part of their sovereignty within the state borders (see Valkonen et al. 2016).

Since the possible ratification of the ILO Convention No. 169 appeared on the political agenda in Finland in the 1990s, with the state taking action to promote the ratification by establishing the Sámi cultural autonomy in 1996, there has been strong resistance by local political movements against the special rights of the Sámi. From the very outset of the establishment of Sámi cultural autonomy, the struggle over Sámi rights has been entangled with the definition of Sámi in the Act on the Sámi Parliament (see footnote 1). On the one hand, the Sámi self-governance argues that subsection (2) of the definition of Sámi, the so-called Lapp clause which refers to historical tax records, is not consistent with Sámi's understanding of themselves. On the other hand, this clause has enabled the local people, who in many earlier cases resisted Sámi rights, to build their own interpretation of indigeneity and Sáminess. The Sámi self-governance, however, consider them to be Finns (Valkonen et al. 2016).

The struggle culminates in the question who, at the individual level, are the Sámi and therefore subjects of indigenous rights, such as rights to the traditionally occupied lands of Sámi. Many other local people may also have long-standing practices of land use and Sámi or tax-Lapp ancestors and, therefore, regard the exclusive indigenous rights of the Sámi as unfair.

Since the 1990s, northern Finland has witnessed the birth of overlapping ethnopolitical movements that are seeking to rebuild, redefine and challenge the prevailing conception of Sáminess and indigenousness in Finland. These include the so-called (neo) Lapp movement and the more recent movement of the so-called non-status and forest Sámi. All these movements challenge the traditional conceptions on Sáminess and the indigeneity of the Sámi themselves, and their conceptions of who belong to the Sámi group—e.g. the practice of ethnic recognition based on kinship (see Lehtola 2012, 31)—by individual-based interpretations of the concept of Indigenous people (article 1) of the ILO Convention No. 169. Who at the individual level fulfil these criteria is regarded as relevant in defining indigenous people. Consequently, the ethnic particularity, groupness and group-based practices of self-identification within the Sámi ethnic group are practically ignored in these interpretations.

The category of (neo) Lapp emerged in 1990s with the simultaneous establishment of Sámi cultural autonomy to refer to people who claim to be indigenous based on their having lived in the region for a long time, often practising traditional livelihoods and having tax-Lapp ancestry. In the situation where the Sámi had achieved indigenous citizenship, they started to call themselves Lapps in public, a former, in some cases pejorative, name for the Sámi given by the majority, and they claimed they were an Indigenous people (Valkonen et al. 2016).

148 *Sanna Valkonen and Jarno Valkonen*

The concept of non-status Sámi has been introduced in a research by Sarivaara (2012) seeking to redefine and recategorize indigenousness and Sáminess. Adapted from the North American (legal and political) concept of "non-status indian", a non-status Sámi is said to be a person who is not included in the Sámi electoral roll, but who has Sámi ancestry and possibly, but not necessarily, identifies as a Sámi (ibid., 23). The category of non-status Sáminess has become a conceptual starting point for the ethnopolitical movements of 2010s, often stressing the historical forest Sáminess as a contemporary indigenous group. The concept of indigeneity has thus become increasingly diversified, complicated and embattled over the period up to 2010.

All these movements—political projects of belonging (Yuval-Davis 2011)—have sought recognition for their Sáminess and indigenousness and thereby the status of political citizenship in contemporary Sámi society. However, these people may not become recognized and identified as Sámi, neither by the kinship-based system of ethnic inclusion of the Sámi society nor by the official policy of the Sámi Parliament (Valkonen et al. 2016; Lehtola 2015). Also the Finnish state earlier considered them to be Finns. There again, some Sámi may support opening the criteria of Sámi subjectivity in order to finish the struggle which has had an influence on people's local social relations. The criteria of ethnic inclusion remains in flux.

Along with the indigenous citizenization of the Sámi, the understanding of the Sámi, Sáminess and indigenousness is in crisis in Finland. The political position of the Sámi is strongly politicized and contested in present-day Finnish political, as well as some academic, debates. The current situation for the Sámi in Finland is thus paradoxical in the sense that laws that were supposed to safeguard the indigenous citizenship of the Sámi and thus assure the full citizenship of the Sámi as Finnish citizens (for instance the right to their mother tongue) have actually problematized and politicized it. For instance, the Finnish state has frozen almost all legislative improvements relating to the Sámi's situation because the question of who the Sámi are is said to be too unclear.

The struggle described above illustrates and renders concrete the highly political nature of the concept of Indigenous people. As Merlan (2009, 306) points out, indigeneity is a social construction which has different uses and consequences depending on the context; it is "something that could be and was formerly otherwise". Although the need for a coherent definition of indigeneity in different global, national and local debates is repeatedly articulated in order to solve the special concerns and problems of these peoples, the concepts—who does it refer to and the particular rights connected to it—are the subject of an ongoing political and academic struggle worldwide (Gausset et al. 2011, 136). Interestingly, Sissons (2009) questions the status of the Sámi as an Indigenous people because the Sámi are not literally victims of settler colonialism. It is ironic that as a more systematic and objective definition of indigeneity is demanded, the more complex the concept tends to come. It is, for instance, far from being self-evident who has right to become defined as indigenous people in the UN system. There is neither a disciplinary consensus about the rights of Indigenous peoples nor about the very notion of indigeneity itself (Gausset et al. 2011, 137).

Conclusion

By analyzing the establishment of indigenous Sámi citizenship in Finland, this article has illustrated that 'indigenous people' is a thoroughly political category and concept. It is the subject of a vigorous ongoing debate which receives different interpretations and practices depending on the context, and by political battles. Indigeneity is also about politicizing self-evident power relations and structures: it is about constructing political space, time and agency from a subaltern position. Even though the concept is often presented and perceived as substantial—as a set of objective criteria defining the "essence" of these peoples—as a political and analytical concept it must be understood like Alfred and Corntassel (2005, 597) point out: "Indigenousness is an identity constructed, shaped and lived in the politicized context of contemporary colonialism".

It is the core idea of conceptual history that concepts do change. This has a dual character. On the one hand, the contents and reference of the concepts change through political debates and battles. As Palonen (1999, 42) writes from a Weberian nominalistic perspective: "The concepts cannot be extrapolated from 'reality' but are to be constructed and constantly revised by human agents in order to better understand the world". On the other hand, concepts generate social change in "real life".

The Sámi have become part of an indigenous citizenization process which has opened new political possibilities for them both globally and nationally. The contemporary Sámi are global indigenous citizens participating in constructing transnational indigenous political systems and wider political partiality of Indigenous peoples. They are also indigenous Sámi citizens within their nation states having their political institutions, political agenda and rights and duties.

Quite unexpectedly, the indigenous non-state Sámi citizenship has problematized the relation between the Sámi ethnos and Sámi demos. The Sámi Indigenous people as it is articulated in current Finnish political debates represents a very different "people" compared to the traditional understandings of the Sámi ethnic group that both the Sámi themselves and state of Finland have held.

Citizenship is always an act of demarcation: citizenship defines both in a legal and political sense the demos in a polity, and therefore draws a border between who is, and who is not, a citizen. Demarcating the Sámi demos has politicized the question "who are ethnic Sámi?" and given

150   *Sanna Valkonen and Jarno Valkonen*

birth to political projects of belonging which struggle for recognition of their alleged indigeneity. This struggle for indigenous citizenship crystallizes how the concept of citizenship is itself a fluid political concept. It can be seen as a political process susceptible to unexpected changes and forms and thus suddenly opening novel horizons of possibility in politics (see also Kurunmäki 2001, 143).

Analyzing the history of concepts enables the elucidation of political conflicts in processes which might otherwise seem uncontested and self-evident. Conceptual history is, therefore, at the core when analyzing contemporary political phenomena (Ball 1988; Kurunmäki 2001, 143). In the case of Indigenous peoples: "Debates over the problem of definition are actually more interesting than any definition in and of itself" (Niezen 2003, 19; Alfred and Corntassel 2005, 607). These debates and struggles actually highlight much more about being indigenous and the political position of these groups in a state-oriented world than any isolated definition ever can.

Note

1 For the purpose of this Act, a Sámi means a person who considers himself a Sámi, provided: (1) That he himself or at least one of his parents or grandparents has learnt Sámi as his first language; (2) That he is a descendant of a person who has been entered in a land, taxation or population register as a mountain, forest or fishing Lapp; or (3) That at least one of his parents has or could have been registered as an elector for an election to the Sámi Delegation or the Sámi Parliament (The Act on the Sámi Parliament 1995/974).

References

Alfred, Taiaiake, and Jeff Corntassel. 2005. "Being Indigenous: Resurgences against Contemporary Colonialism." *Government and Opposition* 40(4): 597–614.

Ball, Terence. 1988. *Transforming Political Discourse: Political Theory and Critical Conceptual History*. Oxford: Basil Blackwell.

Eidheim, Harald. 1997. "Ethno-Political Development among the Sami after World War II." In *Sami Culture in a New Era: The Norwegian Sami Experience*, edited by Harald Gaski, 29–61. Karasjok: Davvi Girji OS.

Eriksson, Johan. 1997. *Partition and Redemption: A Machiavellian Analysis of Sami and Basque Patriotism*. Umeå: Department of Political Science, Umeå University.

Gausset, Quentin, Justin Kenrick, and Robert Gibb. 2011. "Introduction: What Place for Indigenous People in Modern States?" *Anthropological Notebooks* 17(2):5–9.

Hale, Charles R. 2009. "Comment." *Current Anthropology* 50(3):322–323.

The ILO Convention No. 169 concerning Indigenous and Tribal Peoples in Independent Countries. 1989. www.ilo.org/dyn/normlex/en/f?p=NORMLE XPUB:12100:0::NO::P12100_ILO_CODE:C169. Accessed March 24, 2015.

The Non-State Sámi 151

Ingold, Tim. 2000. *The Perception of Environment*. London & New York: Routledge.

Kenrick, Justin. 2011. "Unthinking Eurocentrism: The Political Writing of Adam Kuper and Tim Ingold." *Anthropological Notebooks* 17(2):11–36.

Kingsbury, Benedict. 1995. "Indigenous Peoples as an International Legal Concept." In *Indigenous Peoples of Asia*, edited by R. H. Barnes, Andrew Gray, and Benedict Kingsbury, 13–34. Ann Arbor, MI: Association for Asian Studies.

Kurunmäki, Jussi. 2001. "Käsitehistoria. Näkökulma historian poliittisuuteen ja poliittisen kielen historiallisuuteen." [Conceptual History: An Approach to the Political Aspects of History and the Historicity of Political Language] *Politiikka* 43(2):142–155.

Kymlicka, Will. 1995. *Multicultural Citizenship: A Liberal Theory of Minority Rights*. Oxford: Oxford University Press.

———. 2012. "Responsible Citizenship." *Trudeau Foundation Papers* 4(2): 56–87.

Lehtola, Veli-Pekka. 1997. *Saamelaiset: historia, yhteiskunta, taide* [The Sámi: History, Society, Art]. Inari: Kustannus-Puntsi.

———. 2012. *Suomalaiset saamelaiset* [The Finns and the Sámi]. Helsinki: SKS.

———. 2015. *Saamelaiskiista – sortaako Suomi alkuperäiskansaansa?* [The Sámi Debate – Does Finland Oppress Its Indigenous People?]. Helsinki: Into Kustannus.

Marshall, Thomas H. [1950]1992. "Citizenship and Social Class." In *Citizenship and Social Class*, edited by Thomas H. Marshall and Thomas Bottomore, 3–51. London: Pluto Press.

Martinez-Gobo, Jose. 1986. *Study on the Problem of Discrimination against Indigenous Populations*. www.un.org/development/desa/indigenouspeoples/publications/2014/09/martinez-cobo-study/. Accessed January 20, 2017.

Mathisen, Stein R. 2003. "Tracing the Narratives of the Ecological Sami." In *Nature and Identity: Essays on the Culture of Nature*, edited by Kirsti Pedersen and Arvid Viken, 189–206. Kulturstudier no. 36. Kristiansand: Norwegian Academic Press.

Merlan, Francesca. 2009. "Indigeneity. Global and Local." *Current Anthropology* 50(3):303–333.

Minde, Henry. 2008. "The Destination and the Journey: Indigenous Peoples and the United Nations from the 1960s through 1985." In *Self-Determination, Knowledge, Indigeneity*, edited by Henry Minde, 49–86. Delft, NLD: Eburon Academic Publishers.

Niezen, Ronald. 2003. *The Origins of Indigenism: Human Rights and the Politics of Identity*. Berkeley: University of California Press.

———. 2009. *The Rediscovered Self: Indigenous Identity and Cultural Justice*. Montreal & Kingston, London, Ithaca: McGill-Queen's University Press.

Nyyssönen, Jukka. 2008. "Between the Global Movement and National Politics: Sami Identity Politics in Finland from the 1970s to the early 1990s." In *Self-Determination, Knowledge, Indigeneity*, edited by Henry Minde, 87–105. Delft, NLD: Eburon Academic Publishers.

Palonen, Kari. 1997. *Kootut retoriikat: Esimerkkejä politiikan luennasta* [Compiled Rhetorics: Examples on Political Reading]. Yhteiskuntatieteiden, valtio-opin ja filosofian julkaisuja 11. Jyväskylä: Jyväskylän yliopisto.

152 Sanna Valkonen and Jarno Valkonen

——. 1999. "Rhetorical and Temporal Perspectives on Conceptual Change. Theses on Quentin Skinner and Reinhart Koselleck." *In Finnish Yearbook of Political Thought* 3. Jyväskylä: SoPhi, University of Jyväskylä.

Rodríguez–Piñero, Luis. 2005. *Indigenous Peoples, Postcolonialism, and International Law: The ILO Regime (1919–1989)*. Oxford: Oxford University Press.

Sarivaara, Erika. 2012. *Statuksettomat saamelaiset: Paikantumisia saamelaisuuden rajoilla* [The Non-Status Sámi. Locations within Sámi Borderlands]. Diedut 2/2012, Guovdageaidnu: Sámi allaskuvla.

Selle, Per, and Kristin Strømsnes. 2010. "Sámi Citizenship: Marginalization or Integration." *Acta Borealia* 27(1):66–90.

Semb, Anne J. 2008. *From "Norwegian Citizens" via "Citizens Plus" to "Dual Political Membership"?* Oslo: University of Oslo.

Seurujärvi-Kari, Irja. 2012. *Ale jaskkot eatnigiella: Alkuperäiskansaliikkeen ja saamen kielen merkitys saamelaisten identiteetille* [The Significance of Indigenous Movement and Sámi Language to the Sámi Identity]. Helsinki: Helsingin yliopisto.

Sissons, Jeffrey. 2005. *First Peoples: Indigenous Cultures and Their Futures*. London: Reaction Books.

——. 2009. "Comment." *Current Anthropology* 50(3):326–327.

Stewart–Harawira, Makere. 2005. *The New Imperial Order: Indigenous Responses to Globalization*. London & New York: Zed Books; Wellington: Huia Publishers.

The Act on the Sámi Parliament 1995/974. www.finlex.fi/en/laki/kaannokset/1995/en19950974.pdf. Accessed January 20, 2017.

Tully, James. 2001. "Introduction." In *Multinational Democracies*, edited by Alain Gagnon and James Tully. Cambridge, UK: Cambridge University Press.

United Nations: Declaration on the Rights of Indigenous Peoples. 2007. www.un.org/esa/socdev/unpfii/documents/DRIPS_en.pdf. Accessed January 20, 2017.

Valkeapää, Nils-Aslak. 1985. *Ruoktu váimmus* [Home at Heart]. Kautokeino: Dat.

Valkonen, Jarno, Sanna Valkonen, and Timo Koivurova. 2016. "Groupism and the Politics of Indigeneity: A Case Study on the Sámi Debate in Finland." *Ethnicities* 17(4):526–545.

Valkonen, Sanna. 2009. *Poliittinen saamelaisuus* [Political Sáminess]. Tampere: Vastapaino.

Yuval-Davis, Nira. 2011. *The Politics of Belonging: Intersectional Contestations*. London: SAGE.

Part III

Practising Citizenship

Katja Mäkinen, Anna Björk, Hanna-Mari Kivistö and Claudia Wiesner

Following our reflexive and constructivist approach to concepts, we assume that concepts and changes in them are shaped in and by practices that are influenced by, and also reflected in, changed interpretations of concepts. Citizenship, therefore, is constantly shaped by diverse practices. Thus, in the following section, *Practising Citizenship*, the focus will be on how the practices of a concept influence new interpretations and, vice-versa, how new interpretations of a concept come to be reflected in certain practices—or not. The chapters will take up different practices such as the interplay of diverse actors in developing European Union Citizenship (Wiesner), labour conditions created by posted work (Lillie and Wagner), EU projects as participatory practices (Mäkinen) and electoral practices of external voting (Nyyssönen and Metsälä).

The dimensions of citizenship under investigation in this section are rights and participation. Wiesner traces how Union Citizenship has been developed around rights, Lillie and Wagner focus on market-related rights, Nyyssönen and Metsälä address external voting rights in the context of forming dual citizenship and Mäkinen analyses participation as the active content of Union Citizenship.

The practices discussed will all refer to recent transformations of citizenship. Citizenship in the European Union is the topic of three chapters in this section. Citizenship in the EU context is closely related to the creation of Union Citizenship, which is an example of a conceptual invention as discussed by Joseph Bleicher (1997, 154). According to him, imagining something new is not so much about creating something completely new and original, but rather inventing something different by connecting elements that have earlier been detached from each other. The most obvious new aspect—albeit not unknown in a historical context—in Union Citizenship is the detachment of citizenship from the nation state and its transfer to a new territorial scale and an international economic organisation. What is old about Union Citizenship is that it maintains the connection with national citizenship and uses elements that are familiar from national contexts.

154 *Katja Mäkinen et al.*

Concepts constantly change in an organic way, but in some historical situations, such as revolutions or drafting processes of constitution, they are changed intentionally and through specific activity (Ball and Pocock 1988, 1). The adoption of Union Citizenship in the Treaty of Maastricht in 1992 can be seen as the culmination of such a process. In the treaty, the concept of citizenship was not only re-contextualised, but also new definitions and meanings were given to it. As the nationals of EU member states have been renamed Union Citizens, both the meanings and the scope of reference of the concept of citizen have changed. Adopting Union Citizenship in the Treaty of Maastricht is, hence, an example of a speech act in which saying something produces the thing in question—that is, an issue is made real through linguistic action (Austin 1982; Skinner 2002). In fact, the entire history of EU integration with all its treaties, directives and court decisions can be seen as a collection of speech acts, as Thomas Diez (2001, 88) notes. The redefinitions of the concept of citizenship made in the treaties and other EU discourses are part of a broader conceptual change in which European integration challenges key concepts in political thought and practice.

The concept of citizen had been used in EU documents before the official adoption of Union Citizenship, e.g., in the form of "community citizen". Citizenship was used as a *Vorgriff* (Koselleck 2006)—a concept which refers to future change rather than an already existing state of affairs. The inventors of the concept acted thus as "innovative ideologists" (Skinner 2002, 148–157) who recontextualised the concept and gave it new meaning. The chapters by Wiesner, Lillie and Wagner, and Mäkinen examine these changes and study how the practice of citizenship in the EU has been shaped, thus filling the gap in research focusing on citizenship in the EU from a conceptual historical perspective.

Wiesner investigates the role of conceptual innovation in the development of EU citizenship. Since the 1970s, the development of EU citizenship has concentrated on rights, which is the focus of the chapter by Wiesner. In the Maastricht treaty and in subsequent EU treaties also, Union Citizenship is defined through rights. Citizens' rights are, in fact, used as a justification of Union Citizenship: one goal of the Union is "to strengthen the protection of the rights and interests of the nationals of its Member States through the introduction of a citizenship of the Union" (Treaty on European Union, Article B).

Throughout the conceptual history of EU citizenship, there has been a strong link between the right of mobility and economy, even though political and social rights have been attached to Union Citizenship. Particularly in the discourse about "special rights" in the 1970s, the aim was to promote the internal market and the free movement of people, services, capital and goods. The idea of special rights has its origin in the principle of non-discrimination formulated in the Treaty of Rome in 1957. This principle is one of the conceptual innovations discussed

Practising Citizenship 155

by Wiesner. Through a conceptual analysis of EU treaties and other official documents, the chapter will show how interplay between conceptual innovations, law making and institutional and social practice has formed EU citizenship. Wiesner hints at a crucial problem that is taken up in two other chapters as well: creating citizenship rights in the new EU context represented a conceptual innovation, which then had to be filled with concrete meaning and political practice.

Even though some roots of EU citizenship lie in workers' rights, and EU citizenship rights have been developed precisely to increase workers' mobility, they do not seem to solve all problems of the mobile workers discussed in the chapter by Lillie and Wagner. On the contrary, the chapter shows that EU citizenship established new contradictions and mechanisms for exclusion. The chapter demonstrates as well the tensions characteristic of European integration between market dynamics, democratic politics, national boundedness of citizenship and mobility. It analyses the practices concerning posted workers and the use of rights, or obstacles to claiming rights. Through investigating the potential of industrial citizenship for overcoming some of the contradictions, the chapter contributes to the debates on industrial citizenship.

One attempt to fill EU citizenship with a concrete meaning and political practice is the EU programmes and the projects funded by them. The chapter by Mäkinen focuses on participatory practices at the level of projects funded by EU programmes. She explores the meanings and uses of participation in EU projects as well as the conceptions of citizenship and democracy produced by the conceptual choices related to participation. Participation—a central dimension of citizenship—has become a popular concept and it has been seen as a solution for almost any kind of societal problem. Part of the "participation-boom" is the participatory practices and experiments arranged at various levels of administration for encouraging active engagement. In the EU context, participation is emphasised in, for instance, the Lisbon treaty (2007), the white paper on European governance (2001) and the open method of coordination. Mäkinen's chapter underlines the ambivalence of trying to create new participatory practices with the help of funding programmes. The chapters in the final section show that mutual interaction between practices and concepts have interesting implications for the interpretations and implementation of Union Citizenship.

EU citizenship can be interpreted as a type of multiple citizenship. The notion of multiple citizenship acknowledges that citizenship can be put into many, and sometimes simultaneous, frames and scales, such as towns, substate regions or global frameworks. Multiscalarity of citizenship has been discussed intensively (Bauböck 1994; Delanty 2002; Desforges et al. 2015; Dobson 2006; Faist and Kivisto 2007; Maas 2013; Sassen 2002), and links to different territorial contexts can be seen in the concept of citizenship itself (see Ilyin in this volume).

156   *Katja Mäkinen et al.*

Another type of multiple citizenship is dual citizenship, which is in the focus of the chapter by Nyyssönen and Metsälä. As a legal status and a political instrument, dual citizenship is a contested issue with a number of national variants (Martin and Hailbronner 2004). In Germany, for example, dual citizenship was used as a rhetorical tool in an election campaign of the Christian Democratic Union in Hessen in 1999 (Wiedemann 2004, 340; Björk 2014, 81). The case analysed by Nyyssönen and Metsälä is that of Hungary and the practices and conceptualisations related to dual citizenship and external voting rights. The chapter sheds light on how voting rights—the core category of the political rights attached to citizenship in all democratic polities—can be used for shaping citizenship: who belongs to the national demos and what the (dual) citizens are allowed and expected to do. Nyyssönen and Metsälä examine the connection of dual citizenship and voting rights in Hungary in the period following EU enlargement. Mobility is a key component of Union Citizenship, whereas the Hungarian case exemplifies the return of ethnicity as an instrument of defining citizenship.

Therefore, all the chapters in this part discuss how citizenship is practised in an empirical reality beyond the nation state. Mäkinen examines political participation and EU citizenship by analysing grass-root-level texts of EU projects. Mobile citizens' rights and the possibility of enacting citizenship are discussed in the context of the European Union concerning the free movement of persons, non-discrimination (Wiesner) and the labour market (Lillie and Wagner). Nyyssönen and Metsälä provide a look at external voting in the context of national-level (re)locations in regard to dual citizenship and ethnic kin minorities beyond the state borders. In this case, dual citizenship is not necessarily caused by mobility: some members of the Hungarian minorities in neighbouring countries have lived in their place of residency for their entire lives and even for generations.

References

Austin, John. 1982. "How to Do Things with Words." The Williams James lectures delivered at Harvard University in 1955. Edited by J. O. Urmson and Marina Sbisà. New York: Oxford University Press.

Ball, Terence, and John Pocock. 1988. "Introduction." In *Conceptual Change and the Constitution*, edited by Terence Ball and J. G. A. Pocock, 1–12. Lawrence: University Press of Kansas.

Bauböck, Rainer. 1994. *Transnational Citizenship: Membership and Rights in International Migration*. Cheltenham: Edward Elgar Publishing.

Björk, Anna. 2014. "Accessing Citizenship. The Conceptual and Political Changes of the German Naturalization Policy, 1999–2006." *Contributions to the History of Concepts* 9(1): 74–87.

Bleicher, Joseph. 1997. "Invention and Community: Hermeneutic Politics in Europe." In *Interpreting the Political: New Methodologies*, edited by Carver Terrell and Matti Hyvärinen, 143–157. London & New York: Routledge.

Delanty, Gerard. [2000]2002. *Citizenship in a Global Age: Society, Culture, Politics*. Buckingham & Philadelphia, PA: Open University Press.

Desforges, Luke, Rhys Jones, and Mike Woods. 2005. "New Geographies of Citizenship." *Citizenship Studies* 9(5):439–451.

Diez, Thomas. 2001. "Speaking 'Europe': The Politics of Integration Discourse." In *The Social Construction of Europe*, edited by Thomas Christiansen, Knud Erik Jörgensen, and Antje Wiener, 85–100. London: SAGE.

Dobson, Linda. 2006. *Supranational Citizenship*. Manchester & New York: Manchester University Press.

Faist, Thomas, and Peter Kivisto. 2007. *Dual Citizenship in Global Perspective: From Unitary to Multiple Citizenship*. Houndmills, Basingstoke: Palgrave Macmillan.

Koselleck, Reinhart. 2006. *Begriffsgeschichten: Studien zur Semantik und Pragmatik der Politischen und Sozialen Sprache*. Frankfurt am Main: Suhrkamp Verlag.

Maas, Willem. 2013. "Varieties of Multilevel Citizenship." In *Multilevel Citizenship*, edited by Willem Maas, 1–21. Philadelphia: University of Pennsylvania Press.

Martin, David. A., and Kay Hailbronner, eds. 2004. *Rights and Duties of Dual Nationals: Evolution and Prospects*. The Hague, London, & New York: Kluwer Law International.

Sassen, Saskia. 2002. "Towards Post-National and Denationalized Citizenship." In *Handbook of Citizenship Studies*, edited by Engin Isin and Bryan Turner, 277–292. London: SAGE.

Skinner, Quentin. 2002. *Visions of Politics. Volume I: Regarding Method*. Cambridge: Cambridge University Press.

Wiedemann, Marianne. 2004. "Development of Dual Nationality under German Citizenship Law." In *Rights and Duties of Dual Nationals: Evolution and Prospects*, edited by David A. Martin and Kay Hailbronner. The Hague, London, & New York: Kluwer Law International.

9 Shaping Citizenship Practice through Laws
Rights and Conceptual Innovations in the EU

Claudia Wiesner

The development of EU citizenship has been regularly, albeit not too intensively, discussed in recent decades (see e.g. Besson and Utzinger 2008; Höpner and Schäfer 2012; Bauböck 2007; Bellamy 2008), but it has rarely been analysed as a contested concept (for one exception, see Mäkinen 2015). In fact, the whole field of European integration is one that has rarely been discussed from this viewpoint (Wiesner 2013), even if there are related approaches (see e.g. Lacroix and Nicolaïdis 2010; Wiesner and Schmidt-Gleim 2014). In this context, this chapter will help to fill a gap in research. Its aim is to analyse in detail how, and by whom, EU citizenship has been conceptualised and shaped in order to discuss and answer three crucial questions: How can a conceptual innovation, such as Union Citizenship, be filled with meaning and also with a new institutional practice? Which conflicts, actors and strategies are decisive in these processes? Which particular shape does the concept of citizenship take on in the EU, and which new questions does this new shape give rise to?

It will be shown in the following that, all in all, EU citizenship, and more particularly, EU citizenship rights have been decisively shaped by a typical interrelation between conceptual innovations, lawmaking, implementation conflicts, and institutional and social practice. Moreover, it will be argued that this process differs decisively from how citizenship rights have been shaped in Western nation states. Most of the new EU citizenship rights were initially based on conceptual innovations in the sense that EU actors (e.g., Commission functionaries) behaved as "innovating ideologists" (Skinner 2002, 148) and invented new concepts—for instance, "Citizenship of the Union"—which usually aimed to express some positive and future-oriented meaning. These conceptual innovations were first put on paper, often in the form of policy documents, and then set down in laws. After that, they needed to be put into practice and hence filled with concrete meaning. In the case of EU citizenship rights, this process has been enhanced by lawmaking and jurisdiction of today's Court of Justice of the European Union (CJEU, formerly European Court of Justice, ECJ).

160   *Claudia Wiesner*

After a short introduction to the institutional background, the chapter will exemplify the particularities of these processes with regard to the crucial concepts of non-discrimination and free movement of persons that have a central role in the development of EU citizenship. Analysis will be based mainly on EU documents and law texts. If available, they have been used in their English versions. The concluding part of the chapter will briefly compare the development of EU citizenship practice to the modes of shaping citizenship in Western nation states during their democratisation period, and discuss consequences of these differences for citizenship as a concept more generally.

Institutional Background

The conceptual, legal and practical development of EU citizenship rights is linked to a specific legal background consisting of the treaties of Rome, Maastricht and Amsterdam, and EU laws. The three treaties named are part of the succession of different EU treaties (besides those of Nice and Lisbon and the Single European Act) that take on the role of an EU constitution in that they regulate the EU's institutions, their relations and their competencies, respectively.

EU lawmaking takes place based on the treaties, but the setting behind it is complex and different from most nation states. It is important to take into account the interrelations and power struggles between the different EU institutions, the member states and their bureaucracies in this respect. The documents that will be cited below can also be read as indicators of these power struggles.

Formally, EU law initiatives can only be issued by the European Commission, giving it a key role as a conceptual innovator. In practice, the Council, consisting of the Ministers of the member states, can exercise some influence on the Commission to induce new laws, and today the European Parliament can even cause it to do so (see Tiilikainen and Wiesner 2016).

In the earlier days of integration, EU laws were only voted upon by the Council. After the adoption of the Treaty of Maastricht, in certain policy fields both Council and Parliament co-decided upon new laws, and with introduction of the ordinary legislative procedure following the Lisbon Treaty, the Council currently is the second chamber of legislation besides the EP (Tiilikainen and Wiesner 2016). Decisions regarding Union Citizenship and free movement after 1993 were subject to co-decision by Council and EP, but this was not the case for non-discrimination, which was decided upon solely by the Council.

Most of the EU's law acts are directives which have to be transformed into national legislation to then be applied by the member-state governments and bureaucracies, and regional and local authorities. This means that EU directives are *interpreted* when they are transformed into

Shaping Citizenship Practice 161

national laws, and these interpretations often gave room for different understandings by member state authorities, the EU Commission and the ECJ. Putting into practice newly developed EU citizenship rights in the member states thus revealed several obstacles: some directives were not fully applied and there were other practical problems. Law implementation therefore often led to conflicts related to the interpretation of the newly developed concepts and rights. It became apparent that they interfered with established concepts, competencies, and routines in the nation states. The European Commission at this stage controls the correct implementation of the law and can start infringement procedures against member states before the CJEU in the case of non-compliance. It can also induce new laws in order to change the situation. Finally, after a number of such exchanges, new institutional practices developed.

Analysing these processes reveals a decisive problem in EU integration: newly coined concepts and rights have to be filled with practical meaning; they have to be applied, and the institutional reality in the member states needs to be adapted. Even if this problem may occur with regard to all new legislation it is particularly virulent in EU integration as it is "integration through law" (Cappelletti, Seccombe, and Weiler 1986), i.e., new concepts are created by law and not by social practice.

In the following, I will show that these processes follow a similar model. They essentially have four steps: (1) conceptual innovation, (2) law changes, (3) law implementation and interpretation conflicts and (4) establishment of a new practice.

Market Citizenship and the Treaty of Rome: The Conceptual Dynamics of Non-Discrimination

The Treaty of Rome in 1957 founded the European Economic Community (EEC) and introduced the first set of citizenship-like rights. Those rights concerned the economy and the internal market, among them the right to free movement of employees and service providers (Articles 48 and 59, Treaty of Rome, European Council 1957) and the right to equal payment for women and men (Article 119, Treaty of Rome, European Council 1957). Several of these rights were necessary to realise regulations in the treaty or to guarantee minimum standards for the internal market.

These EEC-related rights, therefore, only concerned market participants: the right to free movement, e.g., was related only to persons working or providing services in another member state, and it was part of the four fundamental freedoms (free circulation of goods, services, capital and labour force) in the internal market. Hence these rights are not citizenship rights in the proper sense, because they do not apply to citizens in their status as citizens of a polity, but only in their status as market participants. The rights can be categorized as creating an "economic citizenship" (Kleger 1995, 39)—or, more specifically, market citizenship.

162   *Claudia Wiesner*

But still, these rights, albeit limited in extent and applicability, created a direct link between nationals of the member states (in their role as market participants) and the EEC, because they were directly applicable, and nationals of the member states could claim them before the ECJ. More importantly, the ECJ interpreted them in its judgements in such a way that over time rights in the areas of work, healthcare or consumer protection developed into an EEC catalogue of rights. The Treaty of Rome thus represented the starting point of a development of EU-related *citizenship* rights—even though the terms "citizen" or "citizenship" were not used in the treaty.

In terms of conceptual innovation, the concept of non-discrimination has been particularly decisive. Once it was introduced, it built the basis for a dynamic interpretation and new conceptual and legal innovations related to citizenship. Important judgements by the ECJ and also further legislation relied on it. To date the EU has decisively contributed to developing a number of new non-discrimination rights that were more far-reaching than most national citizenship rights. As they had to be applied in the member states, they also changed conceptions and practices of national citizenship. In the following, the decisive steps in the related processes of conceptual innovation will be sketched.

The concept of non-discrimination was defined in the Treaty of Rome, first, by interdicting any discrimination based on nationality, and second, by defining the right to equal payment for women and men:

> Within the scope of application of this Treaty, and without prejudice to any special provisions contained therein, any discrimination on grounds of nationality shall be prohibited.
> (article 7, Treaty of Rome, European Council 1957)

> Each Member State shall during the first stage ensure and subsequently maintain the application of the principle that men and women should receive equal pay for equal work.
> (article 119, Treaty of Rome, European Council 1957)

In the subsequent years, EU Commission and ECJ developed into agents of proactive non-discrimination policy by interpreting these rights in the broadest possible way. A crucial case is here the "Defrenne" case: in 1976, the European Court of Justice judged that equal payment and equal treatment of women and men had to be enacted in practice and for individuals. A Belgian stewardess named Gabrielle Defrenne thus successfully claimed her right to equal treatment with regard to retirement age and pension level (European Court of Justice 1976).

The Amsterdam Treaty in 1999 considerably broadened the understanding of the concept of non-discrimination by turning it into a political goal. The following quotation (today it can be found in Article 19 of

Shaping Citizenship Practice   163

the Treaty on Functioning of the European Union, TFEU), highlights the underlying argument. In paragraph 1, the heads of the member states broadened the concept of non-discrimination far beyond equal treatment in the market. In paragraph 2 they provided a new legal foundation for further conceptual and legal innovation.

1   Without prejudice to the other provisions of the Treaties and within the limits of the powers conferred by them upon the Union, the Council, acting unanimously in accordance with a special legislative procedure and after obtaining the consent of the European Parliament, may take appropriate action to combat discrimination based on sex, racial or ethnic origin, religion or belief, disability, age or sexual orientation.

2   By way of derogation from paragraph 1, the European Parliament and the Council, acting in accordance with the ordinary legislative procedure, may adopt the basic principles of Union incentive measures, excluding any harmonisation of the laws and regulations of the Member States, to support action taken by the Member States in order to contribute to the achievement of the objectives referred to in paragraph 1.

(TFEU, Art. 19, European Union 2010)

The European Commission used this new legal base set by the Amsterdam Treaty and once again acted as a conceptual innovator. First, in several policy documents, it further clarified the principle of non-discrimination (see in detail Wiesner 2007, 223–225). Second, to enhance non-discrimination, the Commission suggested a complete policy package in 1999 (see in detail European Commission 1999). It mainly consisted in a proposal of two new EU directives. Referring to the principles of freedom, democracy, human rights, rule of law and the four freedoms of the inner market, the following Commission statement underlines very clearly that the Commission wanted to create an institutional practice that is more far-reaching than in the member states—and it wanted to *force* the member states to change their legal and institutional practices:

In more general terms, a number of Member States do not have comprehensive legislation (other than isolated provisions contained in various labour or criminal codes) to combat discrimination on the grounds of racial or ethnic origin, religion or belief, age and sexual orientation.

(European Commission 1999, 4)

Essentially, the European Commission had thus acted as conceptual innovator by developing a very broad conception of non-discrimination. The principle that had formerly aimed at unimpeded participation in the

164   *Claudia Wiesner*

market had now been extended into one that included most areas of everyday life, and that interdicted discrimination on the basis of a wide range of potential grounds. This conception of non-discrimination was, then, successfully established and put into practice by the new directives passed by the Council that eventually led to changes in the practices of member states once again.

The first new directive (2000/43/EC) interdicts any discrimination on ethnic grounds and fixes equal treatment regarding employment, education, social security and access to products and services (European Council 2000a). The second directive (2000/78/EC) interdicts any discrimination in employment and profession that is based on race, ethnic origin, religion, ideology, age, or sexual orientation. This directive is very concrete because it regards most practical questions related to access, duration and end of education and employment, and it enlarges the legal protection, among others, by a reversal of evidence (European Council 2000b).

These directives show that the European Commission succeeded in rooting its conceptual innovation of non-discrimination via a lawmaking process into the EU's legal *acquis*. Thus it also laid the groundwork to influence institutional and social practices in the member states. But despite the fact that the governments of the member states in the Council had voted for the directives, some of them were very reluctant to apply them. Germany was one of the last states to do so, already under the pressure of an infringement procedure (for more detail, see Wiesner 2007, 223–225). The application of the new directives was therefore pushed forward by Commission and ECJ using their control and sanction authority.

Union Citizenship and the Maastricht Treaty: "Doing Something About Citizenship"

Another crucial step in the development of EU citizenship was taken with the Maastricht Treaty in 1993, which founded the European Union and introduced a new EU-related concept of citizenship, "Citizenship of the Union". Since then, all nationals of an EU member state are citizens of the EU, and the expression "Citizenship of the Union" is explicitly used as a headline in the Treaties (articles 9 and 20, TFEU, European Union 2010).

In Maastricht, a key concept was borrowed from nation state representative democracy and applied to the EU, in an effort to coin a new EU-related key concept. Even if the concept of citizenship has a history that is much longer than that of modern nation states, this move is highly symbolical, especially when considering integration history: during the first decades of European integration, one of its main principles was that the EU should not become something resembling a state but be an intergovernmental entity. This does not go along with the usage of a concept like citizenship, and, vice versa, the fact that this concept was now used

Shaping Citizenship Practice 165

with regard to the EU can be interpreted as a signal of the EU becoming more than an intergovernmental organisation, and maybe even being on its way to becoming a state.

The Treaty of Maastricht combined several of these conceptual shifts and also began to push in the direction of state-like symbolism in other respects. It introduced the term "European Union", and it linked the Union explicitly to an external identity and a Common Foreign and Security Policy (Treaty on European Union, Council of the European Communities 1992, Articles A, B, and new Article 8). It is seldom explicitly stated why the EU treaties thus use key concepts of nation states in such a manner, but it can be supposed that using concepts that have a classical (and mostly positive) meaning within a nation state is seen as a way to add legitimacy to the EU, and to ascribe power to it (on these strategies see Skinner 1999, 66–67; Koselleck 1967).

In addition to having successfully borrowed a concept from its nation state background, the introduction of Union Citizenship represents a decisive conceptual innovation in five more respects.

First, political citizenship rights related to the EU (and not only to member states) were created and applied which clearly exceeded the previous concept of market citizenship. In the history of the concept of citizenship more generally, this is the key innovation of EU citizenship, despite the fact that various forms of federal citizenship predate its use here, such as in the United States.

Today, EU citizenship rights are defined in articles 20–25 of the Treaty on the Functioning of the European Union: the right to free movement and residence all over the EU (but only for EU citizens that can assure the means for living—this is an important aspect, as it formally excludes welfare recipients, which however cannot be further discussed here); active and passive election rights in local and municipal as well as in EP elections in their country of residence; the right to diplomatic and consular protection outside the EU by embassies of all EU member states; the right to petition the EP; and the right to write in one of the 23 official EU languages to EU institutions and receive answers in the same language (articles 20–25, TFEU, European Union 2010).

These rights were not invented spontaneously in Maastricht, but build upon ideas that had been developed over a period of more than 20 years by the Commission, European Parliament and the Council (Wiener 2001, 79–85; Wiener 1998, 84–90). Hence, Maastricht was a window of opportunity to realise existing ideas on EU citizenship. The background lay partly in an EU crisis of legitimacy in the 1990s: the Spanish prime minister Felipe Gonzalez, in the very final stage of the Maastricht negotiations, suggested countering the growing euroscepticism in the population by "doing something about citizenship". The chapter on Union Citizenship, based on the existing preparations, then was drafted in record time (Weiler 1996, 9).

166   *Claudia Wiesner*

The second conceptual innovation linked to Union Citizenship is that, compared to citizenship in nation states, it is a hybrid concept because access is granted automatically for all citizens of EU member states, but there is no independent EU nationality. Therefore, one key feature of Union Citizenship is that it is *derived* from the possession of the nationality of an EU member state. EU citizenship does not endanger the nationality of the respective member states, and the treaties clearly state that the EU does not interfere with the member states' classical sovereign right to determine their nationals (article 9, TFEU, European Union 2010).

But some statements after the conclusion of the Maastricht Treaty underline that Commission and member-state governments held different opinions in that respect. The European Council in Birmingham in October 1992 emphasised the limits of Union Citizenship:

> Union citizenship brings additional rights and additional protection for our citizens, but in no respect takes the place of their respective nationality. [. . .] The nationality of a person will only be ruled by the respective domestic laws of the member states.
>
> (European Union 2001a, 2, translation
> C. Wiesner)

The Commission, in exchange, rather stressed the potentials of Union Citizenship, as the following statement from an official report underlines:

> Citizenship of the Union is both a source of legitimation for the process of European integration, by reinforcing the participation of citizens, and a fundamental factor in the creation among citizens of a sense of belonging to the European Union and of having a genuine European identity.
>
> (European Commission 2001, 7)

The Commission further highlights that EU citizenship concerns both the EU and the member states, even if it also emphasises the fact that EU citizenship does not replace national citizenship:

> Because of its origins and the rights and duties associated with it, Citizenship of the Union is sui generis and cannot be compared to national citizenship in a member state. In this new type of multiple citizenship on different levels, Citizenship of the Union complements national citizenship and does not replace it.
>
> (European Commission 2001, 7)

The third conceptual innovation that is linked to Union Citizenship is a significant conceptual reinterpretation of a formerly nation state based concept, that of sovereignty, which is challenged by the right to free movement. In the EU, nation states no longer have the exclusive authority to determine who may reside within their territory, as today EU citizens can move and reside freely throughout the EU. Member states can hinder them only under extreme conditions. However, as will be shown below, it proved particularly difficult to shape the new EU citizenship practice.

The fourth conceptual innovation linked to Union Citizenship is that, of the four dimensions of citizenship sketched in the introduction to this volume, it is primarily concerned with citizenship rights. No changes occurred in the conditions of access or in the duties of citizens; there are no duties required of the EU citizen. Active EU citizenship, however, was encouraged by specific programmes to some extent (see Mäkinen's contribution) and can be said to be in development (see Wiesner 2007 for a discussion).

The fifth conceptual innovation is that lawmaking had such a decisive role in creating and in putting into practice Union Citizenship. Rather than being obtained in political struggles by EU citizens, it was granted by EU and national politicians and authorities. EU citizenship thus developed a very specific top-down and passive character: it was first a conceptual invention devoid of practical meaning. Once it had been created, it was put into practice by new and further laws.

Struggling with Implementation: The Right to Free Movement

The creation of the concept of Union Citizenship is a case of conceptual change that precedes institutional and social change (see in detail Koselleck 2006, 62). Based on a conceptual invention that applied a key concept to the EU, new laws were created. But this did not mean that institutional and social practice changed as well. Rather, Commission and ECJ had to force the implementation of these new laws after some struggles between member states and the European Commission. These struggles can be delineated by looking at the exemplary processes in the field of the free movement of persons.

In 1997, four years after the introduction of Union Citizenship, 5.5 million EU citizens lived in member states that were not their home countries. In that year, the EU Commission established an expert group which analysed the practice of the application of rights under Union Citizenship. Its report outlines many obstacles in the realisation of the right to free movement. These were often related to unclear, incomplete or contradictory laws. Another problem was that national, regional or local government institutions did not facilitate the implementation, and in some cases even hindered it (European Commission 1997). When looking at the obstacles that are stated in the expert report it becomes obvious that the reactions of the national authorities to the new rights

168 Claudia Wiesner

can be interpreted as a form of conceptual and political struggle around the interpretation of the new Union Citizenship rights—and about the classical sovereign rights of a nation state.

Problems were, e.g., related to the practice of residence permits, acceptance of foreign degrees, employment in the public sector, and social and family related rights. Regarding residence permits, to *enter* another EU member state, i.e., to cross the border, EU citizens needed only a valid ID, however, in order to stay in that member state for more than three months, a residence permit was needed. There was no specific permit for stays between four months and a year—theoretically EU citizens after three months needed to apply for a long-term residence permit. Many in this situation did not do so and hence defaulted into an irregular situation after three months. Students in most cases could not apply for a residence permit that exceeded one year, so they often had serial residence permits, i.e., one permit followed another (European Commission 1997, 17–19).

Unemployed persons had a right to residence only when they did not claim any social assistance in their country of residence (European Commission 1997, 20)—a rule which in principle is valid until today, even if the member states are entitled to grant them social assistance if they decide it is appropriate.

Another source of difficulty was the local authorities. They often interpreted the condition that EU citizens must prove how they gain their living very restrictively. Students often had to hand in receipts when the EU laws only required a formal declaration. In cases where dealing with these obstacles hindered receiving a residence permit, there were occasions where EU citizens were threatened with expulsion, or had to endure difficulties in access to services of general interest like water supply, electricity, heating or telecommunication.

To counter such problems and obstacles, the EU Commission undertook several new moves in its political–conceptual struggle with the member states and their bureaucracies. It first led several infringement procedures before the ECJ against member states. Most of them changed the situation, but only after a number of years (European Commission 2001, 10).

The Commission's second step was to restart the process of conceptual innovation, law implementation and practical enactment. It issued several documents and declarations that claimed improvements: a uniform regulation of the right to free movement and residence for all EU citizens and their family members; a reduction of the requirements for residence permits to a minimum; and more rigid guidelines on the conditions for expulsion (European Union 2001b).

The Commission's third step was to induce new laws. Directive 2004/38/EC (European Union 2004b), voted upon by the Council and the EP, defines unified rules of residence. Among other aspects it declared that Union Citizens may stay in another member state for three months

Shaping Citizenship Practice 169

without any residence permit. After three months, member states may require one. But then employees, self-employed persons, persons in education or studies and their family members, can obtain a permit on the basis of their ID, a working contract or a certificate of training, a proof of self-employed status, a declaration of sufficient means for living and health insurance. Union Citizens can only be expelled in cases of severe threats to internal security, excluding minors and persons that have been resident for more than ten years in the respective state. The directive also requires the member states to inform EU citizens of their rights (European Union 2004a). Thus, free movement has in practice been considerably facilitated by the new directive.

Shaping EU Citizenship Practice by Conceptual, Legal and Institutional Changes

Regarding the leading questions raised in this chapter, what has been said shows a specific picture of how the conceptual innovation of EU citizenship rights was filled with meaning. First, the implementation of the conceptual and legal innovations in EU citizenship rights indeed followed the four-step process sketched above: conceptual innovation, lawmaking, interpretation conflicts and change of social and institutional practice. Second, EU citizenship is not a static concept, but a contested concept in continual development. Third, decisive steps in its development have been brought about initially by treaties and laws. The core actors in these processes have been the Commission, the Council and later the EP. Fourth, key conflicts often appeared in later stages and related to other actors, i.e., when the new EU laws were implemented by the nation states and their authorities. As EU citizenship rules interfered with classical nation state authority, institutional and conceptual struggles around their implementation regularly came about. In several cases the ECJ then intervened, judged and hence created a new legal situation.

The Commission had a clear strategy in all stages, as the policy procedures around free movement highlight: when the new rights were applied, a conceptual and political struggle around their interpretation evolved. In some cases, EU and member state authorities were acting in opposite directions in interpreting the laws. Therefore, the Commission aimed at closing or at least narrowing the space for such conceptual struggles and different interpretations by adding a second set of laws specifying the meaning of the original ones. The Commission thus aimed at shaping institutional practice. Hence, laws in the EU can be said to have a double function in these processes. First, conceptual innovations are transformed into laws. Second, laws also help putting the conceptual innovation into practice, i.e., they lead to social and institutional change.

In sum, the decisive actors in building EU citizenship have been the Commission, ECJ, the EU heads of government or state, or their ministers,

170   *Claudia Wiesner*

and more recently the EP, and the member state bureaucracies, all of them shaping the development of EU citizenship by negotiation, lawmaking and decision making. Thus, EU citizenship has been created by the key institutional actors in the EU system—and not by the citizens themselves. As such, what does this mean for the concept of citizenship more generally?

The setting of actors and processes that pushed EU citizenship rights is quite specific and very different from the settings that were decisive in the processes of citizenship development in national representative democracies (see Wiesner 2007, 251–327). Briefly stated, there is one main similarity and three decisive differences between the development of EU citizenship and national citizenships in Germany and France.

The *similarity* concerns the *institutions and institutional actors* that shaped concepts and institutional practices of citizenship in both nation states. They developed step by step, as did citizenship rights *acquis*, and both were often linked—e.g., the development of parliament and its competences often went along with the development of the right to vote. This is similar to what happens today in the EU, where the institutions gradually evolved towards a representative democratic system (for more detail, see Tiilikainen and Wiesner 2016). The development of the EU in fact shows significant similarities to the "late federal nation state" of Germany.

The differences concern the primary actors involved, the central dimensions of citizenship and the role of the institutions related to identity and community building:

1   In contrast to the EU, where citizenship rights were granted in a top-down way without having been claimed, the development of both conceptual and institutional practices of citizenship in Germany and France was more closely related to *political struggles* led by the citizens-to-be, which were followed by conceptual and law changes, and not the other way around like in the EU (Wiesner 2007, 312–321).

2   Again, in contrast to the EU, crucial issues in the development of nation state citizenship were related to the citizenship dimensions of *access* (Who could become a national? What about women and non-nationals?) and *duties* (military service, school) which both are not objects of debate or political activity in the current EU.

3   In both nation states, citizenship and state institutions have been closely connected to national identity formation. Both in France and in Germany the national governments used their *institutions to shape citizenship* and national identity, or to "create subjects" in the Foucaultian sense (Foucault 1999, 54) through school and military service. As these processes only work if citizens are obliged to attend the respective disciplinary institutions, they went along with the definition of far-reaching citizen duties. In the EU, school and military service cannot be used for this kind of identity building, so other

Shaping Citizenship Practice 171

forms are deployed—this concerns, for instance, the programmes described in the chapter by Mäkinen.

In sum, changes in national concepts of citizenship in Germany and France mirrored or even followed institutional and social changes and also political conflicts, whereas in the EU it often was the other way around, in that conceptual innovation regarding citizenship preceded social and institutional changes, political conflicts being largely absent, so far. And whereas in both Germany and France, the citizens-to-be played a crucial role, in the EU they were merely passive.

Conclusion

This chapter has raised three crucial questions with regard to EU citizenship:

First, there is the question of the emptiness of a new concept: as the discussion showed, a conceptual innovation such as EU citizenship may well be created by lawmaking, but it then has to be filled not only with meaning but also with social and institutional practice. To create such practice, the EU lacks the nation state's institutions that could enforce the creation of "EU subjects", such as schools or military. Whereas we might welcome this absence, it leaves the EU without the means of nation-building which the classical nation states possessed.

Second, there is the question of new mechanisms of exclusion: citizenship, as has been claimed in several contributions to this volume, is per se linked to inclusion and exclusion. At first glance, EU citizenship seems to reduce exclusion considerably. Not only is it granted for nationals of all 28 (or soon 27) member states, it is also explicitly based on the principle of non-discrimination. However, it creates new mechanisms of exclusion that are related to the dimensions that demarcate EU citizenship. First, new differentiations in citizenship status have been created, distinguishing nationals, EU citizens and non-EU citizens, and legal and illegal migrants (see in detail Wiesner 2007, 70, 156, 161–187). Second, market participation creates decisive new mechanisms of exclusion (see Lillie and Wagner in this volume).

Third is the question of democracy: it seems strange that citizenship rights should not be fought for by the subjects, but are deliberately granted. Whereas in nation states democratic and political rights had to be obtained, in part, by bloody fights, in the EU they seemingly come for free. But what does this tell us regarding the fact that democracy requires at least some citizen activity? As has been said, a large part of the development of EU citizenship is due to the fact that the European governments wanted to make the common market function (see also Lillie and Wagner in the following chapter of this volume). Hence, their goal was not primarily to enable democracy, but to enable free market

172   *Claudia Wiesner*

competition. What all this points to is that EU citizenship is currently rather passive, and its link to democracy should grow stronger if it is not to be endangered. One answer has been the EU participation programmes, but they do not necessarily try to enhance bottom-up political activity; rather they activate a kind of guided participation (see Mäkinen in this volume). The question of an active EU citizenry that makes democracy live, therefore, remains open.

References

Law Texts and EU Documents

European Commission. 1997. "Bericht der hochrangigen Arbeitsgruppe zu Fragen der Freizügigkeit unter dem Vorsitz von Frau Simone Veil." www.uni-mannheim.de/edz/pdf/1997/hlpde.pdf. Accessed February 12, 2013.

———. 1999. "Communication from the Commission to the Council, the European Parliament, the Economic and Social Committee and the Committee of the Regions on Certain Community Measures to Combat Discrimination." http://eur-lex.europa.eu/LexUriServ/LexUriServ.do?uri=COM:1999:0564:FIN:EN:PDF. Accessed February 12, 2013.

———. 2001. "Third Report from the Commission on Citizenship of the Union, COM (2001) 506 Final." http://eur-lex.europa.eu/LexUriServ/LexUriServ.do?uri=COM:2001:0506:FIN:EN:PDF. Accessed February 12, 2013.

European Council. 1957. "The Treaty of Rome." http://ec.europa.eu/economy_finance/emu_history/documents/treaties/rometreaty2.pdf. Accessed February 11, 2013.

———. 2000a. "COUNCIL DIRECTIVE 2000/43/EC of 29 June 2000 Implementing the Principle of Equal Treatment between Persons Irrespective of Racial or Ethnic Origin." http://eur-lex.europa.eu/LexUriServ/LexUriServ.do?uri=OJ:L:2000:180:0022:0026:EN:PDF. Accessed November 19, 2013.

———. 2000b. "COUNCIL DIRECTIVE 2000/78/EC of 27 November 2000 Establishing a General Framework for Equal Treatment in Employment and Occupation." http://eur-lex.europa.eu/LexUriServ/LexUriServ.do?uri=OJ:L:2000:303:0016:0022:EN:PDF. Accessed November 19, 2013.

European Court of Justice. 1976. "JUDGMENT OF 8. 4. 197—CASE 43/75." http://eur-lex.europa.eu/legal-content/EN/TXT/PDF/?uri=CELEX:61975CJ0043&from=FR. Accessed October 9, 2015.

European Union. 2001a. "Der Vertrag von Amsterdam: Gebrauchsanweisung Unionsbürgerschaft." http//europa.eu.int/scadplus/leg/de/lvb/a12000.htm. Accessed August 25, 2005.

———. 2001b. "Unionsbürgerschaft: Folgemaßnahmen zu den Empfehlungen der hochrangigen Sachverständigengruppe für Fragen der Freizügigkeit." http//europa.eu.int/scadplus/leg/de/lvb/123032.htm. Accessed August 25, 2005.

———. 2004a. "Berichtigung der Richtlinie 2004/38/EG des Europäischen Parlaments und des Rates vom 29. April 2004 über das Recht der Unionsbürger und ihrer Familienangehörigen, sich im Hoheitsgebiet der Mitgliedstaaten

Shaping Citizenship Practice 173

frei zu bewegen und aufzuhalten." http://eur-lex.europa.eu/LexUriServ/Lex UriServ.do?uri=CELEX:32004L0038R(01):de:HTML. Accessed February 12, 2013.

———. 2004b. "Directive 2004/38/EC of the European Parliament and of the Council of 29 April 2004." http://eur-lex.europa.eu/LexUriServ/LexUriServ. do?uri=OJ:L:2004:158:0077:0123:en:PDF. Accessed February 12, 2013.

———. 2010. "Consolidated Treaties. Charter of Fundamental Rights." http:// bookshop.europa.eu/is-bin/INTERSHOP.enfinity/WFS/EU-Bookshop-Site/ en_GB/-/EUR/ViewPublication-Start?PublicationKey=QC3209190. Accessed February 05, 2013.

Treaty on European Union. Council of the European Communities. http:// europa.eu/eu-law/decision-making/treaties/pdf/treaty_on_european_union/ treaty_on_european_union_en.pdf. Accessed July 17, 2015.

Literature

Bauböck, Rainer. 2007. "Why European Citizenship—Normative Approaches to Supranational Union." *Theoretical Inquiries in Law* 8(2):453–488. www7.tau. ac.il/ojs/index.php/til/article/download/642/603. Accessed February 15, 2017.

Bellamy, Richard. 2008. "Evaluating Citizenship: Belonging, Rights and Participation within the EU." *Citizenship Studies* 12(6):597–611.

Besson, Samantha, and André Utzinger. 2008. "Toward European Citizenship." *Journal of Social Philosophy* 39:185–208.

Cappelletti, Mauro, Monica Seccombe, and Joseph Weiler. 1986. *Integration Through Law: European University Institute/A 2, 1, 2*. Berlin: de Gruyter.

Foucault, Michel. 1999. In *Verteidigung der Gesellschaft: Vorlesungen am Collège de France*. Frankfurt am Main: Suhrkamp.

Höpner, Martin, and Armin Schäfer. 2012. "Embeddedness and Regional Integration: Waiting for Polanyi in a Hayekian Setting." *International Organization* 66(3):429–455. http://journals.cambridge.org/download.php? file=%2F35310_A080427681B69A9BA2B93B1122D6DAF3_journals__ INO_INO66_03_S002081831200015Xa.pdf&cover=Y&code=5735300aaf 4a323c1339879b90c07d0c. Accessed October 25, 2012.

Kleger, Heinz. 1995. "Transnationale Staatsbürgerschaft: Zur Arbeit an einem europäischen Bürgerstatus." In *Transnationale Demokratie: Impulse für ein demokratisch verfaßtes Europa*, edited by Roland v. Erne, 34–59. Zürich: Realotopia.

Koselleck, Reinhart. 1967. "Richtlinien für das Lexikon politisch-sozialer Begriffe der Neuzeit." Archiv für Begriffsgeschichte 11:81–99.

———. 2006. "Die Geschichte der Begriffe und Begriffe der Geschichte." In *Begriffsgeschichten: Studien zur Semantik und Pragmatik der politischen und sozialen Sprache*, 56–76. Frankfurt am Main: Suhrkamp.

Lacroix, Justine, and Kalypso Nicolaïdis. 2010. *European Stories: Intellectual Debates on Europe in National Contexts*. Oxford & New York: Oxford University Press.

Mäkinen, Katja. 2015. "Mobility and Unspoken Citizens' Rights in EU-Documents." *New Zealand Journal of Research on Europe* 9(1):1–62.

174 *Claudia Wiesner*

Skinner, Quentin. 1999. "Rhetoric and Conceptual Change." *Redescriptions (Finnish Yearbook of Political Thought)*, 60–73. www.jyu.fi/yhtfil/redescriptions/Yearbook%201999/Skinner%20Q%201999.pdf. Accessed October 5, 2012.

———. 2002. "The Idea of a Cultural Lexicon." In *Visions of Politics. Volume 1: Regarding Method*, 158–174. Cambridge: Cambridge University Press.

Tiilikainen, Teija, and Claudia Wiesner. 2016. "Towards a European Parliamentarism?" In *Parliament and Parliamentarism: A Comparative History of Disputes on a European Concept*, edited by Pasi Ihalainen, Cornelia Ilie, and Kari Palonen. New York: Berghahn Books.

Weiler, Josef H. 1996. "The Selling of Europe." http://centers.law.nyu.edu/jean monnet/archive/papers/96/9603.html. Accessed February 12, 2013.

Wiener, Antje. 1998. *European Citizenship Practice*. Boulder, CO: Westview Press.

———. 2001. "Zur Verfassungspolitik jenseits des Staates. Die Vermittlung von Bedeutung am Beispiel der Unionsbürgerschaft." *Zeitschrift für Internationale Beziehungen* 8(1):73–104.

Wiesner, Claudia. 2007. *Bürgerschaft und Demokratie in der EU*. Münster: Lit.

———. 2013. "Conceptual Change and European Integration: Introductory Reflections and Research Agenda." Paper held at the ECPR General Conference, Bordeaux, September 5–7. www.ecpr.eu/Filestore/PaperProposal/800bb59a-3736-4309-b86a-41013c15bc26.pdf. Accessed March 16, 2015.

Wiesner, Claudia, and Meike Schmidt-Gleim, eds. 2014. *The Meanings of Europe*. London: Routledge.

10 Practicing European Industrial Citizenship

The Case of Labour Migration to Germany

Nathan Lillie and Ines Wagner

The European Union has its core *raison d'être* in the breaking down of barriers to markets enshrined in its foundational document, the Treaty of Rome. The implementation of this market-constitutional idea brings the EU into conflict with social and democratic principles in many of the policy arenas the EU touches because it implies treating market dynamics as fundamental organizing principles of society which cannot be overturned through democratic politics. Tensions between society and markets have existed as long as there have been markets (Polanyi 1944), but are brought into sharper relief by the current hegemony of market ideas. This article explores how tensions between the conceptual underpinnings of intra-EU free movement and national industrial citizenship reveal this dynamic, using the example of how free movement affects industrial citizenship in Germany. The practices embedded in the concept of European citizenship challenge the normative and practical structures realizing German industrial citizenship as a nationally specific development of German working class capacities, with the result that balance of class power is undermined. In a sense, our argument that globalization undermines labour is hardly a new and original one, but we wish here to show how transnational processes shift interpretations of specifically nationally bounded concepts. Industrial citizenship exists in all modern welfare states but its formulation is always nationally specific. Thus, we focus attention on one example of a process happening all over Europe, specifically how the European project undermines the normative microfoundations of German industrial citizenship.

This chapter shows how one form of labour mobility, unique to the European Union, namely posted work, undermines industrial citizenship in Germany. Posted workers move abroad as part of a dependent work relationship, rather than moving as individuals to take up a job in the host country. Although originally intended as a way for firms to send employees abroad for short periods, posting has become a way to avoid labour regulation and employ low-wage migrants in precarious jobs (Cremers 2013). Whereas industrial citizenship is under pressure in Germany generally (see Brinkmann and Nachtwey 2014),

176 *Nathan Lillie and Ines Wagner*

this chapter focuses on how posted work introducing into the German industrial relations system a class of workers with tenuous relations to the system's regulatory jurisdiction undermines industrial citizenship in Germany. Use of posting avoids contesting the validity of labour rights and industrial citizenship concepts directly, but instead asserts that specific workers under exceptional circumstances are outside the realm of application of those concepts. This works because labour rights, like human rights generally, are exercised via national systems, and posted workers are partially outside of these systems.

Our approach is to examine the contradictions between industrial and market citizenship concepts, and to trace their implications in practice. We first make the case that industrial citizenship developed as a way to socially regulate markets in democratic societies. We then show that EU regulation, and specifically posted work, undermine national industrial citizenship through constitutionalizing markets. Then, the case is made that the key German industrial relations actors are structurally incapable of regulating transnational work relations. Finally, we examine how labour inspectors, who should even in the absence of unions enforce German labour laws, are handicapped by an inability to operate transnationally. We conclude that dominance of market concepts in the EU regulation of posted work circumvents and undermines Germany's industrial citizenship institutions. We rely on interviews of posted workers, trade unionists, managers and policy makers from 2011–2014 in Germany and in the EU context conducted as part of the Transnational Work and Evolution of Sovereignty project (TWES 263782), and on EU and national legal documents.

Conceptualising Industrial Citizenship

Industrial citizenship arose as a Polanyian challenge to capitalism's marketization of the social world as a way of delivering on the promise of national citizenship by recognizing the collective power of the working class in the economic realm. In general, citizenship is both a formal legal status, giving access to rights and protections, as well as a practice of participation in a polity (Zhang 2014). Likewise, industrial citizenship is both a status, granting rights within a defined territorially based (political) community, and a process and relationship between workers and employers. Like other forms of national citizenship, industrial citizenship reflects the societies and communities it is based on, within and bounded by the territories of capitalist states. National industrial relations systems are based on national class identities and capacities, and secure industrial citizenship via mutually interlocking and reinforcing sets of institutions. Industrial citizenship is embedded in the (power) relationship of worker to employer, relying on the creation of structural political power through class-based collectivism and using this power to advance

Practicing European Industrial Citizenship   177

workers' interests. Our chapter therefore examines practices of inclusion and representation via worker organizations such as trade unions and works councils, as well practices and structures of posted worker protection. The first aspect is arguably more important, because it forms the power basis via which the second aspect is achieved (Zhang and Lillie 2015). For posted work, only the second occurs in actual practice, and that only weakly. The concepts underlying industrial citizenship have long been grounded in nationally specific ideas about class, territory and national identity, and as these have changed, so has the expression of industrial citizenship in practice.

In the Marshallian tradition, citizenship is conceived in expansionary terms, with social and economic progress leading to increasing inclusiveness and equality, and ever more substantial and realizable rights (Marshall 1992). Yet contradictions emerge, as modern citizenship is also inextricably embedded in market capitalism. Citizenship's egalitarian and decommodifying implications do not sit well with expanding markets, which produce inequalities and power disparities. Citizenship in capitalist society is undermined by the inability of the impoverished to act as free and autonomous agents (Somers 2008), so that democracy and citizenship depend on structures protecting industrial democracy in the workplace. Furthermore, modern citizenship is spatially grounded and territorially limited, tying individuals to specific nation states. From this came Marshall's notion that industrial citizenship, alongside the closely related social citizenship, served to integrate the working class into the welfare state, supporting the realization of civic and political citizenship (Marshall 1992).

The notion of industrial citizenship serves to explain practices which resolved the tension between class and national identity. Trade unions developed by generating and harnessing class conflict to use collective working-class economic power to establish economic democracy for workers. Industrial citizenship is embedded in the (power) relationship of worker to employer, relying on the creation of structural political power through class-based collectivism and using this power to advance workers' interests. In connecting, integrating and empowering workers in the management of the polity, industrial citizenship is a vehicle for, and an outcome of, class compromise—i.e. its corollary is acceptance of the legitimacy of the polity, and a rejection (or at least deferral) of revolutionary visions of social transformation. This is what C. Wright Mills (1948) meant when he called trade unions "managers of discontent"; unions generate and focus discontent among workers to bargain with capitalists and politicians for the things those workers want (Mills 1948). Unions criticize capitalism and its inequalities to gain power which can only be used under conditions of capitalist inequality. In Gramscian terms, industrial citizenship is an acceptance of the ideological dominance of the ruling class.

178 *Nathan Lillie and Ines Wagner*

Industrial citizenship at once advances the struggle for equality while also embedding it in logics which make achieving complete equality impossible. Within sovereign territories, rights of industrial citizenship are variegated depending on bargaining units and collective agreement; employers also strategize around those cleavages to create groups of workers with less access to rights. Even at its height, access to industrial citizenship was conditioned by ethnic hierarchies, firm boundaries, gender, age and so on, with adult white male workers in stable, union jobs in core industries as the archetype (Zetlin and Whitehouse 2003). Although the precise forms of inequality vary, inequality in industrial citizenship is inevitable, because industrial citizenship is expressed through collective power at work and therefore expresses and reflects inequalities inherent in capitalist societies, even as it (ideally) seeks to lessen them. As a subaltern concept, it finds power in the weakness of the working class and the injustices they are subject to; even in its ideal form, therefore, its logic inherently excludes the possibility of fully achieving its nominal goals.

Industrial citizenship is realized within nation states via national systems of industrial relations made up of employer associations, trade unions and government regulatory agencies. Underlying this superstructure are unions and their structural relations to the national working class; the capacity for mobilization of the working class shapes the resulting class compromise (Wright 2000). There is a functional similarity between systems, and many labour rights are regarded as universal. However, the practical realization and implementation of industrial citizenship is mediated by national institutions and varies from country to country in terms of process and outcomes. Industrial relations practice is based on a strong spatial ontology, reflected in the jurisdictional boundaries of nation states, production sites, worker communities and labour market organizations. Unions articulate the demands of their worker–members from shop floors to bargaining tables and national political settlements, via institutionalized systems of national industrial relations. J. R. Commons (1913), e.g., takes the formation of the national union as the logical endpoint of labour movement development, and the 'systems theory' on which Industrial Relations is based assumes this implicitly (Heery 2008). Rarely using the term 'citizenship', the Industrial Relations discipline has an implicit notion of industrial citizenship, with worker voice, access to interest representation, fair pay, due process and right to strike as key concepts (see Freeman and Medoff 1984).

In recent decades, the ideas underpinning industrial citizenship have come under pressure. Market ideology and notions of market citizenship have eroded worker collective organization and support for industrial democracy (Fudge 2005). The decline of industrial citizenship is related to the declining influence of class-based understandings of workplace relations. Communitarian frames support an organizational logic that grants workers industrial power, allowing them to limit and shape the market outcomes produced by capitalist systems. Industrial citizenship depends on organization, processes and participation, which arise out of class capacities. Class capacities (i.e. the working class's ability to act as a political, economic or social actor) depend ultimately on bonds of solidarity and class consciousness developed from experiences in workplaces and communities. Workers in the same workplace and same geographic space rely on one another at work, share social networks in community and leisure activities and find common cultural reference points (Thompson 1963). The realization of a right of industrial citizenship is highly dependent both on workers' understanding of class conflict and on practising that in specific ways which maximize leverage over employers. Unions engage in identity work (Greer and Hauptmeier 2012), 'building solidarity' to maximize leverage given existing political and economic opportunities; unions have often fulfilled the role of 'schools of class conflict', as part of this process of creating mindsets which generates their power.

Posted Work and the Variegation of EU Citizenship

Free movement has been a foundation stone of European integration since the signing of the Treaty of Rome in 1957. Although contested by ideas such as 'Social Europe', Europe has evolved as a marketization process through the removal of 'barriers to free movement'. Many aspects of national social regulation have been challenged as impediments to free movement, including those relating to industrial and social rights. Intra-EU free movement is central to the construction of a post-national EU citizenship, but its justificatory basis in market norms turns the growth of the pan-EU labour market into a lever to deregulate national industrial relations. This deregulation occurs through differential access to industrial citizenship rights, exploiting the regulatory gaps which emerge as a result of clashes and contradictions between nationally specific concepts of industrial citizenship and globalizing/Europeanizing ideas of market governance (Zhang and Lillie 2015).

The politics of posted work regulation in the EU has been one of policy makers trying to prevent undercutting of wages in host countries, versus policy makers seeking to enable the undercutting of wages in host countries. Much of the contestation had been around the implementation of the EU's Posted Workers Directive (PWD). This directive made explicit that national labour regulations applied to posted construction workers (and to workers in other sectors, if a national government so chooses), but did not provide a harmonized EU level policy. The PWD also limited aspects of national labour regulation that could be applied, as the 2007–2008 *Laval Quartet* of CJEU decisions clarified, in terms of the way standards could be decided on and enforced. Specifically, strike action and minimum wages clauses in public contracts could not be used

180 *Nathan Lillie and Ines Wagner*

on behalf posted workers to compel employers to pay higher wages, because this violates the free movement rights of employers. This is an application of the European Union concept of market making through free movement. The EU expressly seeks to open national territory by constitutionalizing economic mobility rights, and accomplishing this requires suppression of industrial citizenship rights.

The association of market citizenship with EU citizenship is not inevitable; other regulatory paths exist alongside the posted worker path, and indeed have a longer history. The issue of employment and social rights for mobile EU citizens emerged already in the early days of the EU, as the EU sought to promote free movement of labour. Intra-EU mobile workers required rights to social security, mobility of family members and similar, so that over time an individual rights-based approach developed. An EU labour rights framework asserts that mobile workers should be treated equally in their employment and social rights, e.g., the principle of non-discrimination on grounds of nationality is associated with the freedom of movement. Although these began as extensions of the right to work (relying on free movement of labour) they have decommodifying implications (Marzo 2011). However, posted work takes place under the free movement of services rather than labour. The regular free movement rules here do not apply and therefore lack this element of decommodification.

Posted work is a form of temporary labour migration, in which an employer sends a worker abroad to provide 'services' (although often the services they provide involve manufacturing). Regulating post work effectively is, as is shown later, beyond the capacity of host country regulatory institutions, effectively deregulating employment to the extent that in some situations posted work becomes a fig leaf concealing illegal employment arrangements (Cremers 2013). Workers can (and often do) also move as individuals rather than as dependent employees. The difference in legal and organizational position of posted workers vis-à-vis individual migrants is that the laws and organizational practices through which rights are accessed are not native to the territory the worker is in—and therefore in practice are difficult to access. It is thus a further and additional disconnection with territory, relative to individual migrants, and one with a legal basis legitimated by market norms. The promotion of this type of mobility reflects the conceptual shift in the EU, towards promoting markets through deliberate undermining of national labour protections. In this framework of thought, industrial citizenship becomes a barrier to free movement, which can be legitimately circumvented by EU policies making national rules difficult or impossible to enforce.

How Industrial Citizenship is Realized in Germany

We explore the problem of posted work through an examination of the German institutions of industrial citizenship, and their application to

Practicing European Industrial Citizenship 181

posted workers, and find that the insularity and lack of transnational reach of the German industrial relations systems ensures that posted workers fall essentially outside its boundaries. This study explores the German system as an example case. Although treatment of posted workers varies across Europe, this is only a question of degree. Regardless of the details, national specificity and insularity are characteristic of all industrial relations systems.

German industrial relations is characterized by a 'constitutional' approach to firm governance which gives space to industrial democracy, under the idea of a 'social contract' within the firm (Frege 2005). Under principles of 'co-determination', power is exercised not only by management, but also union and works council representatives. Firms are perceived as quasi-public entities. Rather than being the absolute property of their owners, they are social communities, states within the states, or constitutional monarchies, where workers hold democratic rights and the monarch/owner shares power. "The employment relationship is not seen as one of free subordination [as in the US] but of democratization," declared Weimar labour law scholar Hugo Sinzheimer (Finkin 2002, 621).

The German industrial relations system has long been considered a best-practice example, with industrial citizenship realized through a 'dual system' of trade unions outside the immediate workplace, and works councils inside. Lowell Turner argues this produced "democracy at work", closing out the "low-road" of cheap, low-quality production and encouraging German employers to participate in apprenticeship programmes producing workers with high-level job skills (Turner 1991). This ideal picture has been changing since the 1990s, so although the institutional infrastructure still exists and functions for core workers in core firms, there is a large and increasing segment of the workforce excluded from it by labour market dualization (Bosch and Weinkopf 2008). In 2013, only 28 per cent of private-sector workers in western Germany and 15 per cent in eastern Germany were covered both by a collective agreement and a works council.

Both unions and works councils exercise industrial democracy rights in the firm. Within firms, unions in Germany have rights to information and consultation, and in some firms also co-decision (*Mitbestimung*). There is a traditional division of tasks: unions negotiate with employers' associations on a branch level, whereas works councils negotiate with individual employers. Works councillors are elected by all employees of a firm, including the non-union ones, but are often dominated by active trade union members, becoming vehicles for union influence within firms. Works councillors have authority to negotiate on issues such as working hours, working rules, hirings and dismissals, and are in a structurally similar position to shop stewards in other systems.

At the workplace level, works councils are the institutional base for worker representation. Employees in companies with five or more permanent employees can elect a works council; the employer must not interfere with or forbid these elections. Migrant workers who fulfill these requirements may participate in these elections, but few are employed in companies with works councils. Posted workers are by definition excluded because their employers are not incorporated in Germany; the German co-determination act doesn't apply to subcontracting firms that are based outside Germany. Posted workers are employed via foreign subcontractors or agencies; main contractors or agency firms' client may well have a works council, but these have almost no rights to represent workers in subcontracting arrangements and these workers are not permitted to interact with the works council directly. Whether foreign-based subcontractors can elect a works council depends on the regulation of the country where the firm is based. In many countries there is no legal basis to form a works council. More importantly, the reality of employer oversight and pressure is that there is little chance workers of international work agencies would try to form a works council, even if legally entitled to do so. This is not only a problem for posted workers; German workers' traditional institutional arrangements have also been under enormous pressure as firms outsource to smaller firms as a way to avoid works council and trade union power (Doellgast 2009). The difference for posted workers is that they do not even have the *right* to form a works council under German law. Because for German trade unions, works council formation is often the entry into the firm, the possibility to have a works council is an essential expression of German industrial citizenship.

A common regulatory problem under globalization is that the authority of national institutions ends at the border; this is also the case with the authority of German's comprehensive dual system. The free mobility of services and labour, however, enables private actors to extend across territorial borders, reconfiguring relations between actors in ways that inhibit worker access to industrial citizenship (Wagner 2015). These shifting boundaries of regulation facilitate firm strategies to segment the labour market. Whereas immigration generally tends to reduce trade union leverage in the labour market, in the past trade unions have coped by organizing and representing immigrant workers. This has not been without its tensions, but there has nonetheless been a trend toward integration of immigrants into the trade union movement (Marino et al. 2015).

Interaction between posted workers and unions, however, is difficult because both actors are embedded in different normative frameworks. Posted workers, even though physically in the host country, continue to frame their understanding of their employment rights with reference to their home country. One posted worker explains her embeddedness in the home country and her excluded status in the host country:

Practicing European Industrial Citizenship 183

I have been to a union meeting once. There are certain rights, but in vain, because they are not applicable to us 'posted workers' because we are not employed by a German company but by a Romanian company. Our rights are connected to the country and firm where we are employed and pay taxes and social security contributions to, i.e. Romania.

(Bulgarian posted worker interview 2012)

The impression of the worker is that there is a dividing line based on the national context of where the employer is based inhibiting the enactment of certain rights, and preventing her seeking representation from the trade union in the host country. Moreover, many mistrust unions due to negative experiences with home country unions or misunderstanding of the union structure in Germany. The worker leaves the sending country geographically, but in a regulatory and normative sense carries its rules into German territory. The predicament is that whereas unions are understaffed and lack the resources to mobilize posted workers, the workers themselves mostly refrain from seeking help from the union due to fear of employer intimidation and retaliation. This results in a 'catch 22' situation and creates a border between the union and workers (Wagner 2015). Although workers are aware of their agency in this, they also know that changing their situation is difficult and risky because of the multiple mutually reinforcing barriers, and the relative helplessness of the unions to protect them.

Actors play a major role in defining these spaces through their ongoing interactions. There is a mutually constitutive relationship between the material facts of the EU legal framework, the ideas held by actors about organizing these spaces, and actors' practices manifesting those ideas. Searching for ways out of the dilemma, the DGB and its sectoral unions have undertaken various initiatives aimed at integrating migrants into structures of worker representation, e.g., IG Bau has responded by attempting to organize and represent posted workers. One well-known effort was the establishment of the European Migrant Workers Union (EMWU), which attempted to create a transnational union, separate from the IG Bau, from which workers could receive representation in both home and host countries. The EMWU did not establish the independent role initially envisioned due to insufficient union support from unions in Germany and other countries, as well as organizational flaws in EMWU itself, and was eventually reintegrated into the IG BAU (Greer, Ciupijus, and Lillie 2013). Nonetheless, the IG BAU continues to represent the rights of posted workers at the political level and provide information to workers on construction work sites or at worker housing sites and help with legal services in certain dire cases. The same is true for the 'fair mobility' service centres which now exist in large cities across

184   *Nathan Lillie and Ines Wagner*

Germany. In these service centres project workers with relevant language skills inform migrant workers (including posted workers) about labour law and social legislations in their native languages, in an attempt to preserve the norms of the German labour market. The creation of fair mobility service centres interacts with the recognition that migrant workers need also help with housing and other social issues.

The Posting of Workers Law and Collective Bargaining in Germany

Posting is pervasive in the German meat and construction industry. In both industries high levels of subcontracting and international mobility make for a fluid labour market. Subcontracting is used in construction to access specialized knowledge, increase flexibility, manage risk and reduce labour costs, whereas in meat processing it is mainly a cost reduction strategy. Construction consists of large main contractors or building service providers, and numerous small and medium sized subcontractors, who provide the majority of the workers (Bosch and Zühlke-Robinet 2003). Transnational work agencies and subcontractors compete on cost against domestic subcontractors by bringing low-cost migrant workers to high labour cost countries, and preventing them from claiming the wages and benefits demanded by domestically hired workers.

The PWD was translated into German law via the German Posting Act (*Arbeitnehmerentsendegesetz*) in 1996. The German posting law only covers certain sectors. Initially it included construction, building cleaning and mail services, but was amended in 2008 to include slaughtering and meat processing, and in 2009 to include care work (elderly care and ambulant treatment), security services, waste management, training and educational services, laundry services, and special mining work in coal mines. Posted workers in those sectors are covered by German labour law in crucial areas such as wages and job safety, but social security contributions (i.e. sick and pension pay) are paid in the sending country and not in the country where the work is performed. Sending country social security contributions are often much lower than Germany's leading to an overall reduction in labour costs (Fellini et al. 2007). Firms sometimes establish letterbox companies in low cost countries to lower tax and social contributions. For posted workers, this often means they have no effective access to legal remedy if their contracts are violated by the employer, and they can be left with social insurance rights vested in a jurisdiction they will never visit.

The EU's Posted Worker Directive enables national regulation of labour markets, but only in certain ways. Specifically, the *Laval* decision of the Court of Justice of the European Union (CJEU) clarified that host countries can only regulate the working conditions of posted workers through legislative instruments (i.e. not through free collective

Practicing European Industrial Citizenship   185

bargaining), and only in those areas specifically mentioned in the PWD (Kilpatrick 2009, 845–849). In a further CJEU decision, *Rueffert vs. Land Niedersachsen*, the CJEU ruled that public bodies cannot use their purchasing procedures to impose collective agreement wage levels of transnational contractors employing posted workers. In this way, the CJEU explicitly defines posted workers as outside the industrial citizenship framework of host countries, not entitled to the full set of worker rights based on the territory in which they work, but rather to a different, usually lesser, and often inaccessible, set of rights based on the nationality of their employer. In Viking (C-438/05) and Laval (C-341/05) the ECJ ruled that industrial action aimed at representing posted workers from a foreign undertaking could violate the company's freedom to provide services across borders, denying posted workers the right to strike (see Kilpatrick 2009, 845–849), a right available to native workers, and fundamental to the practice of industrial citizenship. These court decisions opened leeway for employers to undermine national regulations and constrained the rights of trade unions to represent posted workers. Prevailing wages or collective agreements in a sector are not (and according to EU jurisprudence cannot be) applied to posted workers, even by unions through free collective bargaining, unless there is a German law generalizing the application of the standard.

Posted Workers and Labour Standards Enforcement

Whereas collective bargaining agreements represent a collective version of exerting workers' voice, enforcement then is responsible for ensuring that these agreements, but also others such as state policies are uphold in order to ensure that industrial citizenship is actually practised. The institution enforcing labour standards for posted workers, the FKS (*Finanzkontrolle Schwarzarbeit*) and its enforcers have police-like powers, including the power to force entry, search persons and premises, confiscate and retain evidence and arrest without warrant. However, the FKS struggles to detect malpractice by transnational subcontractors and to enforce fines for transnationally operating companies (Wagner and Berntsen 2016). In spite of the requirement to provide documents for inspection, according to a FKS representative, inspectors rarely notice discrepancies.

The FKS suspects that many host country documents are manipulated whereas the real accounting book is kept in the home country (FKS interview 2012). To detect malpractice the FKS would need to investigate which wage deductions have taken place and whether the correct amount has been paid to the workers. However, in practice this is almost impossible, because "the investigative power of the labour inspection stops at the German border on the grounds that they have to respect state sovereignty" (NGO interview 2012). In case malpractice is uncovered and

186 Nathan Lillie and Ines Wagner

fines issued, the fine cannot be enforced across the national frontier. Fines and exclusion from public procurement provisions have no dissuasive effect on negligent employers (Zentralverband deutsches Baugewerbe 2006). The cooperation with courts and lawyers in home countries that is required in order to enforce fines is basically non-existent (Sozialkassen der Bauwirtschaft, SOKA BAU interview, 2013). As a result, only 15–20 per cent of the fines are enforced, whereas 80–85 per cent of breaches of the posting of workers regulation have no consequence (Zentralverband deutsches Baugewerbe 2006).

When opportunities to detect malpractice and enforce standards are severely limited, the likelihood of exploitative practices increases. According to a recent government report, many subcontractors do not adhere to minimum standards for posted workers, such as minimum wages or maximum working times (Deutscher Bundestag 2013). The report confirmed that only limited controls take place, because it is time-intensive and complicated. A report from the central association of the German building industry (Zentralverband deutsches Baugewerbe ZdB) reiterates the existence of regulatory gaps. Mechanisms such as double bookkeeping across borders make it difficult for the FKS to detect avoidance mechanisms used by firms (Zentralverband deutsches Baugewerbe 2006, 8).

The persistence of national borders for labour enforcement agencies, but not firms, is reflected in their limited ability to detect malpractice by transnational service providers. The minimal ability of state actors to enforce posted workers' rights renders posted workers disproportionately vulnerable to criminal victimization and workplace exploitation. This de- and re-territorialization of state borders intersects with significant transformations of labour markets in OECD countries since the 1970s (Wagner, 2015). Access to justice is also found to be increasingly difficult for workers employed in atypical employment contexts within Germany (Bosch and Weinkopf 2008), but posted work adds another dimension to the debate by invoking foreign institutional systems.

Conclusion

This chapter exemplifies how an interrogation of the concepts behind European integration and German industrial citizenship reveals contradictions and tensions in the changing territorialities of the European Union. Whereas some (c.f. Habermas 2012) argue that the EU could resolve the contradictions we identify by assuming the prerogatives of nation states on a larger geographic scale, EU institutions for realization of industrial citizenship are not configured to make them equivalent to national industrial relations systems. In EU political circles, but also in the thinking of national policy elites, there has been a shift in understanding how society is and should be organized. Markets have assumed the

Practicing European Industrial Citizenship 187

highest position in the hierarchy of ideas, whereas notions of citizenship based on other principles, such as democratic, social or even sometimes civil rights have been subsumed.

Free mobility is at the heart of the European Union conception of citizenship, yet it is being implemented in such a way as to threaten the industrial citizenship on which modern welfare states have been built. One of the ways this is occurring is through opening avenues for employers to use transnational worker mobility to ignore and subvert national industrial relations institutions. This is nothing new as there has never been a perfect correspondence of nation states to territory, and there have always been grey areas, zones of imperfectly implemented sovereignty, and variegations in status between different groups of people. Modern citizenship is an ideal form which has never been, nor can it ever be, perfectly implemented (Zhang 2014).

European regulations for free movement and the employment relations practices they facilitate reveal a fundamental shift in how industrial citizenship is articulated through the development of new notions of territoriality. Industrial citizenship is itself not directly contested, instead new concepts of territoriality change industrial citizenship's practice— the concepts do not so much change as become irrelevant. While the conceptual history approach shows how the meanings of concepts are subject to interpretation and reinterpretation as part of broader political struggles (see Introduction in this volume), we see in this case that the question of which concept to fight over can also be important, as actors strategically exploit contradictions between basic principles. In this case, those principles are free movement and labour rights; posted workers mobility served as an argument to structurally exclude them from access to industrial citizenship in Germany. As Skinner (1999) notes, certain concepts link meaning and the legitimacy of institutions: i.e. the meaning that is associated with certain kinds citizenships legitimates the practices and structures which regulate that form of citizenship. Contradictions between different conceptions of citizenship reveal fault lines of political conflict.

Cosmopolitan and market-inspired ideas of European Union citizenship are associated with a confused regulatory approach in which actors, practices and legal frameworks extent across national boundaries. The logic and institutional construction of industrial citizenship is grounded on national rights, worker organization and worker protection which end at the national border, and whose authority does not fully extend to extraterritorial employment arrangements. Although unions seek to represent posted workers their employment relationship is designed so that they remain largely outside the scope of union membership and representation, and works council jurisdiction. Industrial citizenship has been declining in Germany for all workers, so in this respect posted workers are not unique. Nonetheless, their circumstances represent the sharp edge

188 *Nathan Lillie and Ines Wagner*

of a wedge. The transnational structure of posted employment puts them outside effective possibility for industrial citizenship, and undermines the power basis which would give posted workers the power to win improvements in their wages and conditions in the German labour market.

References

Bosch, Gerhard, and Claudia Weinkopf. 2008. *Low Wage Work in Germany*. New York: Russell Sage Foundation.

Bosch, Gerhard, and Robert Zühlke-Robinet. 2003. "Germany: The Labour Market in the German Construction Industry." In *Building Chaos: An International Comparison of Deregulation in the Construction Industry*, edited by Gerhard Bosch and P. Philips, 48–72. London: Routledge.

Brinkmann, Ulrich, and Oliver Nachtwey. 2014. "Prekäre Demokratie? Zu den Auswirkungen atypischer Beschäftigung auf die betriebliche Mitbestimmung." *Industrielle Beziehungen* 21(1):78–98.

CJEU. 2007. Case -341/05, *Laval un Partneri Ltd v Svenska Byggnadsarbetareförbundet and Others*, 2007, ECR I-11767.

Commons, John Rogers. 1913. "American Shoe Makers 1648–1895." *Quarterly Journal of Economics* 26:39–83.

Cremers, Jan. 2013. "Free Provision of Services and Cross-Border Labour Recruitment." *Policy Studies* 34(2):201–220.

Deutscher Bundestag. 2013. Mindestlöhne durchsetzen, Qualität der Kontrollen verbessern. Kleine Anfrage der Abgeordneten Beate Müller-Gemmeke, Dr. Wolfgang Strengmann-Kuhn, Brigitte Pothmer, weiterer Abgeordneter und der Fraktion BÜNDNIS 90/DIE GRÜNEN. Drucksache 17/12834. http://dip21.bundestag.de/dip21/btd/17/130/1713009.pdf. Accessed September 28, 2017.

Doellgast, Virginia. 2009. *Disintegrating Democracy at Work: Labor Unions and the Future of Good Jobs in the Service Economy*. Ithaca, NY: ILR Press.

Fellini, Ivana, Anna Ferro, and Giovanna Fullin. 2007. "Recruitment Processes and Labour Mobility: The Construction Industry in Europe." *Work, Employment and Society* 21(2):277–298.

Finkin, Matthew. 2002. "Menschenbild: The Conception of the Employee as a Person in Western Law." *Comparative Labour Law and Policy Journal* 23(2):577–637.

Freeman Richard, and James Medoff. 1984. *What Do Unions Do?* New Brunswick, NJ: Transaction Publishers.

Frege, Carola. 2005. "The Discourse of Industrial Democracy: Germany and the US Revisited." *Economic and Industrial Democracy* 26(1):151–175.

Fudge, Judy. 2005. "After Industrial Citizenship: Market Citizenship or Citizenship at Work?" *Relations Industrielles/Industrial Relations* 30(4): 631–656.

Greer, Ian, and Marco Hauptmeier 2012. "Identity Work: Sustaining Transnational Collective Action at General Motors Europe." *Industrial Relations: A Journal of Economy and Society* 51(2):275–299.

Greer, Ian, Zinovijus Ciupijus, and Nathan Lillie. 2013. "The European Migrant Workers Union: Union Organizing Through Labour Transnationalism." *European Journal of Industrial Relations* 19(1):5–20.

Practicing European Industrial Citizenship 189

Habermas, Jürgen. 2012. *The Crisis of the European Union: A Response.* Cambridge: Polity Press.

Heery, Ed. 2008. "System and Change in Industrial Relations Analysis." In *The SAGE Handbook of Industrial Relations*, edited by P. Blyton, E. Heery, N. Bacon, and J. Fiorito, 69–91. London: SAGE.

Kilpatrick, Claire. 2009. "Laval's Regulatory Conundrum: Collective Standard-Setting and the Court's New Approach to Posted Workers." *European Law Review* 34(6):844–865.

Marino, Stefania, Rinus Penninx, and Roosblad Judith. 2015. "Trade Unions, Immigration and Immigrants in Europe: Union's Attitudes and Actions Under New Conditions." *Comparative Migration Studies* 3(1):1–16.

Marshall, Thomas Humphrey. 1992. *Citizenship and Social Class.* London: Pluto Press.

Marzo, Claire. 2011. "A Dual European Social Citizenship?" In *Before and After the Economic Crisis: What Are the Implications for the European Social Model?*, edited by Marie-Ange Moreau, 170–186. Cheltenham: Edward Elgar.

Mills, Charles Wright. 1948. *The New Men of Power: America's Labor Leaders.* Urbana: University of Illinois Press.

Polanyi, Karl. 1944. *The Great Transformation.* Boston, MA: Beacon Press.

Skinner, Quentin. 1999. "Rhetoric and Conceptual Change." *Redescriptions (Finnish Yearbook of Political Thought)*, Jyväskylä: SoPhi, 60–73.

Somers, Margaret. 2008. *Genealogies of Citizenship: Markets, Statelessness and the Right to have Rights.* Cambridge: Cambridge University Press.

Thompson, E. P. 1963. *The Making of the English Working Class.* London: Victor Gollancz

Turner, Lowell. 1991. *Democracy at Work: Changing World Markets and the Future of Labor Unionism.* Ithaca, NY: Cornell University Press.

Wagner, Ines. 2015. "The Political Economy of Borders in a 'Borderless' European Labour Market." *Journal of Common Market Studies* 53:1370–1385.

Wagner, Ines, and Lisa Berntsen. 2016. "Restricted Rights: Obstacles in Enforcing Labour Rights of EU Mobile Workers in the German and Dutch Construction Sectors." *Transfer: European Review of Labour and Research* 22(2):193–206.

Wright, Erik Olin. 2000. "Workers' Power, Capitalist Interests and Class Compromise." *American Journal of Sociology* 105:957–1002.

Zentralverband deutsches Baugewerbe. 2006. *Hintergrund zum Thema Schwarzarbeit und illegale Beschäftigung.* Berlin: ZdB.

Zetlin, Di, and Gillian Whitehouse. 2003. "Gendering Industrial Citizenship." *British Journal of Industrial Relations* 41(4):773–778.

Zhang, Chenchen. 2014. "Territory, Rights And Mobility: Theorising the Citizenship/Migration Nexus." In *The Context Of Europeanisation*, PhD Dissertation, LUISS Guido Carli University, and Université libre de Bruxelles.

Zhang, Chenchen, and Nathan Lillie. 2015. "Industrial Citizenship, Cosmopolitanism and European Integration." *European Journal of Social Theory* 18:93–110.

11 "All About Doing Democracy"?
Participation and Citizenship in EU Projects

Katja Mäkinen[1]

Participation, citizenship and democracy form a triad that consists of multiple conceptual and practical links in political life and theory. Citizenship is an essential element for democracy (Dahl 2000, 83–99; Tilly 1995), and citizens' participation in decision-making is required if democracy means that people rule. The popularity of the concept of participation and various participatory practices and experiments is growing so strongly that a term "participatory turn" (Saurugger 2010) has been coined to describe the situation. In the administration of the European Union, one way of increasing participation is the EU programmes through which funding is distributed for citizens' cooperation across the member states in different fields. This chapter seeks to investigate conceptualisations of participation at the level of individual projects funded by two EU programmes, Europe for Citizens and Culture, in the programme period 2007–2013. The aim is to analyse the conceptions of citizenship produced through the conceptual choices related to participation. Particular attention will be paid to the links built between participation, citizenship and democracy.

The type of participation examined in this chapter are participatory practices organised by administration. Participatory projects discussed here are funded by EU programmes and organised typically by civil servants of municipalities or third sector organisations. These projects do not primarily involve decision-making, but the aim is rather networking, developing expertise or organising events and activities. Participatory practices may include elements from grass-roots activities, and civil society actors may be involved in them either as organizers or participants. In that sense, despite their position at the borderline between administration and citizens, such practices can be seen as civil society activity and thus central components of a democratic polity.

Administrative participatory projects can and must, I argue, be examined from the perspective of political participation and democratic citizenship. In spite of their complex relation with democracy, such projects can be expected to meet some of the criteria of republican, participatory or input types of democracy. Indeed, promotion of

"All About Doing Democracy"? 191

democracy and active citizenship are mentioned in the Europe for Citizens and Culture programmes (Commission 2005, 27; Decision 2006a, 32; Decision 2006b, 1) and many of the projects funded by them. Both programmes give funding for activities by civil society, which has been seen as one of the key elements of democracy (Dahl 2000; Westholm et al. 2007). It is thus necessary to examine how these goals are interpreted in the projects funded by these programmes: how citizenship—a cornerstone of democracy—and participation—a dimension of citizenship through which citizens' activity contributes to democracy—are discussed in the projects and how they are, in turn, connected to democracy.

Such an analysis provides a practical level contribution to the vivid debate on the quantity and quality of democracy in the context of the emerging EU polity (Bellamy and Warleigh 1998; Blondel et al. 1998; Kohler-Koch and Rittberger 2007; Magnette 2003; Schmitter 2000). Often discussions on democracy at the European level focus on democratising the EU institutions, but transferring the old models of democracy from the nation states to the EU context is not always supported (e.g. Rosanvallon 2006a). Instead, it has been argued that Europe should develop its own original forms of democratic practice and become "one of the laboratories of contemporary democracy—allowing itself to give new forms to deliberation, to representation, to regulation, to authority, to publicity" (Rosanvallon 2006a, 232–233). Analysing EU projects is useful for exploring the extent to which the participatory practices organised by the EU administration may create spaces for new forms of democracy.

I have chosen to analyse six such projects in which participation, citizenship and democracy are explicitly present in their texts. The selected projects are: *Brick—Building Our Community* (2012–2013; hereinafter: *Brick*), *Young Flow—Network on Dialogue Between Young People and Public Institutions* (2011–2013; *Flow4YU*), *I am Europe* (2013); *Celebrating European Cultural Intangible Heritage for Social Inclusion and Active Citizenship* (2013–2015; *Celebrating*), *Eclectis—European Citizens' Laboratory for Empowerment: CiTies Shared* (2013; *Eclectis*) and *European Citizen Campus* (2014–2015).[2]

EU projects like these can be seen as attempts to give practical contents for the concept of Union citizenship. Union citizenship as a conceptual change and a political innovation embodies the complexity of citizenship. Perceiving political innovation as conceptual and conceptual change as political (Ball et al. 1989; Wiesner in this volume) is based on a conception that understands politics as linguistic activity (see the Introduction to this volume). Struggle over concepts is an essential part of politics (Connolly 1983, 30), and analysing concepts is thus central in political research (Farr 1989, 29). This chapter therefore departs from the idea that in the project texts citizenship is created by discussing citizenship and participation and by explicitly using these concepts. This starting point is based on the view that language is not an instrument of description

192 *Katja Mäkinen*

but that states of affairs are produced with language in various texts and speech acts. Hence the texts produced in the EU projects analysed here also contribute to producing and re-interpreting citizenship and citizens through their discursive practices regarding participation. The variety of meanings given to participation in the projects analysed in this chapter demonstrates how contested the concept of participation is which, in turn, reflects the complexity of citizenship.

In what follows, I will first sketch some theoretical points of departure relevant for my reading of participation discussions. After that, I will introduce the research material and the conceptual approach to it. In the empirical section of the chapter, I will discuss how participation is used and interpreted in the projects. The aim is not to define participation, but to explore what kind of activity participation is and what kind of actors the participants are in the project texts. These findings will be mirrored against the ideas of participation, citizenship and democracy suggested by Pierre Rosanvallon (2006b). Finally, I will sum up what implications these conceptualisations of participation have for citizenship and democracy.

Participation, Citizenship and Democracy: Theoretical Points of Departure

During the long history of the concept citizenship (Heater 1990; Pocock 1995; Riedel 1972; Walzer 1989; Ilyin in this volume) conceptions regarding to whom citizenship belongs and what it includes have been changing. Because of the competing interpretations about equality and liberty—the main principles of democracy—there will always be competing interpretations about citizenship (Mouffe 2005, 7, 65–66). Conceptual change and struggle is thus constantly present in both democracy and citizenship.

Common to different forms of participation is that they bring citizens' voices into the public sphere and place new issues on the agenda. This is the relevance of participation for democracy because in democratic systems difference and equal opportunities to use power must be secured (Bauböck 2008). How much and what type of participation is sufficient and suitable for realising democracy in practice is an old question and relates to ideals of citizenship and to understandings of politics (e.g. Martín and van Deth 2007, 305–311; Rosanvallon 2006b, 26). Answers vary from representative democracy to direct democracy and from bottom-up civic activity to participatory practices organised by administration, as well as different combinations of all of these. Participation is understood as a central dimension of citizenship especially in the republican theories of democracy, as well as in the ideas of radical or participatory democracy (Arendt 1998; Aristoteles 1991; Barber 1984; Mouffe 1992; Pateman 1972; Pocock 1975; Rousseau 1988; see also García-Guitián in this volume). Participation can be seen as a necessary element of so called input democracy, whereas in the conceptions of output type democracy, the role of citizens may be less active (about input and output democracy, see Scharpf 1999).

Participation as a dimension of citizenship underlines that citizens' membership in and relationship to a polity is not only a legal status. Participation is a chance to be involved in the public sphere in one way or another and to influence the polity of which citizens are members and the institutions and issues that have effects on the lives of citizens. As such, participation in the public sphere and in decision-making is that dimension of citizenship which makes it active and political. In addition, participation is relevant for the legitimacy of the political system: through their own participation, citizens may feel that the decision-making in the political system is legitimate and give their consent to the use of power in the system (see e.g. Macedo 2005, 4; Michels 2011, 277–279).

In any type of participation, participation itself inevitably formulates the processes of participation from the beginning to the end: who participates, how and in what they participate, and with what results. Moreover, participation has effects on the participants themselves: participation is "not merely representing citizens, but making them" (Turnhout et al. 2010, 2). Conceptually, participation and citizenship intertwine with each other, as "[p]articipation in the practice of public power seems . . . to be the heart of this status [i.e. citizenship]" (Magnette 2005, 7) across times. Therefore, "[c]onceptions of what citizens are and how they are supposed to behave are deeply implicated in how participation is organized and put into practice" (Turnhout et al. 2010, 3). All this applies also to the participatory practices organised by administration, such as the EU projects discussed here.

Participation has been classified in various ways (Arnstein 1969; Verba and Nie 1972; Westholm et al. 2007). Participatory practices organised by administration, such as the EU programmes, can be recognised as a distinct category of participation, which may share aspects of other forms of participation. In this type of participation the question is not directly about grass roots engagement or civic activism. Instead, these practices include the involvement of citizens in auditions, projects, partnerships or other activities organised by the administration at different levels. Participatory practices are anything but new, but they have been generated increasingly within so called new governance or multilevel governance. In some of them, citizens are involved in decision-making, for instance through participatory budgeting. In others, the main aim is rather to 'hear' citizens' views. The relationship of participatory practices with democracy is contested: participatory practices may offer opportunities for more direct democracy, but they may also mean participation under the conditions defined by the administration (Cruikshank 1999; Lindgren and Persson 2011; Michels 2011; Moini 2011; Newman 2005; Newman and Clarke 2009; Nousiainen and Mäkinen 2015; Papadopoulos and Warn 2007).

194 *Katja Mäkinen*

In order to address the links between participation, citizenship and democracy in the participatory practices in the EU projects, I refer to the multifaceted idea of democracy discussed by Pierre Rosanvallon (2006b), according to which democracy is not only a system but includes various types of acts that vary from one context to another. The ideas of Rosanvallon (ibid.) intertwine participation, democracy, citizenship and politics, which helps to examine how conceptualisations of participation produce various understandings of citizenship in EU projects. Rosanvallon (2006b, 26) sees participation as an instance through which citizens interact with politics, and differentiates expression, involvement and intervention as three ways of participation. For him, these are simultaneously forms of citizenship, and also democracy is articulated around them. In the empirical section, it will be investigated to what extent the EU projects as participatory practices include aspects of expression, involvement or intervention.

Research Material and Method

The material analysed in this chapter is produced in six projects funded by Europe for Citizens and Culture programmes. The citizenship programmes of the EU have a central role in implementing Union citizenship. Through the Europe for Citizens programme, funding can be given to town twinning, citizens' projects and support measures, civil society organisations, European public policy research organisations, events, information and dissemination tools as well as preservation of the main sites and archives associated with the deportations and the commemoration of the victims (Decision 2006a, 34–35). In the subsequent programme period of Europe for Citizens, 2014–2020, similar kinds of activities are funded (Council Regulation 2014).

For their part, the programmes regarding culture are central actors in implementing the common cultural policy of the EU. The Culture programme aims at supporting cooperation projects, bodies active at European level in the field of culture, analyses and the collection and dissemination of information (Decision 2006b, 4). In the programme period 2014–2020, funding is continued under the programme title Creative Europe (Regulation 2013). A close link between participation and citizenship is made in the proposal for the Culture programme: "encouraging direct participation by European citizens in the integration process" is seen as a way "to make European citizenship a tangible reality". Fostering cultural cooperation and diversity contributes to this end, according to the proposal (Commission 2004, 10). In the course of European integration, culture has indeed been seen as a central field of the production of citizenship, and both citizenship and culture were made official fields of European governance in the Treaty of Maastricht in 1992. They are both crucial for democracy: citizenship is one criterion for democracy and cultural diversity can contribute to the plurality and equality required by democracy.

"All About Doing Democracy"? 195

The material includes websites, project descriptions and reports of the projects or events included. Most of the material analysed here has been found at the websites of the projects or at the websites of institutions involved in the projects, organising the project or one part of it—such as art organisations, cultural institutions or non-governmental organisations. The authors of the texts are not often mentioned but they can be expected to be the coordinators of the projects or the members of the advisory boards. Some texts have been written collectively by the participants in the workshops or other meetings of the projects. I see these texts as representations of the projects: they show what the projects wish to look like in these public arenas.

In all these texts, concepts such as participation, citizenship and democracy are frequently used but not often defined. From the viewpoint of conceptual history, it can be seen that a concept and its usage is significant even when the meaning and function of the concept are not explicated. In order to investigate the understandings of participation and citizenship, I take a conceptual look at the project texts and examine the vocabulary referring to participation: the terms that are used, meanings given to them and the relations built between terms. Rather than mapping the entire variety of meanings and uses related to participation, the focus will be on how participation, citizenship and democracy are conceptualised together.

"Actively Involved in the Democratic Life": Conceptualising Participation in the EU Projects

Common to the texts produced in the projects is that participation means acting in the framework of the projects themselves. Other arenas of participation are local politics (*Flow4YU*), European politics (*I am Europe, European Citizen Campus*), community development (*Brick, Celebrating*) and urban environment (*Eclectis*). In the projects funded by the Culture programme, participation is connected with concrete ways of acting within the projects, such as practising skills of conservation and restoration (*Celebrating*), making art (*European Citizen Campus*) and investigating one's living environment with practical equipment (*Eclectis*). Also in the projects funded by the Europe for Citizens programme, participation takes concrete forms such as visiting local decision-makers (*Flow4YU*), writing a blog (*I am Europe*) or designing a game on community development (*Brick*).

Flow4YU is a project aiming at promoting dialogue between young people and public authorities and institutions. The objective is to promote "active involvement and participation of young people in the life of the community" and "active participation in the civil society and public life". Participation of young people is seen as part of "active citizenship". The main instruments for improving the dialogue are increasing knowledge and developing communication channels. Young

196   *Katja Mäkinen*

people need more knowledge about "public life and institutions [. . .] as well as the democratic principles which are the basis of our civic society" and about "administrative systems and organisation at local and European level". Also, the authorities' knowledge about young people must be increased (About. *Flow4YU*). Such conceptualisations refer to ideals of active citizenship. The field of participation is the public arena of local administration and decision-making.

Also in *I am Europe*, a political aspect of participation and agency is present, the field of participation here being EU policies. Participation is tightly linked with citizenship and with attempts to concretise the conceptual innovation of the Union citizenship:

> I am Europe (iEU) is an exploratory expedition into the heart of the European Citizenship concept. Through this project, we want to learn what citizens' participation can mean in a European context, and find out what is needed so that European citizens get more involved in EU policymaking.
>
> (About. *I am Europe*)

Participation is understood as involvement in decision-making and policymaking. Citizens and their participation are seen as having an influence, as the objective is "to exchange, explore, evaluate and (re-)invent participation tools to enlarge the influence the citizens can have on EU policies" and to "maximize their [i.e. citizens'] impact on European policy and in the public domain" (About. *I am Europe*).

Concrete examples of this kind of participation are citizens' assembly and citizens' president—two innovations developed in a fictional report about the future of Europe (*I am Europe* blog 2013) to institutionalise the role of citizens in the European Union—as well as European Citizens' Initiative addressed in the *I am Europe* magazine (2013, 3). In addition, lobbying is discussed as the citizens' way of participation at the EU level in the *I am Europe* blog (2013). Lobbying representing different fields of industry is seen in the blog as a threat to democracy. Citizens' potential, in contrast, is yet unexploited, even though citizens would have legitimacy and credibility, according to the text. From the viewpoint of democracy, lobbying can be seen as a controversial form of participation, which is neither representative democracy nor direct democracy, requiring plenty of resources that not all citizens can have.

Another project explicitly focusing on the concept of citizenship at the European level is *European Citizen Campus*, aiming at "a creative process on different vision(s) of the European citizenship concept" (Detailed Description, p. 3) among students. In it, participants are invited to "actively engage in social and political life" and to "contribute to the promotion of active European citizenship and the creation of an ever-closer Europe" (ibid., 1). These ideas refer to political participation in

"All About Doing Democracy"? 197

which participants have a chance to become part of political debates and influence issues.

Political dimensions of participation are mentioned also in *Brick*, in which community planning and community development are the fields of participation. Participation has an explicit role in the project, as citizens' participation in community planning is used as a defining label of the project.

> Brick—building our community was a European project about citizens' active participation in community planning. [. . .] The aim of Brick was that citizens would get wider understanding of community planning and become a more active part of the community development processes. [. . .] Brick's main theme was Active participation in community development.
>
> (Project Description)

The scope of the action is mainly participants' own living environment. Under the sub-theme "Ethnic inclusion in democracy", participation is linked with democracy and decision-making. The aim is "to encourage citizens, and especially people from ethnic minorities, to get more actively involved in the democratic life, and by this, achieve more equal opportunities in decision-making". The "urban planning process" is seen as part of "the democratic process", and the participants should become aware of this process and their own channels of impact on it (Project Description).

Political aspects of participation are emphasised in *Eclectis*, which concentrates on the urban environment and its development through different fields, such as art, architecture and new technologies. Participation is one of the stated goals of the project. The aim of *Eclectis* is "to facilitate citizens' knowledge and action potential on urban environment" and "to empower citizens to drive local change" (Eclectis). As a central aim of *Eclectis*, participation also means "creating a direct link between citizens and political stakeholders" (A Contribution).

In addition, *Celebrating* focuses on participants' living environment, which is attached to citizenship. Activities regarding cultural environment and built heritage are seen as a way "to enhance a sense of European citizenship" and to promote social inclusion (Celebrating). This kind of participation can be categorized as small-scale democracy meaning action in specific roles mainly regarding citizens' own lives (Westholm et al. 2007). Also in *Brick* and *Eclectis* participants are expected to act in the role of residents who aim at influencing their own living environment. This type of involvement is not only "an important aspect of citizenship in its own right", but it also "may have important implications for other, more directly political realms of citizenship, e.g. by having a spillover effect on political participation" (Andersen and

198 *Katja Mäkinen*

Rossteutscher 2007, 221, 225–227). On the other hand, if participation focuses only on private interests, there is a risk that participants develop particularistic orientations and become too individual, narrow-minded consumers (ibid., 227).

Information, Networks and Proximity as Keywords of Participatory Projects

Common to many projects is an emphasis on the dissemination of information about public issues and other themes. In them, as well as in the programme documents, it is even seen as a solution to problems of democracy. Related to information, communication between citizens and decision-makers was in focus in *Flow4YU*, *I am Europe* and *Eclectis*, and briefly in *Brick* and *European Citizen Campus*. Opening communication channels and connections between citizens and decision-makers offers potential for those activities, which Rosanvallon (2006b, 26) includes in "democracy of expression": in the projects, participants may improve their ability to express opinions, make judgements about decision-makers and their actions, as well as to make claims. In some of the projects, it is explicated that policy recommendations will be given as a result of the project (Antwerp Declaration; A Contribution; Project Description), which may imply articulating collective sentiments, also included in the democracy of expression by Rosanvallon (ibid.). On the other hand, the flood of information and conflicting messages at the EU website are mentioned as hindrances to citizen participation at the EU level (*I am Europe* blog 2013).

Cooperation, networks, dialogue and exchange are keywords in both projects and programme documents. Following the programme documents, all the projects share the conception of participation as a way of generating vertical proximity between the EU and citizens as well as horizontal proximity among citizens from different member states. Cooperation within projects—together with information—is seen as an instrument for creating the proximity in practice. In the projects, the EU seems to come close to citizens, and networks are built between the project participants. As such, these EU projects could be seen as contribution to the "democracy of involvement", which, defined by Pierre Rosanvallon (2006b, 26), includes the ways citizens gather together and create mutual relations in order to produce a common world. The EU projects analysed here are indeed about coming together and creating common bonds, as exemplified by *Brick*.

The objectives were that the citizens would: [. . .]

- Share good practice of community development and work on common challenges with the European partners, to together build a better Europe in relation to our themes. [. . .]

"All About Doing Democracy"?   199

- Create networks both among different target groups in their society and between the European partners.
- By the experience of cooperating with a diverse European group, get a sense of European identity and feeling ownership of the common European work we are doing.

(Project Description)

Rosanvallon (2006b) emphasises the public dimension of the common world—issues must be brought to the public space to be seen and discussed by anyone—whereas in the projects, activities sometimes seem to remain in the private sphere. Moreover, participants in the projects are often people who are already active in the fields of the projects, such as professionals, students or members of NGOs. Hence, it can be asked what kind of common world do participatory practices create and whose world is it.

The third type of participation and democracy defined by Rosanvallon (2006b, 26) is "intervention" and consists of modes of collective action to achieve the desired outcome. The project texts do not reveal, how the goals are formulated and by whom. Intervention, according to Rosanvallon (ibid.), includes forms of political activity, but in the EU projects it is not quite clear to what extent the goal is to intervene in politics and decision-making and what kind of intervention is targeted through participation. Political participation with an attempt to influence broader outcomes, which Westholm et al. (2007) see as characteristic of large-scale democracy, is clearest in *Flow4YU* and *I am Europe*. The editorial of the *I am Europe* magazine (2013, 2) declares that *I am Europe* is "all about doing democracy", investigating "how citizens may truly participate in the process of EU decision-making". According to the editorial (ibid.), "[l]iving democracy is a way of life, a civic culture in which citizens participate creatively in public life". This implies a democratic conception of citizenship. Democratic ideas of participation and citizenship were also present to varying degrees in other projects discussed here, but it is not always explicated in the projects how these ideas will be realised. In some projects, moreover, it is not the highest priority to frame participation as democratic influencing or enhance it as public activity aiming at change. Instead, the main focus may lie in networking or developing participants' expertise and capacities in the subject area of the project.

Conclusions

If citizens' participation is one of the cornerstones of democracy, then participatory practices may also contribute to the development of democracy. In the programme documents regarding Europe for Citizens and Culture programmes, however, democracy is merely mentioned as a principle and a goal rather than discussed explicitly. Democratic aspects

200 *Katja Mäkinen*

of participation are nevertheless included in some of the EU projects funded by those programmes, and this chapter has focused specifically on them.

In the texts produced in the EU projects, conceptions of participants vary from active agents to a more passive audience. Participants are seen as team workers and their participation is mainly located in the framework of the projects themselves, but also in municipalities and the participants' own living environments, and in some cases at the European level. The agency of the participants is thus mostly seen as local but also European. To some extent, participants are seen as political agents and democratic citizens acting, deliberating and using power in the public sphere. In *Brick*, *Flow4YU*, *I am Europe* and *European Citizen Campus*, underlining public activity which aims at change refers to republican and participatory conceptions of citizenship. In some projects, however, citizenship is conceptually linked with identity and the notion of 'European identity' (see Wiesner in this volume). It is connected to the abstract idea of being involved in the construction of the EU as a community and thus means membership in the European Union. When the term 'European citizenship' is used in the project texts it is understood as a 'European identity' and as transnational cooperation between member states rather than a membership or agency in a political community.

The conceptual reading of the project texts shows that participation is primarily conceptualised as networking, cooperation and exchanging information. All of them can be seen as prerequisites for democratic action, but this understanding of participation does not seem to meet the ideas of republican, radical, participatory or input types of democracy. It also lacks many of the forms of participation which are typically viewed as central for democracy. For instance, a list of democracy indicators (Borg 2013) based on European Social Survey, World Values Survey and various statistical data includes a wide range of activities from voting and party attachment to public demonstrations and writing to newspapers, and from strikes and work place democracy to consumption choices and civil disobedience, but such types of participation are not discussed in the EU projects. This represents a depoliticised conception of both participation and citizenship and a conceptual discontinuity from understanding them as instruments of change and sources of democracy.

Rather, participation in EU projects can be interpreted as social participation. As such, EU projects can "indirectly [promote] the quantity as well as quality of [citizens'] participation in small and large scale democracy" (Westholm et al. 2007, 8–9). This kind of participation is important for citizenship, as "[t]he realisation of citizenship is not merely a matter of how democracy operates on a larger scale but also of how individuals or small groups of citizens are able to influence in their situation within various social roles and domains" (ibid., 1).

"All About Doing Democracy"?   201

Because the participatory practices in the EU projects discussed in this chapter are funded by the EU and organised and coordinated by administration at different levels, there is a risk that participation in these practices may become a de-politicised instrument for legitimising the goals of the authorities. Simultaneously, however, they can be seen as political participation to the extent that they offer the potential for the participants to use power and change power structures. In the discussions on participation in the texts produced by the projects, both risks and potentials can be found. As such, they exemplify the complex relations to democracy and politics typical for participatory governance (see Nousiainen and Mäkinen 2015).

A similar dualism characterises participation in a more general way, according to Rosanvallon (2006b, 28–30, 257–268): the greatest problem of our time, for him, is that the strengthening of the indirect democracy has lead into weakening of politics. Rosanvallon (2006b, 260) calls this unpolitical democracy. The increase of modes of participation means that citizens have more ways to be involved in politics, but simultaneously, together with the fuzziness of governance, it may mean that the political field becomes weaker. Paradoxically, the more active, better informed and more interventionist civil society has been accompanied by the unpolitical (ibid., 312). It is striking that the idea about the possibility of an alternative has been eroding, even though the civil society is increasingly active and participatory (ibid., 258).

In principle, then, administrative participatory practices such as the projects examined here may aim at democratisation of the European Union but if they encourage consensus rather than controversies and do not bring their discussions into the public debate, the result may be "unpolitical democracy" (Rosanvallon 2006b), at best. If the projects do not create space for contestation and struggle over power and rather turn political questions into practical problems to be solved, participation does not become political.

Notes

1 The chapter is based on two research projects: Politics of participation and the democratic legitimation of the European union, funded by the Kone Foundation (grant number 46–11423) and Legitimation of European cultural heritage and the dynamics of identity politics in the EU (EUROHERIT), funded by the European Research Council (grant number 636177).
2 The home countries of the organisations and municipalities participating in the projects were as following (the country of the coordinator party mentioned first): *Brick* Finland, Denmark, Slovenia, Spain (participants also from Czech Republic, Germany, Hungary, Italy, Portugal, Romania and Sweden); *Flow4YU* Finland, Croatia, Italy, Sweden; *I am Europe* Belgium, Bulgaria, France, Germany, Poland, Romania, Spain, Sweden; *Celebrating* Romania, Belgium, France; *Eclectis* Netherlands, France, Portugal, Slovenia, Spain; *European Citizen Campus* Germany, Belgium, France, Italy, Luxembourg, Portugal.

202 Katja Mäkinen

References

Project Texts

About. *Flow4YU*. www.flow4yu.eu/index.php/about. Accessed April 8, 2016.

About. *I am Europe*. www.iameurope.eu/about. Accessed February 1, 2017.

Antwerp Declaration for a Stronger Promotion of Student Culture. Distributed in the European Citizen Campus dissemination conference and opening of the global ECC exhibition. June 25–26, Antwerp, Belgium.

Celebrating. Celebrating European Cultural Intangible Heritage for Social Inclusion and Active Citizenship—CECIH. www.transylvaniatrust.ro/index. php/en/programs/celebrating-european-cultural-intangible-heritage-for-social-inclusion-and-active-citizenship-cecih/. Accessed February 1, 2017.

A Contribution from Cultural and Creative Actors to Citizens' Empowerment. European Citizens' Laboratory for Empowerment: Cities Shared. http://waag. org/en/news/eclectis-publication. Accessed February 1, 2017.

Detailed Description of the Project. Received from the coordinator of the European Citizen Campus project via e-mail May 15, 2014.

Eclectis—European Citizens' Laboratory for Empowerment: CiTies Shared. www.expeditio.org/index.php?option=com_content&view=article&id=1008 :eclectis-european-citizenslaboratory-for-empowerment&catid=82&Itemid= 300&lang=en. Accessed February 1, 2017.

I am Europe blog. 2013. Blog entry June 20, 2013. http://iameurope-ef.blogspot. fi/. Accessed February 1, 2017.

I am Europe Magazine. 2013. www.iameurope.eu/. Accessed February 1, 2017.

Project Description. *Brick*. http://brickeurope.org/about/general-information/. Accessed April 8, 2015.

Policy Documents

Commission of the European Communities. 2004. "Proposal for a Decision of the European Parliament and of the Council Establishing the Culture 2007 Programme (2007–2013)." July 14, 2004, COM (2004) 469. http://eur-lex. europa.eu/LexUriServ/LexUriServ.do?uri=COM:2004:0469:FIN:EN:PDF. Accessed February 1, 2017.

———. 2005. "Proposal for a Decision of the European Parliament and of the Council Establishing for the Period 2007–2013 the Programme 'Citizens for Europe' to Promote Active European Citizenship." July 12, 2005, COM (2005) 116 final. http://eurlex.europa.eu/LexUriServ/LexUriServ.do?uri=CO M:2005:0116:FIN:EN:PDF. Accessed February 1, 2017.

Council Regulation. 2014. "No 390/2014 of April 14, 2014 establishing the 'Europe for Citizens' programme for the period 2014–2020." Official Journal of the European Union L 115, 17.4.2014, 3–13. http://eur-lex.europa.eu/ legal-content/EN/TXT/PDF/?uri=CELEX:32014R0390&from=EN. Accessed February 1, 2017.

Decision. 2006a. "Decision No 1904/2006/EC of the European Parliament and of the Council of 12 December 2006 Establishing for the Period 2007 to 2013 the Programme 'Europe for Citizens' to Promote Active European Citizenship."

"All About Doing Democracy"? 203

Official Journal of the European Union L 378, December 27, 2006. http://
ec.europa.eu/citizenship/pdf/lexuriserv_en.pdf. Accessed February 1, 2017.
———. 2006b. "Decision No 1855/2006/EC of the European Parliament and of
the Council of 12 December 2006 Establishing the Culture Programme (2007
to 2013)." Official Journal of the European Union L 372, December 27, 2006,
1–11. http://eur-lex.europa.eu/LexUriServ/LexUriServ.do?uri=OJ:L:2006:372
:0001:0011:EN:PDF. Accessed February 1, 2017.
Regulation. 2013. "No 1295/2013 of the European parliament and of the council
of 11 December 2013 establishing the Creative Europe Programme (2014 to
2020)." Official Journal of the European Union L347, December 20, 2013,
221–237. http://eur-lex.europa.eu/legal-content/EN/TXT/PDF/?uri=CELEX:3
2013R1295&from=EN. Accessed February 1, 2017.

Literature

Andersen, Jörgen, and Sigrid Rossteutscher. 2007. "Small-Scale Democracy:
Citizen Power in the Domains of Everyday Life." In *Citizenship and
Involvement in European Democracies: A Comparative Analysis*, edited by
Jan W. van Deth, José Ramón Montero, and Anders Westholm, 221–254.
London & New York: Routledge.
Arendt, Hannah. 1998. *The Human Condition*. Chicago, IL: University of Chicago
Press.
Aristoteles. 1991. *Politiikka* [Politics]. Helsinki: Gaudeamus. Finnish translation
by A. M. Anttila.
Arnstein, Sherry A. 1969. "A Ladder of Citizen Participation." *Journal of the
American Institute of Planners* 35(4):216–224.
Ball, Terence, James Farr, and Russell L. Hanson, eds. 1989. *Political Innovation
and Conceptual Change*. Cambridge: Cambridge University Press.
Barber, Benjamin. 1984. *Strong Democracy: Participatory Politics for a New
Age*. Berkeley, Los Angeles, & London: University of California Press.
Bauböck, Rainer. 2008. "Beyond Culturalism and Statism. Liberal Responses to
Diversity." Eurosphere Working Paper Series. Online Working Paper no. 06.
Bellamy, Richard, and Alex Warleigh. 1998. "From an Ethics of Integration to an
Ethics of Participation—Citizenship and the Future of the European Union."
Millennium 27:447–470.
Blondel, Jean, Rochard Sinnott, and Palle Svensson. 1998. *People and Parliament
in the European Union: Participation, Democracy, and Legitimacy*. Oxford:
Clarendon Press.
Borg, Sami, ed. 2013. *Demokratiaindikaattorit 2013* [Democracy Indicators
2013]. Helsinki: Oikeusministeriö.
Connolly, William. 1983. *The Terms of Political Discourse*. Oxford: Martin
Robertson.
Cruikshank, Barbara. 1999. *The Will to Empower*. Ithaca, NY: Cornell University
Press.
Dahl, Robert. 2000. *On Democracy*. New Haven & London: Yale University Press.
Farr, James. 1989. "Understanding Conceptual Change Politically." In *Political
Innovation and Conceptual Change*, edited by Terence Ball, James Farr, and
Russell L. Hanson, 24–49. Cambridge: Cambridge University Press.

204 Katja Mäkinen

Heater, Derek. 1990. *Citizenship: The Civic Ideal in World History, Politics, and Education.* Essex & New York: Longman.

Kohler-Koch, Beate, and Berthold Rittberger. 2007. *Debating the Democratic Legitimacy of the European Union.* Lanham, MD: Rowman and Littlefield.

Lindgren, Karl-Oskar, and Thomas Persson. 2011. *Participatory Governance in the EU.* Basingstoke: Palgrave Macmillan.

Macedo, Stephen. 2005. *Democracy at Risk: How Political Choices Undermine Citizen Participation, and What We Can Do About It.* Washington, DC: Brookings Institution Press.

Magnette, Paul. 2003. "European Governance and Civic Participation: Beyond Elitist Citizenship?" *Political Studies* 51(1):144–160.

———. 2005. *Citizenship: The History of an Idea.* Colchester: ECPR Press.

Martín, Irene, and Jan W. van Deth. 2007. "Political Involvement." In *Citizenship and Involvement in European Democracies: A Comparative Analysis,* edited by Jan W. van Deth, José Ramón Montero, and Anders Westholm, 303–333. London and New York: Routledge.

Michels, Ank. 2011. "Innovations in Democratic Governance: How Does Citizen Participation Contribute to a Better Democracy?" *International Review of Administrative Sciences* 77(2):275–293.

Moini, Giulio. 2011. "How Participation Has Become a Hegemonic Discursive Resource: Towards an Interpretivist Research Agenda." *Critical Policy Studies* 5(2):149–168.

Mouffe, Chantal. 1992. "Preface: Democratic Politics Today". In *Dimensions of Radical Democracy: Pluralism, Citizenship, Community,* edited by Chantal Mouffe, 1–14. London & New York: Verso.

———. 2005. *The Return of the Political.* London & New York: Verso.

Newman, Janet. 2005. "Participative Governance and the Remaking of the Public Sphere." In *Remaking Governance,* edited by Janet Newman, 119–138. Bristol: Policy Press.

Newman, Janet, and John Clarke. 2009. *Publics, Politics and Power: Remaking the Public in Public Services.* London: SAGE.

Nousiainen, Marko, and Katja Mäkinen. 2015. "Multilevel Governance and Participation: Interpreting Democracy in EU-Programmes." *European Politics and Society* 14(2):208–223.

Papadopoulos, Yannis, and Philippe Warn. 2007. "Are Innovative, Participatory and Deliberative Procedures in Policy Making Democratic and Effective?" *European Journal of Political Research* 46:445–472.

Pateman, Carole. 1972. *Participation and Democratic Theory.* Cambridge: Cambridge University Press.

Pocock, John. 1975. *The Machiavellian Moment: Florentine Political Thought and the Atlantic Republican Tradition.* Princeton, NJ: Princeton University Press.

———. 1995. "The Ideal of Citizenship Since Classical Times." In *Theorizing Citizenship,* edited by Ronald Beiner, 29–52. Albany: State University of New York Press.

Riedel, Manfred. 1972. "Bürger, Staatsbürger, Bürgertum." In *Geschichtliche Grundbegriffe: Historisches Lexikon zur politisch-sozialen Sprache in Deutschland,* 672–725. Stuttgart: Ernst Klett Verlag.

"All About Doing Democracy"? 205

Rosanvallon, Pierre. 2006a. *Democracy: Past and Future.* New York: Columbia University Press.

———. 2006b. *La contre-démocratie: La politique à l'âge de la dèfiance.* Paris: Seuil.

Rousseau, Jean-Jacques. 1988. *Yhteiskuntasopimuksesta* [Du Contrat Social]. Finnish translation by J. V. Lehtonen. Hämeenlinna: Karisto.

Saurugger, Sabine. 2010. "The Social Construction of the Participatory Turn: The Emergence of a Norm in the European Union." *European Journal of Political Research* 49:471–495.

Scharpf, Fritz W. 1999. *Governing in Europe: Effective and Democratic?* Oxford: Oxford University Press.

Schmitter, Philippe C. 2000. *How to Democratize the European Union—and Why Bother?* Lanham, MD: Rowman & Littlefield Publishers.

Tilly, Charles. 1995. *Citizenship, Identity and Social History.* Cambridge: Cambridge University Press.

Turnhout, Esther, Severine van Bommel, and Noelle Aarts. 2010. "How Participation Creates Citizens: Participatory Governance as Performative Practice." *Ecology and Society* 15(4):26.

Verba, Sidney, and Norman H. Nie. 1972. *Participation in America: Political Democracy and Social Equality.* New York: Harper & Row.

Walzer, Michael. 1989. "Citizenship." In *Political Innovation and Conceptual Change,* edited by Terence Ball, James Farr, and Russell Hanson, 211–219. Cambridge: Cambridge University Press.

Westholm, Anders, José Ramón Montero, and Jan W. van Deth. 2007. "Introduction: Citizenship, Involvement, and Democracy in Europe." In *Citizenship and Involvement in European Democracies: A Comparative Analysis,* edited by Jan W. van Deth, José Ramón Montero, and Anders Westholm, 1–32. London & New York: Routledge.

12 Dual Citizenship and Voting Rights

Domestic Practices and Interstate Tensions

Heino Nyyssönen and Jussi Metsälä

Events in the Caucasus, Crimea and Ukraine have shed new light on the question of the different understandings and political uses of citizenship and dual citizenship. One of the justifications given by the Russian government to the (possible) use of armed force in Crimea was the protection of its own citizens and related populations. Another relatively recent example of the dangers of using citizenship as an excuse for military action was the 2008 war between Georgia and Russia over Abkhazia and South Ossetia; e.g., Szabolcs Pogonyi (2014, 122–140) states, that in this case Russia 'misused external citizenship' to its own ends.[1]

The situation between Russia and Ukraine is no doubt extreme but there are also other cases in which the concept has caused interstate tensions. In April 2014, ethnic Hungarian dual citizens[2] residing outside of Hungary were able to cast their votes in Hungarian parliamentary elections for the first time. Essentially, this was just a domestic manifestation of a longer internal debate, as it is within the sovereign authority of individual states to decide on whom to naturalise and to whom it grants (dual) citizenship. Then again, the contentious nature of the whole concept of citizenship is revealed by the fact that there are also relevant international dimensions in the matter as this kind of policy can cause interstate tensions. There are numerous actors involved in matters concerning a diaspora, like the kin state, host state and the minorities themselves.

Nevertheless, surprisingly little attention has been paid to these questions, although citizenship—particularly in Central and Eastern Europe—necessarily concerns issues such as states, borders and territories, thus intensifying questions of identity, belonging and even loyalty.[3] This is partly caused by the historical realities and differing circumstances between Western and Eastern Europe; in many cases the dramatic contemporary and historical changes in the power relations of the area can be still seen in daily politics. According to Pogonyi, Kovács and Körtvélyesi (2010, 4) the process of establishing legislation allowing external citizenship for kin minorities has been, in a sense, unilateral, as many states would like to endorse their kin minorities living in other states, but at the

Dual Citizenship and Voting Rights 207

same time are highly critical about the policies of other states related to their own minorities.

The focus of this chapter is to examine the controversial connection of dual citizenship and voting rights with power politics, i.e. how dual citizenship can be used as a power resource for political actors and for different purposes. Our purpose is to address the contested character of citizenship, not only between states, but also within states. Therefore, special attention is given to the case of Hungary, which we consider as a striking example of politicking with citizenship as a concept and practice, both on a national and international level. In the Hungarian case, aspirations of maintaining political power are an important factor, as our analysis will clearly show. The chapter is based on the source material provided mainly by articles in various Hungarian newspapers.

What makes Hungary particularly interesting is its large ethnic kin minorities just beyond its national borders. Subsequently, there are over two million people just outside of the existing borders—in the Hungarian state there are circa 9.9 million inhabitants (cf. Kovács and Tóth 2007; Népszabadság, March 10, 2012). While post-Trianon Hungary itself is ethnically quite homogenous, 'Hungarians are neighbours of Hungarians', as all neighbouring states have a Hungarian minority. Also, it is worth remembering that for the purpose of this chapter the question is not merely of groups of migrants, but of people who have largely lived in their countries of residency for their whole lives, and even for generations. The new Hungarian citizenship is an alternative political construction, an add-on to these already existing citizenships. In Bauböck's (2009, 480, 481, 493) words, the Hungarian case can be seen as example of an ethno–national understanding of belonging to a community, i.e. those with shared past or linguistic contiguity are to be included in the 'national body'.

Although our case, the Hungarian diaspora, has existed at least since the First World War, we concentrate mainly on the period following the enlargement of the European Union because it appears that the entrance to the Union has not removed the question from the agenda but, instead, led to dual citizenship being a potential problem even inside the EU. There are two particularly significant Hungarian events to be studied. First, in December 2004 the citizens had to decide in a referendum whether the parliament should accept dual (multiple) citizenship, without the right to vote. Second, there is the debate that has been under way since spring 2010 when the parliament unilaterally guaranteed Hungarian citizenship for non-domiciled Hungarians. On one hand, the possibility of multiple citizenships has been seen as a long overdue passing of the old Westphalian state system, but as political examples in Europe and elsewhere show, other perspectives are also possible, some of them clearly being a question of power politics.

Our approach aims to study dual citizenship on three levels. First, we explicate the conceptual background of the concept from the point

208   Heino Nyyssönen and Jussi Metsälä

of conceptual history. There our claim is that despite Western, liberal and postmodern views of citizenship as an individual right[4] and the effects of migration, our case seems to bring the ethnic principle—*ethnos* instead of *demos*—back to the limelight in European politics. Second, we understand that establishing dual citizenship and voting rights are related and serve power political interests. On the third level we focus on the practicalities of establishing voting rights (see Gil in this volume) and representation (see Lietzmann in this volume) and in the kin state parliament.

The Concepts of (Dual) Citizenship

Globalisation and the erosion of state power has been a continuing theme for decades and it is clear that political entities are no longer seen as exclusive but overlapping in many ways (Blatter 2011, 791). Or, as Miles Kahler (2006, 1, 18) notes, the meanings of territorial borders might have changed—especially after the end of the Cold War—but they have most certainly not gone away. The reality of borders separating 'Us' from 'Them' is still very much alive and globalisation processes have also resulted in the reaffirmation of certain forms of borders, old or new (Newman 2006, 101–103; Paasi 2003, 475; see also Spiro 2011, 736–738).

Interestingly, most of the new international borders emerging (between 1900 and 2002) through state partition or secession are situated on old existing administrative boundaries and not, e.g., along ethnic or cultural divisions (Goemans 2006, 28, 52; cf. also Pogonyi 2014, 130). In fact, it should be noted, that many states have been extending their sovereignty well beyond their borders for a long time such as, e.g., by proclaiming the validity of domestic laws outside their geographical borders for their own citizens and permanent residents (Raustiala 2006, 219, 222–223).[5]

Therefore, dual citizenship has become an issue particularly for modern multicultural societies characterised by growing migrant populations (Bron 2002, 34–41; Grace 2007; cf. Dahlin and Hironaka 2008, 55–56, 68; Nyyssönen and Korhonen 2010, 134). However, this is not the whole story, as our case study shows. Here the concept is used in a context which is neither migration nor multicultural. Despite stories of individuals with several passports the idea of dual (or multi) citizenship, as such, is rather new, e.g., The Oxford Encyclopædic English Dictionary (1991, 269) does not recognise the concept at all. When depicting citizenship, however, there is an expression 'citizen of the world', which the dictionary links to cosmopolitanism. The international disinclination towards dual citizenship, exemplified by the 1930 League of Nations convention stating, that everyone should have only one nationality, has been forcefully transformed by the pressures of globalisation. We have outpaced the idea that both territory and those living inside of it are a part of the

Dual Citizenship and Voting Rights 209

sovereign state and of that state alone (Blatter 2011, 771; Kahler 2006, 15, 17; Spiro 2010, 111–130).

Practicalities labelled under the umbrella of dual citizenship vary in the world: in present (2016) day Europe countries like Finland, France, Italy, Portugal, Sweden, Switzerland and the UK accept the principle of dual citizenship, but Germany, e.g., obligates individuals to decide on citizenship at the age of 23. Yet, there are also prominent countries like Austria, the Czech Republic, Estonia, Holland, Norway, Spain or Ukraine, which have not tolerated multiple citizenship at all, although even in some of these states there might not be any penalties imposed for actually holding dual citizenship.

There are also several different layers in the formation of dual citizenship. It can be a result of birth or naturalisation and also re-naturalisation. There are also several different ways—some more preferential than others— for one state to grant (dual) citizenship or residency, all dependent on the actual circumstances of the case. Equally important are the actual, concrete ways of exercising the rights associated with citizenship(s). That is because possessing dual citizenship does not automatically guarantee participation in political decision making, one of the main features of the whole concept. A useful portrayal of this is found in Jussi Ronkainen's study, which examines dual citizens in Finland and their identification with different citizenships (Ronkainen 2011, 258–259; Bauböck 2009, 475).

Ronkainen's classification of different types of attitudes towards dual citizenship can be paraphrased with the use of his terms 'either–or', 'both–and' and 'neither–nor' citizens. The first group sees themselves entirely as members of only one political entity, the second as members of many entities simultaneously, and the last group as 'non-traditional' form of transnational political belonging, as sort of outsiders without a 'continued tie to any state/society' (Ronkainen 2011, 254–257). Based on this, political rights are an important part of the concept of citizenship, even if someone happens to live in a foreign state, but the actual political participation and voting behaviour is largely depended on the level of attraction felt towards the state granting citizenship (Pogonyi 2014, 125). A crucial question remains, however: is citizenship something 'external' referring to benefits and ethnicity or 'internal', which means full participatory rights in a given community (see also García-Guitián in this volume).

Concepts of citizenship (citizen) and nationality (national) are often used as synonyms. However, from the point of conceptual history both concepts have a different etymology. Citizens have rights to participate in the political life of the state, whereas nationals need not to have these rights, although normally they do.[6] It might be useful here to distinguish nationality from citizenship, as in several non-English-speaking countries

210 Heino Nyyssönen and Jussi Metsälä

nationality is often used as a synonym of ethnicity, e.g., the identity cards of the former Soviet Union separated nationality (Armenian, Estonian, Jew, etc.) from the citizenship of the Soviet Union. However, here we are content with the term citizenship when we refer to Hungarian *állampolgarság* (citizenship) and *kettős állampolgarság* (dual citizenship).

Whereas customarily the state has been free to decide to whom it grants citizenship—and states have been quite successful in incorporating the legal status as a member of the society with the idea of national identity—the topic has implications for relations between states (Spiro 2011, 694, 697, 715–716). It is quite important to recognise that citizenship and the territorial nation state are no longer synonymous—a misconception created by 'methodological nationalism' in political science—if they ever were. The argument that long standing nationalistic thinking like 'one nation for one country' has, for the most part, run its course could very well be accurate (Bauböck 2009, 475–476; Goemans 2006, 40–41).

External Voting Rights

Whereas external voting is not a new phenomenon by any means, a somewhat revealing position on the matter of regulating external enfranchisement can be found in the report titled *Code of Good Practice in Electoral Matters—Guidelines and Explanatory Report*[7] composed by the Venice Commission of the Council of Europe in 2002. This report maintains that citizens living abroad could be given 'the right to vote and to be elected', although states could impose restrictions and qualifications based on residency. Consequently, the formalization of international normative rules regarding the rights of migrants and expatriates to exercise their rights by voting has not been a particularly successful process, predominantly only states with large diaspora populations have favoured such an arrangement, whereas in general the international community has not been very concerned about the matter (Grace 2007, 40–41; Bauböck 2009). Still, the number of people eligible for external voting has doubled in the last 40 years (Pogonyi 2014, 122). According to Michael Collyer (2014, 66) only South Africa and Macedonia have implemented new legislation in order to inhibit external voting.

The extent of voting rights for external citizens, dual or otherwise, can be seen in the fact that globally states allowing some form of external voting number between 115 and 120 from the total of 214. In Europe almost all of the current 28 EU member states have provided at least some access to voting rights for their citizens residing in other states. Only Cyprus, Greece, Ireland (see e.g., Honohan 2011), Malta and Slovakia do not have, or have not implemented, provisions for external voting. Furthermore, there are four states (Croatia, France, Italy and Portugal), which have enacted legislation to allow their non-resident citizens to have separate legislative representation (Pogonyi 2014, 123; Collyer 2014, 62;

Dual Citizenship and Voting Rights   211

Pogonyi, Kovács and Körtvélyesi 2010, 13; see also Annex A in *Voting from Abroad: The International IDEA Handbook* 2007).

The important issues of citizenship itself are, to paraphrase Jussi Ronkainen (2011, 248), what the degree of citizenship is (who belongs and to where, and who doesn't belong and where don't they belong), what are the implications of citizenship (the privileges and obligations associated with the status) and what is the penetration of citizenship (what is the individual's level of attachment to the political system and society, and vice versa). Accordingly, a citizen is, or should be, someone having a stake in the future of that particular political entity (Bauböck 2009, 478–479, 481). Consequently, granting citizenship and voting rights to a population utterly detached from the 'national' framework of a state is most likely to produce rather little, as the connections between the population and political processes are not strong enough to generate an affirmative reaction. It can be argued that actual ties are essential to participation in political life in one or several countries (Ronkainen 2011, 258–259; cf. also Elena García-Guitián's chapter in this volume).

Therefore, guaranteeing voting rights for external citizens does not necessary lead to a strengthening of any particular government but rather to speculation about its political advantages and disadvantages. Indeed, there are numerous examples showing the impressive potential influence and power that voting rights might produce for external citizens in 'cases of large-scale enfranchisement of trans-border ethnic kin groups' (Pogonyi, Kovács and Körtvélyesi 2010, 15). As an indication of the aspirations of maintaining political power, the idea suggested by the former Hungarian Minister of Health István Mikola in 2006, that it could be possible to remain in power even for decades with the help of the votes of the non-domiciled Hungarians, reveals that ultimately the case is not about supporting brothers and sisters, but about political power (e.g., Pogonyi 2011, 697). By granting external voting rights Hungary has increased its 'potential citizenry' considerably, and the absolute number of the external voters—potential or actual—is in an entirely different category when compared, e.g., with many migrant diasporas with the same rights (Pogonyi 2014, 133).

The Hungarian Case

The Hungarian diaspora traces its roots to the collapse of the Austro-Hungarian Empire and the harsh conditions of the peace treaty of Trianon in 1920. Despite the demands for revision of the situation, the room for political manoeuvring ranged from limited to non-existent during most of the remaining 20th century (see Gerner 2007). The first post-1989 attempt to deal with the question of non-domiciled Hungarians concerned basic treaties to confirm present state borders. In particular, treaties with Ukraine, Slovakia and Romania caused

212   Heino Nyyssönen and Jussi Metsälä

debate, as some MPs demanded guarantees for minority treatment in neighbouring countries—then the socialist Foreign Minister could argue that acceptance of those bilateral treaties, in particular, will end allegations of revisionism (*Az Országgyűlés hiteles jegyzőkönyve 1994–1996*: 23390–23391). A second, and still current, topic was the question of regional autonomy openly backed by the Hungarian parliament in the mid-1990s as a softer alternative compared to contesting state borders themselves (see e.g., Blatter 2011, 783–784). Third, a particular Status Law was an attempt to lower the Hungarian state border for ethnic Hungarians on the threshold of EU accession. On the basis of an idea of belonging to the same homogenous 'nation', Hungary aimed to subsidise and grant benefits to Hungarians in neighbouring states, except in Austria, the only neighbouring EU member. The law was modified after domestic political changes and after consultations with neighbouring countries, like Romania and Slovakia, and the Council of Europe in 2003. At that time, Fidesz, the main opposition party, and two radical minority organisations did not sign the amendment to the law.

A formal proposal for dual citizenship emerged outside the state actors: a few months after the modification of the Status Law in 2003, minority organisations in Serbia and Romania took the initiative—as at that time it seemed plausible that Hungary's membership in the EU would lead to the closure of the borders to Hungarian minorities. With the help of the Hungarian World Organisation 474,000 signatures were gathered by July 2004 and a referendum was organised. The result committed the parliament to act if at least half of the whole electorate participated in the referendum.

Domestic party political emphasis was present in the referendum campaigns, as pro and contra arguments were divided mostly on the basis of party, with the government against and the opposition favouring dual citizenship. When looking at the arguments of the socialist–liberal government it is clear that they opposed dual citizenship, favoured republicanism and civil nationalism—i.e. Hungarians inside the Hungarian state—and also that economic arguments prevailed. Furthermore, historical arguments were used as the then socialist Prime Minister Ferenc Gyurcsány surmised, that the proposal will empty regions beyond the borders, i.e. trigger immigration, and lead to a 'second Trianon' (Magyar Hírlap, November 3, 2004; Népszabadság, November 10, 2004; Magyar Hírlap, November 27, 2004). The worst scenario seemed to include an axiom that 'our' land exists only as far as people live there, and ethnic minorities beyond the borders were a constant reminder of the existence of the nation. As such, a territorial principle was present in the debate: the philosopher János Kis condemned PM Gyurcsány's scenario by arguing that if people leave their land as a consequence of the law, the question is not about people but of land. Instead of using nationalist language and clichés from the extreme right, the government should

Dual Citizenship and Voting Rights 213

condemn the proposal because it would lead to postponing rational solutions for many years (Magyar Hírlap, November 27, 2004).

The biggest party in the opposition, Fidesz, with more communitarian views, took a completely different stance. Statistically, the number of ethnic (non-domiciled) Hungarians had been decreasing since the 1990s, and now dual citizenship was to stop migration. They estimated that dual citizenship would not empty regions, and aimed to maximize rights for ethnic Hungarians, even at the cost of a domestic political confrontation. The leader of the party, Viktor Orbán, re bordered Hungarians as a nation of 15 million and argued, that dual citizenship had already been carried out in many European countries, and 'only Hungarians are made to believe that they should be small' (Magyar Nemzet and Népszabadság, November 29, 2004). However, Fidesz's conception of dual citizenship was narrow from the very beginning: it excluded the right to settle in Hungary and the right to vote or run as a candidate in parliamentary elections. Dual citizenship linked the concept to the thematic of nation as it meant 'reuniting of the nation'.

Thus, on 5 December 2004 voters decided whether the parliament should enact a law regarding the citizenship of persons who claim to be Hungarian but are not citizens, do not live in Hungary and could prove their (Hungarian) nationality on the basis of the Certificate of Hungarian Nationality or by other means defined by the law (Magyar Nemzet, December 4, 2004; Népszabadság, December 6–7, 2004). The referendum was not valid, as only 37.5 per cent of the whole electorate participated. Evidently a domestic controversy was stressed in the end, and neither side was able to present a coherent interpretation of international norms and practices supporting their respective positions (Kovács 2005, 72). In addition, Romania opposed the idea in public claiming that Romanian Hungarians would have to give up their citizenship in the case of applying for Hungarian citizenship.

In 2010, as one of its first actions, the new conservative government established dual citizenship, with a passport, but without the right to vote (see *A magyar állampolgárságról szóló*, 2010). Fidesz followed a policy line presented during the 2004 referendum; failure of which was now labelled as national treason (Magyar Nemzet, August 18, 2010). According to vice PM Zsolt Semjén, the question was about national solidarity and the need to repair the injustice of Trianon. The bill divided the socialists, now in opposition, as a slight majority supported it whilst the remainder did not participate in the final vote.

Concurrently, the Slovakian parliament accused its neighbour of 'Greater Hungarian revisionism' and modified the State Citizenship Act. The majority, including a number of opposition parliamentarians, decided to withdraw citizenship from those Slovakian citizens who wished to apply for Hungarian citizenship. This law is still valid, although the number of cases has not been significant. Yet, in February 2011 the

214 *Heino Nyyssönen and Jussi Metsälä*

parliament rejected a proposal which would have rendered Hungarian dual citizenship on Slovakian soil invalid and would have prevented dual citizens from joining certain offices such as the military or police (Magyar Nemzet and Népszabadság, February 11, 2011). Here, Slovakia was not alone: after Romania's membership in the EU, Moldova imposed restrictions concerning public positions on those having dual citizenship. Similar considerations took place in Lithuania, this time against those of Polish heritage (Pogonyi, Kovács and Körtvélyesi 2010, 11).

Instead of minority protection the discourse shifted more to 'nation policy' and towards the notion of 'reunification of the nation'. According to the foreign policy strategy of Fidesz domestic, foreign and nation policies were closely intertwined. Under the subtitle 'Nation Policy' they argued how it is peculiar for Hungarian foreign policy to have to fulfil two interests at the same time: Hungarian state and nation. Partly this means securing international tasks for Hungarian citizens and partly supporting Hungarians beyond borders to 'strengthen the stability of the area' (*Következetes Külkapcsolatok: Magyarország külkapcsolati Stratégiája*).

The new Hungarian Constitution (2012) begins provocatively: 'We, the members of the Hungarian nation' (Hungarian Constitution 2011). The formulation does not refer to citizens, or dual citizens, but to a nation, which in the Hungarian context is not the same as the (current) state. The basic law was accepted only after a few weeks of debate, and without the full support of all parliamentary parties, which either opposed or boycotted the whole process. To the extent that the 1989 constitution declared that Hungary shall bear a sense of responsibility for Hungarians living outside the borders, the 2011 paragraph is more detailed. At first article D defines the cause: 'Motivated by the ideal of a unified Hungarian nation, Hungary shall bear . . .'

In general, Slovakia and Romania, the countries in which the largest Hungarian minorities live, were the most critical but they also partially accepted the principle of dual citizenship and their criticism lost much of its prominence. The latest dispute has dealt with the *Székely* flag (an autonomous area during 1952–1968), as Romania restricted the use of the flag, which was then hoisted above the parliament in Budapest as a 'symbol of national solidarity'. However, these hegemonic acts were only partially successful: e.g., in the Slovakian elections of 2010 and 2012, two rival Hungarian parties emerged but the traditional Party of the Hungarian Coalition (*Magyar Koalíció Pártja*), which had drifted towards a close cooperation with Fidesz, failed to pass the required threshold. Instead a new party, the *Most-Hid*—the name means 'bridge' both in Slovakian and Hungarian—with ethnic Slovakian members gained seats. The Fidesz-KDNP is strongly opposed to the party, and even the vice premier Semjén has expressed how 'ethnicity' instead of 'assimilation' should be the criteria of support.

Dual Citizenship and Voting Rights 215

In 2010, Hungary was the only country in the European Union having a two-thirds super majority won by an electoral bloc with 52.73 per cent of the votes, whereas Romania, also with a mixed electoral system, followed suit in 2012. Thus, Fidesz was able to introduce electoral reform without a broader consensus and in 2011, despite earlier standpoints, guaranteed voting rights also to non-domiciled Hungarians. One of the main differences compared to the old electoral system inspired by the German model was that in 2014 a majority of MPs (106 out of 199) were elected by a first past the post system, and the rest by a proportional vote. According to the Chairman of the Parliament, László Kövér, in practice the new voting rights completed the unification of the nation in legal sense (Népszabadság, September 3, 2013).

The new electoral act offers voting rights for Hungarian citizens without permanent residence in the country. The first draft of the bill included the preregistration of all voters, heavily criticised by the domestic opposition, and finally ruled unconstitutional by the constitutional court. Currently non-resident (new) citizens need to register to be eligible to vote for party lists, not for single seat candidates, unless they can prove their permanent address in Hungary. The government expected a vast majority of new dual citizens—ca. 500,000 including children and other non-registered voters—to support the government, whilst the opposition expected expats—another relevant group outside Hungary with up to 500,000 people—to favour the opposition. However, according to the critics, 'Some are more Equal than Others', namely new dual citizens were in a privileged position as they could register on the Internet and vote by mail ballot, but ordinary citizens staying abroad during the elections had to be personally present in the Hungarian Embassy or consulate (cf. Népszabadság, January 5, 2013; Népszabadság, February 27, 2014; Lane Scheppele 2014; Magyar Nemzet, March 4, 2014).

In April 2014 Fidesz-KDNP won 133 seats out of 199 with 2,198,489 votes. The number of non-domiciled Hungarian votes remained smaller than expected, at 128,712, but of those votes Fidesz gained 95 per cent. Compared with the 2010 outcome (2.7 million votes) the party *de facto* lost several hundred thousand voters. Nonetheless, because of the new electoral system the government could maintain its huge two-thirds super majority—this time with only 45.23 per cent of the votes. Contrary to expectations, the 'ethnic card' was overshadowed by other current foreign political topics, like Ukraine and nuclear energy. Yet, in Slovakia local nationalists covered up Jobbik party's election posters, which they considered provocations on Slovakian territory (*Nemzeti Választasi Iroda* 2014; Magyar Nemzet & Népszabadság, April 2, 7, 8, 2014).

Soon after the elections Fidesz announced that their national list for EU elections will contain Hungarian representatives beyond borders, i.e. from neighbouring countries as well. Actual 'campaigning' had reached those states even earlier: e.g., in 2012 the Speaker of the National

216 Heino Nyyssönen and Jussi Metsälä

Assembly visited ethnic Hungarians despite the wishes of the Romanian authorities to postpone the visit until after the Romanian parliamentary elections. Also socialists have been active particularly in Romania, largely in territories belonging to pre-Trianon Hungary. Arguably, domestic politics has had an influence on political the reasoning of ethnic minorities and the Hungarian foreign policy. Whereas in Europe state borders have been lowered, or 'de-bordered', at the same time the structure of the nation has become more visible, or been 're-bordered' (Magyar Hírlap, April 11, 2014; Népszabadság, June 5, 2012; Nyyssönen 2011).

Conclusions

We have analysed citizenship, and dual citizenship, on three levels. By sharing views of conceptual history, we have showed different and contested meanings in its content and usage. There, the question is not only if a particular country tolerates dual citizenship but how it uses the concept and what kind of rights and duties it demands from its new citizens. In as much as dual citizenship is still understood as a phenomenon and a consequence of multiculturalism and migration, this is not the case here. Paradoxically, Hungary is a (historical) case in which national borders have moved, not the people themselves. Instead new citizens do not even need to move to the kin state. Here, of course, Hungary is not alone and could be a potential forerunner to other states, like Russia and their minorities abroad after the collapse of the Soviet Union. For those who think juxtaposing Russia and an EU member state is misguided we may say that both are indeed successor states and have, e.g., used historical arguments recently.

Second, the question of establishing dual citizenship and voting rights is related to power political interests. 'Nation policy', completed with an electoral reform, is the newest conceptual attempt and neologism in the long story of Hungarian nationalism. Despite its individual nature, it seems that our case is bringing the ethnic principle back into politics: During the last twenty years we have witnessed a discursive change, from minority protection to more radical 'nation policy' in the Carpathian Basin. In this sense, dual citizenship is no longer simply a question of an individual but also of regional and global issues which can be easily politicised for nationalist purposes.

Third, there is the question how much the diaspora de facto makes or should make an impact on particular policies of a kin state. This is related to citizenship practices and how they shape citizenship. Some countries have established separate representation in the parliament for their external citizens. In the Hungarian case, it seems plausible that limiting the representation only to party lists dispelled the worst fears of those not living in the country or not paying taxes having too much weight in national politics. Nevertheless, we think that an idea of a

Dual Citizenship and Voting Rights   217

particular quota, or a special constituency, might still be a better option to avoid these fears. In addition, it would place the expectations and the influence of the 'diaspora card' into its rightful place—perhaps like the national minorities, who in 2014 were also guaranteed representation, and non-domiciled Hungarians are also definitely a minority. Thus, time will tell if some sort of a quota arrangement might also be favourable in the Hungarian case. Likewise, what remains to be seen, are the responses and concrete actions of the very populations so recently officially nationalised or 'Hungarianised'.

Notes

1 On 1 March 2014, the President of Russian Federation, Vladimir Putin, requested the Russian parliament to authorise the use of military forces on Ukrainian territory, because of the 'threat to citizens of the Russian Federation, our compatriots'. The official translation of the request can be found at http:// eng.kremlin.ru/news/6751. For a more nuanced description of the Georgian situation and consequences of Russian policy of 'passportisation' in the areas, see Artman 2013.

2 The term *dual citizen* is used in this chapter interchangeably with the term *multiple citizenship* to emphasise the possibility of being a citizen of more than one polity at the same time, with full participatory rights. For the use of the term *external citizenship* see Bauböck (2009, 475–478).

3 While there are a lot of studies depicting minorities and polices towards minorities in a particular country, practical forms and policies dealing with 'kin states' and their relations to 'kin minorities' are less studied. Extensive analysis of the Hungarian Status Law can be found in English in *The Hungarian Status Law Syndrome: A Nation Building and/or Minority Protection* (Kántor et al. 2004). Moreover, Maria Kovács (2005) has studied the 2004 referendum; Nyyssönen and Korhonen (2010) focused on Hungary, particularly observing how these policies affect geopolitics and borders. Citizenship laws in the new EU member states were analysed in *Citizenship policies in the New Europe* (Bauböck, Perchinig and Sievers 2009), whilst Myra Waterbury (2010) has studied Hungarian diaspora politics and kin state nationalism.

4 An often-used characterisation of citizenship (originally used by Hannah Arendt) is 'the right to have rights' (e.g., Blatter 2011, 771; Spiro 2011, 719, note 167; Bauböck 2009, 478). According to Spiro there just might be developing an international normative stand towards citizenship legislation on the basis of international human rights. Hereby, citizenship would become, for individuals, 'the right to have the right to have rights'. What the long-term effects of this sort of development are going to be remains to be seen (Spiro 2011, 719–720, 745). See also Amanda Nielsen's chapter in this volume.

5 Extraterritorial legislation—efficient or not—concerning various forms of financial transactions and especially taxation (e.g., FATCA in the United States) is rather common, but the forms of 'territorial extension' are various, even in the EU (Scott 2014; see also Bean and Wright 2015). Another good example of widely applied extraterritorial legislation are the laws on sexual crimes, especially those concerning children. Several states (over 40 in 2008) have enacted some forms of ET legislation on this matter (see e.g., Beaulieu 2008.). Legislation and/or jurisdiction in these cases are not bound only to territory, but to citizenship and residency also, i.e. national laws can follow citizens/ residents even while abroad.

218 *Heino Nyyssönen and Jussi Metsälä*

6 For Aristotle, a citizen was the 'one who is a partner in the legislative and judicial process', and thus a member of the political community, *polis*. The world nation is derived from Latin and built on the past participle form *natus* 'having been born' of the verb *nasci* 'to be born'. Cicero, e.g., referred to all races (*omnes nationes*), which were able to bear enslavement, but Rome, our community (*nostra civitas*) cannot. Nationality is a product of the 19th century (see also Ronkainen 2011, 249–250).

7 Full text of the report is available at www.venice.coe.int/webforms/documents/default.aspx?pdffile=CDL-AD%282002%29023rev-e. Accessed February 20, 2017.

References

Documents

A magyar állampolgárságról szóló. 2010. www.parlament.hu/internet/plsql/ogy_naplo.naplo_fadat_aktus?p_ckl=39&p_uln=4&p_felsz=107&p_felszig=174&p_aktus=19. Accessed February 19, 2017.

Az Országgyűlés hiteles jegyzőkönyve. 1994–1996.

Hungarian Constitution (The Fundamental Law of Hungary). 2011. www.kormany.hu/download/e/02/00000/The%20New%20Fundamental%20Law%20of%20Hungary.pdf. Accessed February 15, 2017.

Következetes Külkapcsolatok Magyarország külkapcsolati Stratégiája. http://static.fidesz.hu/download/210/FideszSzpF1_belivek_148x210.pdf. Accessed August 21, 2013.

Nemzeti Választasi Iroda. 2014. www.valasztas.hu. Accessed February 15, 2017.

Literature

Artman, Vincent M. 2013. "Documenting Territory: Passportisation, Territory, and Exception in Abkhazia and South Ossetia." *Geopolitics* 18:682–704.

Bauböck, Rainer. 2009. "The Rights and Duties of External Citizenship." *Citizenship Studies* 13:475–499.

Bauböck, Rainer, Bernhard Perchinig, and Wiebke Sievers, eds. 2009. *Citizenship Policies in the New Europe*. Amsterdam: Amsterdam University Press.

Bean, Bruce W., and Abbey L. Wright. 2015. "The U.S. Foreign Account Tax Compliance Act: American Legal Imperialism?" *ILSA Journal of International and Comparative Law* 21(2):334–368.

Beaulieu, Catherine. 2008. *Extraterritorial Laws: Why They Are Not Really Working and How They Can Be Strengthened*. Bangkok: ECPAT International.

Blatter, Joachim. 2011. "Dual Citizenship and Theories of Democracy." *Citizenship Studies* 15:769–798.

Bron, Agnieszka. 2002. "Demos and Ethnos in European Citizenship: Possible Connections and Challenges for Adult Education." In *Active Citizenship and Multiple Identities in Europe: A Learning Outlook*, edited by Danny Wilderneersch, Veerle Stroobants, and Michal Bron Jr., 33–47. Frankfurt am Main: Peter Lang.

Collyer, Michael. 2014. "A Geography of Extra-Territorial Citizenship: Explanations of External Voting." *Migration Studies* 2:55–72.

Dual Citizenship and Voting Rights   219

Dahlin, Eric C., and Ann Hironaka. 2008. "Citizenship Beyond Borders: A Cross-National Study of Dual Citizenship." *Sociological Inquiry* 78:54–73.

Gerner, Kristian. 2007. "Open Wounds? Trianon, the Holocaust and the Hungarian Trauma." In *Collective Traumas: Memories of War and Conflict in 20th-Century Europe*, edited by Conny Mithander, John Sundholm, and Maria Holmgren Troy, 79–109. Bruxelles & New York: P.I.E. Peter Lang.

Goemans, Hein. 2006. "Bounded Communities: Territoriality, Territorial Attachment, and Conflict." In *Territoriality and Conflict in an Era of Globalization*, edited by Miles Kahler and Barbara F. Walter, 24–61. Cambridge: Cambridge University Press.

Grace, Jeremy. 2007. "Challenging the Norms and Standards of Election Administration: External and Absentee Voting." In *Challenging the Norms and Standards of Election Administration*, 35–58. International Foundation for Election Systems.

Honohan, Iseult. 2011. "Should Irish Emigrants Have Votes? External Voting in Ireland." *Irish Political Studies* 26:545–561.

Kahler, Miles. 2006. "Territoriality and Conflict in an Era of Globalization." In *Territoriality and Conflict in an Era of Globalization*, edited by Miles Kahler and Barbara F. Walter, 1–21. Cambridge: Cambridge University Press.

Kántor, Zoltán, Hokkaidō Daigaku, Surabu Kenkyū Sentā, 21-seiki COE Puroguramu, eds. 2004. *The Hungarian Status Law: Nation Building and/or Minority Protection*. Sapporo: Slavic Research Center & Hokkaido University.

Kovács, Maria. 2005. "The Politics of Non-Resident Dual Citizenship in Hungary." *Regio – Minorities, Politics, Society* 8:50–72.

Kovács, Mária, and Judit Tóth. 2007. "Kin-State Responsibility and Ethnic Citizenship: The Hungarian Case." In *Citizenship Policies in the New Europe*, edited by Rainer Bauböck, Bernhard Perchinig, and Wiebke Sievers, 135–159. Amsterdam: Amsterdam University Press.

Lane Scheppele, Kim. 2014. "Hungary, An Election in Question, Part 1–5." *The Conscience of a Liberal*. http://krugman.blogs.nytimes.com/2014/02/28/. Accessed February 15, 2017.

Newman, David. 2006. "The Resilience of Territorial Conflict in an Era of Globalization." In *Territoriality and Conflict in an Era of Globalization*, edited by Miles Kahler and Barbara F. Walter, 85–110. Cambridge: Cambridge University Press.

Nyyssönen, Heino. 2011. "De-Bordering the State, Re-Bordering the Nation." In *De-Bordering, Rebordering and the Symbols on the European Boundaries*, edited by Jaroslaw Janczak, 53–66. Berlin: Logos.

Nyyssönen, Heino, and Pekka Korhonen. 2010. "Contemplating Hungarian Borders." In *East and the Idea of Europe*, edited by Katalin Miklóssy and Pekka Korhonen, 119–142. Cambridge: Scholars Publishing.

The Oxford Encyclopaedic English Dictionary. 1991. Edited by Joyce M. Hawkins and Robert E. Allen. Oxford: Clarendon Press.

Paasi, Anssi. 2003. "Region and Place: Regional Identity in Question." *Progress in Human Geography* 27:475–485.

Pogonyi, Szabolcs. 2011. "Dual Citizenship and Sovereignty." *Nationalities Papers* 39:685–704.

———. 2014. "Four Patterns of Non-Resident Voting Rights." *Ethnopolitics* 13:122–140.

220 *Heino Nyyssönen and Jussi Metsälä*

Pogonyi, Szabolcs, Maria Kovács, and Zsolt Körtvélyesi. 2010. *The Politics of External Kin-State Citizenship in East Central Europe*. Robert Schuman Centre for Advanced Studies/EUDO Citizenship Observatory Comparative Report.

Raustiala, Kal. 2006. "The Evolution of Territoriality: International Relations and American Law." In *Territoriality and Conflict in an Era of Globalization*, edited by Miles Kahler and Barbara F. Walter, 219–250. Cambridge: Cambridge University Press.

Ronkainen, Jussi Kasperi. 2011. "Mononationals, Hyphenationals, and Shadow-Nationals: Multiple Citizenship as Practise." *Citizenship Studies* 15:247–263.

Scott, Joanne. 2014. "The New EU 'Extraterritoriality'." *Common Market Law Review* 51:1343–1380.

Spiro, Peter J. 2010. "Dual Citizenship as Human Right." *International Journal of Constitutional Law* 8:111–130.

———. 2011. "A New International Law of Citizenship." *The American Journal of International Law* 105:694–746.

Voting from Abroad: The International IDEA Handbook. 2007. Stockholm & Mexico City: International IDEA & Federal Electoral Institute of Mexico.

Waterbury, Myra. 2010. *Between State and Nation: Diaspora Politics and Kin State Nationalism in Hungary*. New York: Palgrave Macmillan.

Newspapers

Magyar Hírlap
Magyar Nemzet
Népszabadság

Conclusion
Contested Conceptualisations of Citizenship

Claudia Wiesner, Anna Björk, Hanna-Mari Kivistö and Katja Mäkinen

The chapters in this book have shown how citizenship and its dimensions have been shaped and challenged in different settings in contemporary Europe in, and by, theory, debate and practice. They discuss themes that have both contemporary as well as historical relevance, such as inclusion, exclusion, and intersectionality and their implications in terms of access, rights, duties and the active content of citizenship. These issues relate to classical questions linked to the concept of citizenship addressed in citizenship theory and citizenship studies, but the chapters also indicate significant challenges to citizenship today—representative democracy and its future, political participation, migration, mobility, multilevel citizenship, dual citizenship, ethnic rights, only to name some of the main examples. Currently, these topics are being intensively debated (e.g. Clarke et al. 2014; Maas 2013; Rosanvallon 2006).

The reflexive and constructivist perspective on the concept of citizenship taken in this book contributes to bringing new insights to these debates. The approach has a clear added value in exploring different conceptions of citizenship and thus is a crucial theoretical and methodological gain and tool for a better understanding of the concept of citizenship and its meanings and usages in political science, conceptual history and citizenship studies.

The investigations led throughout the book are here summarised through three broad fields of discussion: First, citizenship is approached through *historical linguistic* analysis; and second, it is viewed from the perspective of *representative democracy*. Third, a considerable number of concluding remarks refer to *relocations* of citizenship in the context of migration, beyond and between nation states and in the framework of the European Union. The chapters allow us to draw conclusions about the shifting conceptions of citizenship and their implications for the changes in the idea of the political community and particularly the role of nation states as scenes of citizenship.

First, different conceptions of citizenship can be approached by looking at how they are constructed and understood *linguistically* (Koselleck 2006), as Ilyin shows in his opening chapter. Conceptual historical

222   *Claudia Wiesner et al.*

approaches (Pocock 1998, Skinner 1993) bring added value in analysing the different historical interpretations of the concept of citizenship systematically. They allow exploring not only long term changes of concepts but also their "prehistorical" construction and contestations. This is exemplified in the analysis by Ilyin, which shows how the shifting frameworks and conceptions of citizenship have been constructed and understood linguistically during the long history of the concept in various languages.

Second, in current *democratic theory,* citizenship is reflected in debates about political *participation* (García-Guitián; Mäkinen; Nyyssönen and Metsälä) and *representative democracy* (García-Guitián; Gil; Lietzmann). In democratic theory, topical questions concern elections, the shape of representation, classical and modern forms of participation, and ways to enhance participation. Regarding the link between citizenship and representative democracy, the chapters by García-Guitián, Gil and Lietzmann in the first part discuss the frequently used notion of a "crisis" of representative democracy. But is representative democracy really in crisis or is it rather facing new challenges and transformations? In a similar way, questions are raised with regard to participatory democracy: Should it be seen as a challenge, as a new chance, or rather as an over-emphasised concept? With regard to these questions, the chapters help to relativise the diagnosis of a crisis. They highlight challenges that representative democracy and democratic theory should address and suggest that the idea of a general crisis of representation might be misleading. Furthermore, there is enough reason to re-think the concept of representation in theory and practice, as is suggested in the chapter by Lietzmann. Similarly, low voter turnout has often been regarded as a sign of a crisis of democracy, but Gil demonstrates that abstention from voting does not have any self-evident implications for democracy and citizenship. Perhaps, as Elena García-Guitián argues, instead of asking when one is a good citizen it might be worthwhile to ask simply after the good-enough citizen.

Third, all chapters in parts two and three discuss various forms of what can be called *relocations of citizenship.* These chapters emphasise that citizenship has multiple contexts, diversifications and internal divisions. The complexity of citizenship becomes visible by examining the edges of citizenship and the intersections between citizenship and other factors. This relocation of citizenship is, first, discussed in the chapters by Björk, Kivistö, and Nielsen, in which immigrants are conceptualised as non-citizens. Second, citizenship "beyond" or "between" nation states is discussed in the chapters by Nyyssönen and Metsälä as well as by Valkonen and Valkonen. Mobile citizenship in the transnational context of the European Union, which is the third form of relocation discussed here, is addressed in the chapters by Lillie and Wagner as well as by Mäkinen and by Wiesner. These chapters show how citizenship is in a process of continual diversification, always including different kinds of demarcation.

Conclusion 223

The chapters in part two have shown that *migration* is a key issue for citizenship in several respects. Migration once more raises the question of access to both the status and rights of citizenship. Historically, citizenship status has often been seen as the basis for rights, but admission criteria to citizenship and its associated rights have changed over specific periods of time: In the Greek polis, citizens enjoyed broad political rights and the practice of citizenship was very intense, but only a small part of the population was admitted to citizenship and hence possessed full citizenship rights. Such exclusions from citizenship continued to exist although later they have concerned different groups. The chapters show that parallel to many historical situations, political struggles and debates around access to citizenship and/or to rights are frequent in today's representative democracies. These struggles may be fought on behalf of, but also be led by non-citizens. Here we find another parallel to the historical development of democratisation of western nation states, where many struggles on access to citizenship and rights were led by persons without the status of full citizenship (e.g. women and their fight for the electoral rights). This illustrates how there are forms of political agency outside of the status of citizenship (Isin and Nielsen 2008).

The importance of the formal status of citizenship for rights is emphasised in the chapters in part two as well. The chapters of Björk, Kivistö and Nielsen focus especially on citizenship and access, rights, and non-citizenship. These chapters have hence analysed conceptual struggles over access to citizenship rights and the recognition of rights, and dealt with arguments, claims and the articulation of rights. The accounts raise the question of the conditions for obtaining rights and problematise the difference between human rights and citizenship rights. The questions about access to citizenship and rights, as well as concerning the legal and political status of the individuals, are particularly visible currently in regard to irregular migration, as Nielsen demonstrates. Furthermore, the discussion has shown that the criteria for access to citizenship are contested still today, as especially Björk argues, and differ from case to case: Migrant workers and asylum seekers face different situations in this respect. Asylum as a right of political refugees, which is discussed by Kivistö, is another example of a hotly debated question that has direct implications for how access to citizenship is conceptualised. Another question concerns the responsibilities of states towards non-citizens, i.e., towards asylum seekers, refugees and undocumented persons. These issues are topical today, but they also resonate historically: Similar questions of both access to and rights of citizenship have been decisive in the history of democratisation for centuries.

Citizenship beyond and between states is discussed through the cases of dual citizenship and indigenous citizenship. Both emphasise the role of ethnicity in shaping citizenship as well as the importance of territorial borders. Dual citizenship, addressed by Nyyssönen and Metsälä, refers

224 Claudia Wiesner et al.

to both national and transnational citizenship: National Hungarian citizenship with its voting rights is extended to people living outside of state borders which makes it citizenship "between" nation states. The indigenous Sámi people, discussed by Valkonen and Valkonen, reside on the territories of several states. However, nation state-based citizenship has not guaranteed the Sámi full political rights to decision-making in matters concerning themselves, and the concept of indigenous citizenship has been introduced as a solution to this problem. Both chapters have shown that in the cases of dual citizenship and indigenous citizenship ethnos and demos are intertwined and struggles on citizenship are centred around ideas of linguistic unity and a shared past.

European integration has been creating new types of citizenship and new layers within existing conceptions, thus having a diversifying effect on citizenship. A number of new EU-related rights have been developing during the decades of European integration. Moreover, the new status of "Union Citizen" has been created. EU citizenship is often taken as an example of a transnational or even a form of cosmopolitan citizenship but, as the chapters in this volume have underlined, there are ambivalences and pitfalls in these developments: New second, third and fourth class citizens in the EU have been created not only with regard to legal status but also in regard to class—posted workers bear significance to a new rightless and transnational proletariat.

The role of European integration in the reorientation processes of citizenship is, therefore, Janus faced. The chapters by Wiesner and Mäkinen discuss EU citizenship as a conceptual innovation in which the concept of citizenship has been given new meanings. Wiesner shows how in the EU the concept of citizenship has been developed, first, at the conceptual level, and then later at legal and institutional level, and how the process has included conflicts in the interpretation and implementation of the new concept. Whereas this process has brought new benefits for well-educated EU citizens, posted workers, as discussed by Lillie and Wagner, are in a situation in which neither the workers' original citizenship, nor Union Citizenship, nor the legislation in the host country can guarantee sufficient rights while working in another country. The study demonstrates how the tension between market dynamics and democratic politics that is characteristic for the EU expresses itself in citizenship practice through the situation of posted workers.

A closer look at the political practice of the new space of the European Union shows that the jump from theory to practice is not simple, as the new concept of EU citizenship needs to be filled with a meaning and political practice. An attempt to give concrete meaning to citizenship in the EU context, and more specifically to the conceptual innovation of Union Citizenship, are the participatory projects organised in the context of specific EU programmes. In these projects, discussed by Mäkinen, citizens' participation is mainly understood in the sense of networking

Conclusion 225

among project participants and regarded as part of European integration. This leads to an understanding of citizenship relating to more transnational exchange and "European identity" formation, rather than to political agency. The various interpretations of "participation" in EU projects often lack some central aspects of active democratic participation, which should be self-organised and reflect the citizen´s interests. This refers to the shortcomings of participatory practices organised by administration in general. Adapting a quote by Eugen Weber (1979), the question in these top-down participatory projects is how to "make active EU citizens".

The discussions on citizenship in the context of both current transformations of democracy and the relocations of citizenship have shown that different conceptualisations of citizenship have important implications for the conceptions of *political community*, especially through questions of access and participation. This has been the case also in earlier times, as demonstrated by the linguistic analysis of the concept of citizenship in different languages (Ilyin). Conceptual analyses of the inclusions and exclusions related to citizenship (Björk; Kivistö; Nielsen; Lillie and Wagner) improve our understanding of constructions of political communities and the boundaries of their membership. The analysis on external voting rights of dual citizens by Nyyssönen and Metsälä refers to the political community (demos), or at least an "election day demos". Simultaneously, however, it refers to an ethno–national type of belonging to a community, as citizenship is discussed as an "ethnic" principle concerning those living outside the Hungarian borders but considered "ethnic" Hungarians. In the debates investigated by Valkonen and Valkonen, membership criteria in the Sámi community are crucial themes of dispute. The analyses by Lillie and Wagner as well as by Mäkinen and by Wiesner on citizenship in the context of European integration show that the European Union cannot yet be seen as a fully-fledged political community of citizens.

One of the main conclusions to be drawn from the investigations on citizenship in different settings carried out in this volume concerns the question whether *nation state citizenship* is an intermediary result of an epoch that will ultimately end. Manifold changes to nation state citizenship have been discussed: The new questions in representation and participation (García-Guitián; Gil; Lietzmann; Mäkinen), struggles about defining the demos in theory and practice, and the development of new citizenship practices outside the nation state. But the chapters presented here have shown that, despite the changes, the ideal of nation state citizenship remains central and is an important touchstone of political struggles all over Europe. This concerns the whole nexus of conceptualisation, policy making, and practical implementation of policies on the domestic level, and foreign policy. EU citizenship also carries within it traces of national citizenship (Mäkinen; Wiesner), and the Hungarian

226 Claudia Wiesner et al.

case (Nyyssönen and Metsälä) bears witness to how the links between nationality and citizenship are re-established.

Hence, the interplay between the national, international and supranational brings about challenges and opportunities for conceptual analyses where the micro and macro levels can be effectively taken into account. This contributes to the deconstruction of oppositions that are frequently made: national interest vs. international and transnational relations and networks. We do not experience oppositions here, but rather a number of entangled and related processes of exchange. Therefore, the chapters in this volume suggest that it seems to be premature to think about an end of the concept of nation state based citizenship. Rather, they underline that citizenship is a changing concept and that, more importantly, nation states are not the only reference point for citizenship. Citizenship is, and has always been, attached to various communities and frameworks.

In sum, this book has demonstrated that citizenship is always changing and contested, but that the concept is also used as an elusive and useful political tool. The chapters powerfully show how ambiguous, contradictory and changing the concept of citizenship indeed is, hence emphasising the concept as a locus of controversy—or, as a script, as termed by Spanakos (2015, see also the introduction to this volume). The book also has indicated that changing political contexts and realities influence how citizenship is politically contested. Several chapters manifest how the concept of citizenship gets new meanings and usages particularly in the relocations of citizenship. There, the concept of citizenship has worked as a lens (ibid.) through which new aspects of reality have become visible. In some chapters, concepts have been used as building blocks (ibid.). For instance, the concept of non-citizenship has deepened our understanding of asylum as a right (Kivistö), the concept of indigenous citizenship has enabled making sense of the rights of the Sámi (Valkonen and Valkonen), and the concept of industrial citizenship is examined as a potential solution to the problems of the posted workers (Lillie and Wagner). All this demands for rethinking the concept of citizenship and its function as a lens, building block and script (ibid.) of political analysis. The reflexive and constructivist approach to concepts proposed in this volume brings an important contribution to this rethinking.

Exploring these changes and their contestation through our reflexive and constructivist approach to concepts has proven to be a promising endeavour. The concept of citizenship, as shown here, has been shaped in theory, debate and practice by, or in relation to, struggles over the concept. Be it the challenges related to migration, European integration, multilevel governance or the changing role of nation state—all of them have given rise to new conceptualisations aiming to shape citizenship.

The reflexive and constructivist approach to concepts, as well as the insights and heuristic tools of conceptual history used throughout the

Conclusion 227

book have allowed for a focus on how those new conceptualisations have been created, debated, and succeeded or failed. Seeing the multiplicity of the meanings of citizenship as an asset and a starting point for analysis has enabled a broadening of the analytical perspective on different aspects of the politics of citizenship.

To study how a concept, as in this case the concept of citizenship, can be interpreted differently, and how and why it is contested, not only enables a more precise view of the possibilities, but also the limits and ambivalences, of using the respective concept as an analytical category: Any such usage needs to be aware of the diverse possible meanings and contents of the concept and make explicit which understandings it uses. To interpret a concept and category as reflexive and socially constructed, therefore, can be enormously beneficial. It allows us, as political scientists, to be more precise and reflective in the use of our analytical apparatus.

References

Clarke, John, Kathleen Coll, Evelina Dagnino, and Catherine Neveu. 2014. *Disputing Citizenship*. Bristol: Policy Press.

Isin, Engin F., and Greg M. Nielsen, eds. 2008. *Acts of Citizenship*. New York: Palgrave MacMillan.

Koselleck, Reinhart. 2006. "Drei bürgerliche Welten. Zur vergleichenden Semantik der bürgerlichen Gesellschaft in Deutschland, Frankreich und England." In *Begriffsgeschichten: Studien zur Semantik und Pragmatik der politischen und sozialen Sprache*, 402–463. Frankfurt am Main: Suhrkamp.

Maas, Willem, ed. 2013. *Multilevel Citizenship*. Philadelphia: University of Pennsylvania Press.

Pocock, John. 1998. "The Ideal of Citizenship since Classical Times." In *The Citizenship Debates: A Reader*, edited by Gershon Shafir, 31–41. Minneapolis: University of Minnesota Press.

Rosanvallon, Pierre. 2006. *La contre-démocratie: La politique à l'âge de défiance*. Paris: Seuil.

Skinner, Quentin. 1993. "Two Concepts of Citizenship." *Tijdschrift voor Filosofie* 55: 403–19.

Weber, Eugen. 1979. *Peasants into Frenchmen the Modernization of Rural France, 1870–1914*. Stanford, CA: Stanford University Press.

Index

abstention 20, 71–4, 76–7, 79–84, 222
access 8, 13, 17–18, 29, 32–3,
  83, 87–90, 95, 102–5, 108–12,
  114–17, 120, 123–5, 128–9,
  131–3, 143, 164, 166–8, 170, 176,
  178–80, 182, 184, 186–7, 210,
  221, 223, 225
Arendt, H. 77, 89, 94–5, 98–9, 103,
  192, 217
asylum *see* right of asylum
asylum seekers 88–9, 93–7, 99,
  102–3, 105, 115–18, 120, 123,
  129–36, 223
Austin, J. L. 154

Basic Law; Grundgesetz 94–5, 99,
  102–4, 214
belonging 10, 17–18, 23–4, 27, 35,
  37, 90, 95, 97–8, 119–20, 126,
  138, 148, 150, 206–7, 209, 212,
  216, 225
Brennan, J. 20, 71–83

categories 1–2, 9–11, 13, 52, 88–90,
  95, 97, 111, 118, 126, 128,
  130, 132
citizen participation 19–20, 40, 43–7,
  50–2, 198
citizenization 141, 144–6, 148–9
citizenship 1–3, 6–13, 17–20, 23–9,
  31–2, 34–7, 39–40, 50, 55–8, 65,
  71, 77, 83, 87–90, 94–9, 108–15,
  117–20, 123–7, 133–4, 138–41,
  144–50, 153–6, 159–62, 164–72,
  175–82, 185–8, 190, 200, 206–14,
  216–17, 221–7
citizenship rights 9, 11, 89, 98, 124,
  126–32, 134–5, 155, 159–62, 165,
  167–71, 179–80, 223
civic rights 34, 72
cognitive schemata 23–4, 26

colonialism 139, 148–9
communitarianism 17
comparative politics 1–3, 8, 10–11
concepts 1–8, 12–13, 18, 20, 23, 25,
  27, 35, 39, 52–8, 64, 84, 87–8,
  95–6, 110–11, 117, 120, 124–5,
  127–8, 131–2, 134–5, 138, 143–4,
  148–50, 153–5, 159–61, 165,
  170–1, 175–9, 186–7, 191, 195,
  208–9, 222, 226
conceptual change 4–7, 10, 36, 60,
  64, 66, 95, 124, 128, 134, 154,
  167, 191–2
conceptual history 3–6, 11, 13, 23–6,
  71, 84, 109–10, 124, 127–8, 139,
  143, 149–50, 154, 187, 195,
  208–9, 216, 221, 226
conceptual invention 153, 167
constitution 47, 60–1, 94–5, 140,
  145, 154, 160, 214
crisis 19–20, 39–43, 45–7, 52, 55,
  59–61, 66, 93, 148, 165, 222

Dahl, R. A. 11, 39, 43, 49, 190–1
definition 3, 7–8, 12, 17–18, 36, 46,
  71, 87–8, 95, 97–9, 103, 139–41,
  144, 146–50, 154, 170, 182
deliberation 43, 50, 76, 79–81, 83,
  96, 99–100, 145, 191
demarcation 11, 87–90, 95–6, 101,
  105, 110–12, 118, 124, 132, 135,
  138, 149, 222
democratic theory 8–9, 17–20, 40, 48,
  55, 222
dichotomies of citizenship 18, 20
dual citizenship 153, 156, 206–10,
  212–14, 216, 221, 223–4
duties 8–9, 13, 17–19, 20, 25, 30,
  32, 34, 36, 71–3, 75, 77, 81, 94,
  99, 118, 139, 149, 167, 170,
  216, 221

Index   229

electoral rights *see* voting rights
epistocracy 76–7
ethnicity 9–10, 90, 156, 209–10, 214, 223
EU institutions 160, 165, 186, 191
EU law 160, 168–9
EU programmes 155, 190, 193, 224
European citizenship 119, 154–6, 159–61, 164–72, 175, 179–80, 194, 196–7, 200, 224–5
European Union 8, 11–13, 111, 118, 138, 153–4, 156, 159, 163–6, 169, 175, 180, 184, 187, 190, 196, 200–1, 207, 215, 221–2, 224–5
exclusion 8, 10, 13, 23, 28, 79, 87, 89, 108, 110, 115, 124–6, 129, 134, 155, 171, 186, 223, 225
external voting 153, 156, 210–11, 225

Federal Republic of Germany 94
free movement of persons 156, 160, 167

Germany 4, 35, 89, 94, 99, 102–5, 119, 156, 164, 170–1, 175–6, 180–4, 186–7, 209
good-enough citizen 40, 48–9, 222

health care *see* right to health care; right to medical care
human rights 89–90, 93–6, 98–101, 104–5, 123–35, 146, 163, 176, 223
Hungary 156, 206–7, 211–16

iconological representation 20, 59, 62, 66
identity 18, 26, 37, 90, 112–13, 139, 149, 165–6, 170, 177, 179, 199–200, 206, 210, 225
ILO Convention No. 169. 140, 145, 147
immigration 11, 88, 101, 108–10, 112–13, 115–20, 129, 182, 212
inclusion 8, 10, 13, 23, 27–37, 83, 87, 108, 110, 125–6, 146, 148, 171, 177, 197, 221, 225
indigeneity 10, 138, 141–4, 146–50
indigenous citizenship 12, 87, 90, 138, 140–1, 146–8, 150, 223–4, 226
Indigenous people 90, 138–50
industrial citizenship 155, 175–82, 185–8, 226
integration 8, 10–11, 31, 33, 108–10, 112, 114, 116–19, 126, 154–5, 159–61, 164, 179, 182, 186, 194, 224–6
interviews 176

irregular migrants 11, 89–90, 124–6, 128–32, 134–5
irregular migration 125

kin minorities 156, 206–7
Koselleck, R. 3–6, 59, 110–11, 154, 165, 167, 221

labour migration 125, 175, 180
labour mobility *see* labour migration
labour rights 176, 178, 180, 187
legitimacy 6, 19–20, 39, 50–1, 57–8, 65–6, 75–6, 80, 134, 138, 141, 146, 165, 177, 187, 193, 196
liberalism 17, 50

margins; marginalised 13, 88, 90, 97, 138–9, 142–3
market citizenship 161, 165, 176, 178, 180
Marshall, T. H. 8–9, 17, 90, 139, 177
membership 23–4, 27, 34, 36, 48, 88, 90, 95, 97–8, 105, 123, 126, 132, 134, 139–40, 187, 193, 200, 212, 214, 225
migration 11, 17, 89, 93, 111, 113, 115–17, 125–6, 129–30, 134, 175, 180, 208, 213, 216, 221, 223, 226
Mill, J. S. 71, 74–5, 77–80
minority 45, 133, 139, 145, 207, 212, 214, 216, 217
morphological method 27
multiple citizenships 18, 36–7, 207

nation state 127
nation state citizenship 8, 23, 34, 89, 95, 139, 170, 225
nationality 8, 87, 94, 98, 108–10, 112–13, 115–16, 119–20, 162, 166, 180, 185, 208–10, 213, 226
Nationality, Immigration and Asylum Act 108–10, 112–13, 115–16
naturalization 94
non-citizenship 10, 223, 226
non-discrimination 132, 154, 156, 160–4, 171, 180
non-state citizenship 87, 90, 138–9

operationalisation 1, 57
order 23, 26, 28–34, 36–7, 60, 80–1, 104, 138, 142, 144

Palonen, K. 4–6, 58, 65, 96, 111, 143–4, 149
parliament 20, 37, 47, 63, 75, 87, 111, 118, 123–4, 130, 133, 140–1,

230 *Index*

145, 147–8, 160, 163, 165, 170, 207–8, 212–16
Parliamentary Council; Parlamentarischer Rat 96, 99, 103
parliamentary debates 13, 113, 118, 120, 129
participation 9–13, 17–21, 23, 30, 36, 39–40, 43–52, 55, 72, 74, 76–9, 81–3, 88, 108–10, 117–20, 139–40, 146, 153–6, 163, 171–2, 176, 179, 190–201, 209, 211, 221–2, 224–5
participatory democracy 19, 39, 42–3, 52, 192, 222
participatory governance 11, 13, 201
patrimonialism 31
polis 18, 23, 26–7, 29, 31–5, 223
political activity 2, 8–9, 19–20, 87, 170, 172, 199
political community 36, 98, 127, 176, 200, 221, 225
political concepts 3, 5, 25, 84, 96, 109
political movements 42, 147–8
political participation 11, 13, 20, 39, 72, 76, 78–9, 139, 146, 156, 190, 196–9, 201, 209, 221–2
political representation 19–20, 40–1, 50–2, 55–66
political theory 4, 7, 9–10, 17, 20, 40, 42, 59, 111
posted workers 88, 155, 175–6, 179–88, 224
postwar 89, 93–4, 97–9, 103–4, 125, 145
power politics 207
prototypes and invariants of concepts 26–30

refugees 11, 88–9, 93–105, 113, 115–20, 223
representative democracy 9, 13, 19–20, 39–43, 45–6, 51–2, 60, 164, 192, 196, 221–2
republicanism 17, 212
rhetoric 4–6, 111, 115–16, 118, 119, 156
right of asylum 99, 101–3, 115
right to health care; right to medical care 89–90, 128–30
rights 8–9, 11–13, 17–21, 25, 30, 32, 34, 36, 72, 77, 87–90, 93–105, 108, 110, 115–18, 123–35, 139–49, 153–6, 159–71, 176–87, 206–11, 213, 215–17, 221, 223–6

Rosanvallon, P. 61, 191–2, 194, 198–9, 201, 221

Sámi 12, 87–8, 90, 138–50, 224–6
Sámi Parliament 140–1, 145, 147–8
Schumpeter, J. A. 18, 40, 43, 46, 52, 80
Skinner, Q. 3–7, 17–18, 35, 154, 159, 165, 187, 222
social rights 9, 90, 123–5, 132–3, 154, 179–80
sovereignty 39, 59–60, 94–5, 97–8, 100, 102, 105, 127, 139, 147, 167, 176, 185, 187, 208
speech act 95, 154, 192
state borders 12, 111, 147, 156, 186, 211–12, 216, 224
state sovereignty 95, 97–8, 100, 105, 185
status 18, 25, 41, 57, 88–90, 94, 96–9, 104, 108–10, 114–20, 123–6, 129, 131–3, 141, 145–8, 156, 161, 169, 171, 176, 182, 187, 193, 210–12, 223–4
suffrage 9, 47, 71–2, 76–82
Sweden 89–90, 123–35, 140, 144, 209
symbolic representation 31, 56

temporality 108–11, 118–19
trade unions 48, 61, 177–8, 181–2, 185
Treaty of Maastricht 154, 160, 165, 194
Treaty of Rome 154, 161–2, 175, 179

undocumented migration 89, 128–34, 223
Union citizenship 8, 140, 153–6, 159–60, 164–8, 187, 191, 194, 196, 224
United Kingdom 26, 100, 108, 110, 114
United Nations 94, 99, 140, 143
United Nations Declaration on the Rights of Indigenous Peoples 140
Universal Declaration of Human Rights 94, 96, 99

voting 12, 18–20, 39–40, 43, 46, 48–9, 52, 71–84, 153, 156, 200, 206–17, 222, 224–5
voting rights 20, 153, 156, 206–8, 210–11, 215–16, 224–5

welfare state 11, 123–6, 132, 145, 175, 177, 187
Westphalian state system 207
workers' rights *see* labour rights